CHANGE AND
THE CHURCHES
An Anatomy
of Religion in Britain

David Perman

CHANGE AND THE CHURCHES
An Anatomy
of Religion in Britain

THE BODLEY HEAD
LONDON SYDNEY
TORONTO

© David Perman 1977
ISBN 0370 10329 7
Printed and bound in Great Britain for
The Bodley Head Ltd
9 Bow Street, London WC2E 7AL
by W & J Mackay Limited, Chatham
Set in Monotype Ehrhardt
First published 1977

CONTENTS

Foreword

'*The Churches . . . An Anatomy* . . . it sounds like a prophetic title,' wrote an Anglican vicar in Lincolnshire. But, despite the fact that anatomy is normally studied from corpses, this book is not written on the assumption that the Christian churches in Britain are already dead or about to expire. It may well be that some of them will sooner or later disappear, either through institutional decay or ecumenical merger. But the Church (as distinct from the churches) is still remarkably alive. No body which is active in so many different ways, even if some of the activity is at time rather feverish, can be pronounced a corpse. On the other hand, nobody would claim that all is well with the churches, not even as well as it was a mere decade ago in the hopeful sixties. Some people say that the churches are now in crisis; others do not know what to say about the parlous state of institutional religion. But all commentators agree that there is widespread bewilderment and demoralisation in the churches of the seventies and that this is associated with the climate of constant change, both inside and outside the churches themselves.

The aim of this book is to survey that change and to try to explain to bewildered church people and puzzled outsiders alike just what is going on. None of the churches' professional diagnosticians—the clergy, the theologians, the administrators or sociologists—have attempted such a sweeping survey across the denominational boundaries. Perhaps they know the ground with all its pitfalls too intimately to attempt a broad-horizoned survey. But now is the time when the common experiences and problems of the different Christian denominations need to be brought together in a factual survey, with only as much digression into theology as is needed to explain the changes on the ground. The full intellectual and theological exploration of the climate of change through which the churches are passing is left to other books and other writers, like David Edward's stimulating *Religion and Change* (SCM Press, London 1974). This is a layman's book by a mere journalist. But it could not have been written

7

without the enormous help, generosity and patience of a large number of clergy and other specialists in church affairs. They are too numerous to mention and many of them would possibly find it embarrassing to see their names recorded. To them all, I express deep gratitude. A special debt is owed however to the few who laboured through parts of the text and drew attention to errors of fact or judgement—to Desmond Day, Michael Harper, John Habgood, Hugh Kay and David Martin in particular. Needless to say, the errors which remain and the views which are here expressed are the sole responsibility of the author.

Ware, Herts   *October 1976*

I

Church and Nation

On 15 October 1975, the Archbishop of Canterbury called an 'important' press conference at Lambeth Palace, his Tudor residence just
across the Thames from Westminster. The media arrived in force.
What Dr Donald Coggan had to tell them was that he and his brother-
archbishop at York were issuing a pastoral letter to be read from
Anglican pulpits on the following Sunday. Nothing very important
about that! But the reason for the ballyhoo and the strict instructions
for everyone to observe the archiepiscopal deadlines (including clergy)
was that this was a pastoral letter with a difference. It was an appeal to
the nation.

The appeal was couched in simple terms and at first sight was not
the sort of statement that anyone could reasonably take exception to.
Britain was drifting into chaos, said Dr Coggan. The tide of envy and
selfishness had to be stemmed; 'each for himself and the devil take the
hindmost' leads to chaos. Materialism offered no real alternative;
moral and spiritual issues were at stake. The common belief that
individuals were powerless to stop the drift was a lie, for the voice and
vote of each man and woman counted. The archbishop therefore
appealed to 'the great body of seriously-minded people' inside and
outside the churches to make themselves heard. And he suggested they
might do three things. They might consider the creed: 'God first—
Others second—Self last'. They might ask themselves the questions:
'What sort of society do we want?' and 'What sort of people do we
need to be in order to achieve it?' And they might write to him at
Lambeth Palace with their answers.

Twenty-four thousand people did write within four weeks of the
appeal. In the wake of a steep rise in postal charges, that was fairly
remarkable. But no one would now seriously suggest that Dr Coggan's
appeal proved to be a turning-point, or even a significant milestone at
which the nation paused in mid-career towards 'chaos' and gave
thought to its economic and social priorities. It would be splendid to
report that it had, for there could be no more appropriate event in that

case with which to open a book about the state of the churches. It would not really matter if the various denominations were being turned upside down, their members attempting desperately to keep abreast of the successive waves of liturgical, ecumenical, spiritual and organisational change that were hitting them—so long as the Church could speak with authority to the world about the world's problems. This after all is what Christians mean by 'mission' and effective mission has usually entailed religious upheaval. St Francis of Assisi, John Wesley, William Booth and many other saints of the Church brought religious change in their wake as they expanded the frontiers of mission. Nearer our own time, Archbishop William Temple called the Malvern Conference in 1941 to try to find a better answer for postwar Britain than the capitalism of the thirties, but implicit in that search was the Church's desire to put its own house in order.

Archbishop Coggan's appeal was the first of its kind since Temple's and he had advantages denied to his predecessor—a fat, peacetime press and television too. But it is doubtful if Dr Coggan's appeal will merit even the footnote in the history books which Temple achieved, at a time when there was certainly no shortage of world news. So why begin this anatomy of the contemporary churches with what appears to be a non-event? First, because the perspective of this book is the present and, although there may have been other recent church events which are destined to have a greater long-term impact, none of them attracted the immediate attention and debate of Dr Coggan's appeal. Secondly, it was an event which has proved to be unusually rich in clues to what the churches and their members are thinking, not just about their attitudes to national issues but indeed about the justification for their very existence. And, thirdly, where else could we begin a book about the churches than with some such attempt to relate their life to the non-Christian world outside? The popular demand that the churches should be 'relevant' is now endorsed by the theologians, and by no means only the radicals. As one of Britain's foremost Roman Catholic thinkers, Bishop Christopher Butler, has written: 'the Church is necessarily outward-looking, not primarily introspective and conservative, but primarily an indomitable adventurer into new fields. What else could she be, since she is, as St Augustine taught us, the incorporation of Christian love or charity.' (*Searchings*, 1975.) Perhaps one reason why Dr Coggan failed to stir the nation was that he (not necessarily as a person but because of his office) could not be an indomitable adventurer.

The archbishop admitted that his was only a modest initiative. He had set out, he said, not to launch a campaign but 'to initiate a debate at a deeper level than is common about what our country needs in order to get on its feet.' It was better to ask questions, therefore, than to produce authoritative answers, better to give the individual some confidence in his own contribution to the debate than to launch into a critique of ill-defined social forces. For many people, clearly the archbishop had pitched his appeal about right. He saw the letters he received (ultimately over 27,000) as 'encouragement for the Church's continuing entry into the socio-political arena, provided that entry is seen not to be aligned with any one sector of society and not to be to the detriment of the Church's primary task of worship and Christian proclamation, but rather as an outcome of it.' As a newcomer to a position of national leadership, for he had been enthroned at Canterbury only nine months before, Dr Coggan was made aware of the special restrictions under which leadership and authority laboured in the mid-seventies, particularly in the aftermath of two general elections in a single year. People desired a firm lead, but they did not trust those who offered simple answers to problems that everyone knew to be complex. And perhaps this is where Dr Coggan had begun to fail. He was only asking questions, but his critics detected behind the questions what they took to be a simplistic view of the national predicament and of the Church's proper response to it. The time was past when a church leader could say, like Pope John: 'some people always want to complicate simple matters; I wish to simplify complicated matters.'

Where for example was the 'chaos' into which the archbishop alleged that Britain was drifting? Was it to be found in Britain's economic situation, which in some important respects, like inflation, had begun to improve, although it is true that unemployment was on the increase? Was there 'chaos' in the social and political divisions of Britain? Here too there had been some improvement, for confrontation between the Government and the trades unions had been replaced by something called the 'social contract'. Or was the archbishop referring to some more diffuse malaise, perhaps associated with his reference to materialism? On this, some of the archbishop's critics pointed out that materialism could be another name for the redistribution of the affluence of the few among the many, and perhaps the Church should be cautious about criticising this since it had not been conspicuous in the past in its concern about concentrations of wealth. A leading article in the *Daily Telegraph*, a paper not normally hostile to the Anglican leadership, summed up these doubts about the appeal to the nation. It pointed out 'with respect' that it was an over-simplification to suggest that the present situation in Britain could be explained in terms of the moral and spiritual decline of the nation. 'Of course,' it went on, with a nice sense of irony, 'if all workers and managers were devout Christians, our industrial relations, presumably, would be better than they are, and this would be a real gain—to put it mildly. Yet this would be crying for the moon.' The Church however cannot speak with any special authority on the economic problems of the nation and nor should it bother—'it should leave to Caesar the things that are his.'

It was an unusually critical comment; the media were on the whole well disposed towards Dr Coggan's initiative. Indeed, the archbishop may have delivered himself too blithely into the hands of the media, particularly the BBC, which gave him almost constant exposure in the week following the appeal. And perhaps the deliverance went further back. It was reported that the archbishop had been told by his advisers in the media that if he wished to repeat the 'Call to the North' (which he had launched as Archbishop of York) on a national scale, then he should do it in the year of his enthronement, rather than later. Lack of consultation with other churchmen was one result of that advice.

So was there in fact a national moral crisis? An interesting indica-tion of the Christian answer to that question was provided, in the week following the archbishop's appeal, by a straw poll carried out among delegates to the annual assembly of the British Council of Churches. 'The picture is of insecurity and anxiety verging on fear, disillusionment and tiredness bordering on hopelessness, perplexity and bewilderment leading to a sense of powerlessness,' said the survey. And it seemed to bear out Dr Coggan's basic thesis that the nation was in chaos. 'The disillusionment, at least among older people, seemed frequently to be a deep disappointment at the apparent failure of their earlier idealisms and hopes in social reforms—the ills of affluence and its fragility, the elusiveness of social justice or the threats to social order. For both young and old, it was expressed in a retreat from politics. The perplexity seemed to have come because everything now is so big and so complicated, with so much that is new, so much change and such an unmanageable glut of information.' And yet the survey did not reveal any significant support for the view that Britain's problems were due to materialism or, surprisingly, any great desire to return to 'Christian standards' of morality or to specifically 'Christian solutions'. The survey went on: 'there was some sense of improvement particularly in the view that many of our problems are at least in parts products of a new enrichment, notably the heightening of expectations and the enlargement of consciousness whereby we are richer in information and more conscious of the wider world.'

This then was no shocked Christian reaction to a 'drift into chaos', but the fumbling realisation of a new style of social change, bringing with it new problems of assessment for everyone, not only Christians. It was certainly not all black and white. And there was another and perhaps more fundamental questioning of the archbishop's underlying assumptions. It came from the Bishop of Southwark, Dr Mervyn Stockwood, a veteran radical on the episcopal bench. Using the somewhat surprising platform of the Communist daily, *Morning Star*, the bishop took his archbishop to task for neglecting to mention that 'a man's character be it good or bad is partly if not largely determined by his environment, by the social and economic circumstances in which he is placed'. It struck right at the basis of Dr Coggan's appeal which was built upon the premise of personal responsibility. For good measure, Dr Stockwood added that 'an economic system which is based on selfishness and greed and which leads to class divisions, injustice and unemployment, is bound to produce social chaos. It is this system, more than any other single factor, that is producing the evils that Dr Coggan so greatly deplores. If he is right in thinking that our country is heading for disaster let him draw the attention of the nation to the system that is largely responsible for it.'

It was the classic Christian Socialist retort to the archbishop's assertion of the old Evangelical ethic of personal responsibility for the society that people live in, and it put a great deal more substance into the debate than the original pastoral letter had done. Dr Coggan later admitted as much. But here was a major division within the Anglican leadership. It bore out the earlier reports, which had been strenuously denied, that the bench of bishops was split over the way in which the pastoral letter had been conceived and even the need for it at all. Thus one effect of the appeal to the nation was to reveal to all that the Church of England was in two opposed minds about its approach to national affairs. On the one hand, there was a traditional view, held particularly by Evangelicals but finding favour with many Catholics too, that the Church's primary task was to speak to the individual. As Dr Coggan wrote in a column in the *Guardian*, 'in the last resort it is the kind of people we are that is responsible for the kind of society we get.' On the other hand, there was a radical view that it was no longer worthwhile to appeal to the finer feelings of individuals, when they were so much the creatures of the social environment. This was not a new view, for the founding father of the 'social gospel' in America, William Rauschenbusch, had written before the First World War that 'an unChristian society makes good men do bad things; a Christian one makes bad men do good things'. So what should the Church do about society's problems? Should it go on trying to convert individuals or should it concentrate on converting society itself? Should it blame 'Them' for the ills in modern Britain, or 'Us'? It was one of the major divides within the churches, approximating in some ways, although not completely, to the left-right division within society itself.

So, despite the large personal mail which had arrived at Lambeth and at the archiepiscopal palace at Bishopsthorpe, York, the appeal to the nation was not an unqualified success. The nation itself did not agree that it was drifting into chaos, although just where it was going was not clear to many people. The essential point of divergence between the archbishops and their critics was that to the latter Britain's predicament was a secular one, and a complex one, deriving from many different economic and political causes. It was a highly cross-grained and essentially new situation, to which the application of old remedies like 'doing a good day's work' or paying more regard to family life, although helpful, could not be in any way conclusive. In any case, the link between national crisis and personal responsibility was widely rejected. This could hardly have been more evident than at the Lord Mayor's Banquet in the City of London later in the year when Dr Coggan, who had himself taken a recent salary cut, suggested that across-the-board, progressive cuts of five per cent or more for those earning over £6,000 a year might be used to help the homeless. His audience clapped politely, the newspapers duly reported it, but the suggestion fell on deaf ears. So the national debate 'at a deeper level than is common about what our country needs to get it on its feet' scarcely got off the ground. And of course one would not put the blame for this entirely on Dr Coggan, Dr Stuart Blanch of York, or their advisers.

Within the churches, however, the appeal did initiate widespread debate which still goes on with varying degrees of intensity. It can be seen in the large number of local groups—Roman Catholic and Free

Church as well as Anglican—who took up the archbishops' diagnosis and tested it against their own experience. It can also be seen in national exercises, like the two-year study on national affairs initiated by the British Council of Churches. In the light of the debate that had already taken place in the national press, particularly after Dr Stockwood's intervention, all of these study groups had more to get their teeth into than the original pastoral letter. Indeed the two archbishops, in an 'appendix' to the letter, had fed into the discussion a number of more specific topics, like unemployment, and the conflicting claims in society of law and order, of power and powerlessness and of ambition and integrity. But the agenda is not closed even yet. Nor could it be. For what all of these groups have been doing is enlarging their consciousness of themselves as Christians by posing questions drawn from the national situation, rather than the traditional questions drawn from the Bible, from theology or from personal experience. The appeal to the nation thus became an exercise in Christian re-education. It was also incidentally a safety valve through which a large number of churchpeople, clerical and lay, were able to release the pent-up feelings they had been harbouring for so long about their relevance in the modern world.

The reasons for this are not difficult to appreciate. In the mid-seventies, the churches as much as the political institutions of Britain were going through a leadership crisis. A few months after Dr Coggan's appeal, the death of Cardinal Heenan (who was genuinely and deeply mourned for his personal qualities) revealed the leadership crisis which had been building up beneath the surface of English Catholicism. The Vatican appeared to endorse this view by going outside the entire English and Welsh hierarchy to choose as Heenan's successor a little-known Yorkshire abbot, Dom Basil Hume. In the Church of England, the leadership crisis had been around for some time. It was often said that Lord Fisher—Dr Coggan's predecessor but one—was the worst thing that had befallen the Church in this century and even Lord Ramsey, though not at all an institutional churchman in the Fisher mould, was in early 1976 confessing the errors of his own leadership at Canterbury. And of course the problems of leadership ran right down the scale in all of the churches, and were one obvious reason for the demoralisation of many clergy. Materialism was also a Church problem, as the various denominations wrestled with the host of moral and practical difficulties created by inflation. And as for 'chaos', well there was certainly a confusing diversity of opinion and practice in a wide area of the churches' life—from their forms of worship and the motley state of ecumenical relations, to the variety of often contradictory teaching they were giving on moral and social issues and more fundamental ones, like the meaning of sin or of the Holy Trinity. The appeal to the nation came, therefore, at a time when Christians in Britain were as aware of the deep malaise within their own ranks as they were of that in the secular society. In many instances, the symptoms were the same.

This gives a new relevance to the famous dictum of the World Council of Churches, that 'the world provides the agenda for the Church'. It has become the motto of a growing number of Christians who now pursue their religion in secular activities like politics, social work or mass communications. They do so in the belief that Christ is calling them out of the safety of institutional religion to discover him afresh in non-religious situations and among religionless people. Dietrich Bonhoeffer, the German pastor who coined the phrase 'religionless Christianity', pointed out that the Greek word for Church, *Ekklesia*, meant 'those who are called forth'. This is one interpretation of the World Council's dictum and it is a heartening one: the picture is of Christians as confident and spiritually well-equipped people who are ready and able to seize the challenges thrown up by a spiritually confused world. But, of course, that is only half of the story. The Church is in many ways as confused about its basic values and as compromised over them as the world is, often more so. It discovers this as soon as it attempts to embrace some major cause in the world. No sooner do its bolder members take up the challenge of racism, for example, than they are forced to tackle the racism within their own ranks. No sooner do they set out to change the less acceptable faces of capitalism than they find them, as bold as brass, leering out from the finance and investment committees of institutional religion. They begin to look for the deeper causes of social division and they come up against the class question, which is a crucial one for the churches themselves. The world may provide the agenda for the churches, but it is also constantly setting the examination papers on which the modern churches are forced to test themselves.

This is not wholly a bad thing. It does, to be sure, often lead to an introverted form of Christianity, to a preoccupation with the need to carry through internal reforms before the Church can turn outwards again. Many people feel that this is essentially what has gone wrong with the efforts that have been made to heal Christian disunity and to bring up to date the liturgies, legal canons, constitutions of government and so on of the churches. This can be paralysing for mission and is an obvious symptom of the malaise that afflicts the churches in Britain today. And the conviction that the Church must first cast the mote out of its own eye before it can tackle the world's blindness also induces feelings of guilt. The guilty conscience of Western Christians is particularly evident in the way some of them have taken up the causes of racism and social injustice in the Third World. But how, some people ask, can the churches proclaim a gospel of freedom when they are weighed down with the burden of their own guilt? On the other hand, the days of self-confident Christian proclamation may be over, for the time being at least, and we may now be in an era where proclamation is possible only by example. Thus the churches' concern with setting their own house in order could in itself be an effective form of mission. It could be their best chance of becoming society's mentors when older habits of authority and leadership are unacceptable. Church spokesmen often complain that 'the world no longer listens to us'. It is true—the world does not listen—but it does watch and watch very critically. The space now given to church affairs by newspapers and particularly the new 'current affairs' approach to religion on television and radio are evidence of the world's scrutiny. So a new situation arises with the Church as a pattern for the world, its 'paradigm' as the theologians call it, rather than its schoolmaster. There are numerous instances of Christians in Britain already working on this assumption. There is the new emphasis on the Church as a 'caring community', which has led to a diversity of experiments in local community, many of them blessed by officialdom, some decidedly not. Another instance of the Church as society's pattern may be found in the stipendiary policies being pursued by the Church of England. It is proposed that all parish priests throughout the country should receive the same income and that differentials, arising from size of congregation, parish generosity (including the customary Easter offering) and extra earnings, should in time be ironed out. If successful—and there are obvious organisational and other difficulties to the scheme—it would be a far more valuable piece of Christian proclamation about incomes policy, than any number of sermons and pastoral letters on the subject.

This is an important development, but it cannot completely replace the Church's need to speak out, to retain a prophetic role. But the prophet must know what he is talking about and, when it comes to

Christian proclamation on national affairs, one is struck by the churches' lack of expertise. The appeal to the nation suffered greatly in this respect. Dr Coggan had no 'think-tank' of experts available to him either at Lambeth (where his personal staff consists of three chaplains and a press officer) or elsewhere in the Church. This is a strange state of affairs for, as the subsequent debate in the national press revealed, there is certainly no shortage of clergy or lay people who possess the extensive knowledge and experience to advise an archbishop about national problems. But they are not organised to do so. The nearest thing that the Church of England possesses to a 'think-tank' is the Board for Social Responsibility, but that body is stretched to the full in reviewing ethical-social issues like abortion, divorce, euthanasia and so on. Indeed, when the Board was required to provide a position paper for a General Synod debate on the state of the nation, it had to commission one from the chaplain to the Speaker of the House of Commons. Not a bad choice, as it turned out, but it was only one man's work. And this is not a peculiarly Anglican problem. The resources of the Methodist Church are as stretched as Anglican resources are. In the Roman Catholic Church, the Justice and Peace Commission now operating in many dioceses has neither the money nor even the authority to provide their bishops with clear advice on the national drift.

One church which does possess the machinery for national comment is the Church of Scotland. For the past fifty-seven years, the Kirk has had in its Church and Nation Committee, a standing body of expertise to comment on a wide range of national, economic and social questions. Some of these, like Third World poverty, North Sea oil, unemployment and devolution for Scotland, have appeared in many of the Committee's annual reports to the General Assembly (the Committee first reported on devolution in 1946). It is worth noting that the Committee has had to fight off a number of attempts to restrict its scope to those topics which directly affect Kirk life, but it has seldom had much difficulty in doing this. The reason why the Church of Scotland alone among the British churches should possess the machinery for full-dress national comment derives as much from the close identity of Church and nation north of the Border as from any deliberate denominational policy. The sense of remoteness from the centre of government in London and the common experience of unemployment and economic depression have given Scottish church-men a concern for national affairs which their English cousins clearly do not share. The English churches are either too close, both in geography and culture, to the ruling establishment of London to be able to put government into a critical perspective or, like the Roman Catholics, they fear that their intervention in national affairs might create divisions both among their own people and among outsiders. But it is essentially to the Church of England that other churches look for a national lead in the sort of comment the Kirk makes for Scotland. They feel that the Church of England, as the Established Church, ought to play a more vigorous role in the nation's life instead of using its state connection for largely internal benefits. This is a point made forcefully in a book by a United Reformed Church minister, Daniel Jenkins, which appeared at about the same time as the archbishops' appeal. 'When the wraps are taken off it, the state connection which, despite all they say to the contrary, most Anglicans cherish as the most important thing about their church, is a way of ensuring that the Church is always managed by people who are likely to be more loyal to English self-interest than to Christ, and to the traditional "ruling class" conception of that self-interest at that.' (*The British: Their Identity and Their Religion*, 1975.) It is an extreme statement, of course, but Daniel Jenkins feels that it has to be made in order to make Anglicans aware of their 'historical vocation' to act as a national church on behalf of all Christians in Britain.

Mention of the Scottish experience and of Free Church criticisms of the Anglican stance, brings us to a curious feature of the arch-bishops' appeal which was ill-reported at the time. As an appeal to the nation, it was narrowly English and Anglican in its base. As we have noted, many other Christians have in fact taken up Dr Coggan's challenge and it has been made the subject of action by the British Council of Churches. But the non-Anglican churches played little or no part in the planning of the appeal and, officially at least, they took a back seat in commending it to their people. There was clearly resentment in Free Church circles at the lack of prior consultation. In the Roman Catholic Church, it may have come as a relief that the bishops were not invited to take a more active, ecumenical role, for that could have set up divisive tensions. In the event, Cardinal Heenan supported the appeal with his prayers. But this lack of cooperation among church leaders, on what should have been a relatively easy matter for cooperation, is curious when one remembers that this is supposed to be the new age of Christian entente, the ecumenical age in which the churches of Britain are said to be closer than they have been for 400 years. It was made all the more curious by the fact that church leaders in Scotland, where ecumenical relations are far less advanced than in England, were able to cooperate in a national appeal. At exactly the same time as Dr Coggan's press conference, the leaders of the Church of Scotland, the Roman Catholic and Scottish Episcopal (Anglican) churches were putting before their members a detailed study and prayer programme about national affairs. The issues they covered were certainly comprehensive: unemployment, drinking, gambling, promiscuity, advertising, inflation, homelessness, Third World problems and the unrestrained power of some sections of business, the financial institutions and the trades unions. It had a typically Scottish sweep to it and made the Anglican appeal look vague by comparison. And as for the Englishness of the archbishops' appeal, it certainly seemed odd to some observers that an appeal to the nation omitted all mention of Northern Ireland. It bore out another of Daniel Jenkins's criticisms: 'many Anglicans still have to be made to see that they really do have a serious problem in their relations with other Christians, especially Christians within these islands.'

If we draw together all these lines of enquiry originating in the appeal to the nation and use them to construct a sort of montage of today's churches, the picture we get is rich in contrasts and contradictions. We cannot pretend that it is a definitive or comprehensive picture, but that is probably no longer possible anyway. The time is past when the churches could plausibly be regarded as uniform and easily comprehensible bodies—even the Roman Catholic Church which fitted that description more recently than the others has changed dramatically in the decade since the end of the Second Vatican Council. Indeed, it is now difficult to grasp just what constitutes the identity of a particular church, or even sometimes of Christian as distinct from non-Christian 'humanists'. One outstanding feature of our picture may offer some explanation for this. It is the decline in the churches' authority, both among their members and in society at large. The erosion of authority is by no means confined to the churches: it affects government, the police, the professions, especially teachers, as well as most parents. But authority is a matter of special concern to the churches, for they are ordered bodies, for whom democracy has seldom been congenial, and in any case they claim that their authority derives ultimately from Jesus Christ. We can see in our picture some of the ways in which authority has declined—the greater openness to ideas from outside the Christian tradition, the closer identity of Christians with the world's problems, the questioning of the older social and personal values proclaimed by the churches.

Another outstanding feature of our instant ecclesiastical montage is the new diversity of opinions and practice which now seems to be compatible with church membership. Everyone is not quite yet doing his own thing, but it is getting very near to it in some areas. And diversity means divisions. The old divisions of the churches ran along denominational lines or were between church parties, like Catholic and Evangelical which were a sort of hidden denominational lines. These dividing lines are still there. Although they are no longer the source of open discord and may now be widely recognised to be less doctrinal in substance, than social, cultural and ethnic, yet the denominational divisions have not been as easy to eradicate as some enthusiasts for church unity would have people believe. But the more significant divisions in the churches now cut across the denominational boundaries and are to be found within different churches. The divergent views of Dr Coggan and Dr Stockwood, at least as they were expressed in the debate on the pastoral letter, were one such fundamental division within the Church of England about its attitude towards the world. At roughly the same time, Christians in Britain were in open disagreement about many other issues of basic concern to them—Northern Ireland, aid to liberation groups in southern Africa, birth control and abortion law reform, homosexuality and other 'moral' questions, the ordination of women, ecumenical relations, doctrine and the liturgy. Not all of these forms of 'pluralism' are to be found in the same churches (there are few declared Catholic pro-abortionists, for example) and nor is Christian pluralism as representative as that in our secular society. But the recognition of the fact that the Church is now pluralist to an extent never known before has brought a new dimension to the life of the churches. How to contain that pluralism within communities that can still claim to have a common Christian identity is a major problem for today's Church leaders. It is one of the aspects of the debate about authority.

Many writers are tempted to formalise this diversity into a clear division of the Christian churches into two camps—progressive and traditionalist, perhaps, or Left and Right. But the picture of the churches that we have does not lend itself easily to that sort of interpretation. The modern Christian diversity is truly pluralistic. It does not follow party lines in Disraeli's description of parties as 'organised opinion', for this pluralism is essentially not a matter of organisation, but of motivation, even of temperament. If one has to split the Christian community in Britain into two, then the most satisfactory division is between those who find the present climate of change invigorating, and those who find it deeply perplexing and something to be resisted. The division is between those who see modern life as enriched by the wealth of new information and the enlargement of expectations and consciousness, as some respondents to the British Council of Churches' survey saw it, and those who experienced 'insecurity and anxiety verging on fear, disillusionment and tiredness bordering on hopelessness'. The Church, as much as society itself, is under continual assault from change. How it will react is, of course, dependent on the nature of the changes in question. But how should it prepare itself psychologically for this new environment of change? Should it set out to be 'an indomitable adventurer into new fields' as Bishop Butler put it? Or should it see its role as holding fast to the unchanging verities of life, as preserving and defending the old faith and the older moral values, come what may? There is no one modern answer and in fact it is not just a modern problem.

Churchmen were asking much the same questions in the 1840s, when the challenge of new scientific knowledge and of new philosophical alternatives to Christianity were beginning to be felt. In 1847, the West Country vicar and hymn-writer, Henry Lyte, gave one view: 'Change and decay in all around I see. O thou, who changest not, abide with me.' But two years earlier, John Henry Newman, in his *Essay on the Development of Christian Doctrine*, had given a very different answer: 'Here below to live is to change and to be perfect is to have changed often.' Newman was referring to the individual's pilgrimage, which in his case was to take him into areas which he could not have imagined in 1845. But today, it is not only the individual Christian who is the pilgrim: the Second Vatican Council sanctioned the idea of the 'pilgrim church'. And this is at the heart of the churches' present psychological difficulties, for pilgrimages can be strenuous and unsettling. In the past decade, the churches' pilgrimage has become identified with unceasing change, with constant reform and reappraisal of doctrines and attitudes. Many older churchpeople find this profoundly dispiriting and undoubtedly it is a major cause of disaffection from the institutional churches. However logical and well-intentioned specific church reforms may be, they often lead to a drop in the churches' influence and adherents.

2

The Drift from the Churches

One of the most notable changes in church life in Britain since the second world war has been the decline in regular churchgoing—the 'drift from the churches' as it is popularly and fairly accurately described. Although this has not been a uniform change between the different denominations, and it is certainly not the same for all parts of the United Kingdom or even between the towns and rural areas of southern England, it can be seen as a coherent and steady process now affecting all churches. This is amply borne out by the statistics. It is also a useful antidote to the periodic talk of 'crisis' in church circles which is associated with the fall-off in churchgoing. It is rather pointless to speak of a current crisis in relation to the decreasing proportion of the population who attend Anglican services, for example, when their decline has been progressing steadily for more than a century. In fact, the talk of crisis derives from something other than the statistical evidence. It arises partly from the fact that the new statistical awareness of the churches has provided fuel for the reformism of younger clergy and the masochism of some older men, and partly from the new problems that declining attendances have created for the maintenance of existing church buildings and traditional ministries. It is the effects of inflation as much as declining church attendances that have made the present situation one of crisis for the churches.

The reasons for the decline itself are many and complex, and anything but a brief, impressionistic look at them is beyond the scope of this book. Clearly, most of the reasons are the result of social change which is outside the control of the churches. There is migration into and out of the country. There is the continuing and relentless fragmentation of settled communities, especially those in rural areas, in the face of urbanisation and greater social and job mobility. Physical mobility is also a potent force. The family car has become a major rival to regular churchgoing, as has the television set. The churches long ago lost their monopoly over mass communications, whether from the pulpit or the parish door, as well as their monopoly over education, social care, a great deal of culture and even ethics. Whatever influence they still held in these fields thirty years ago has been considerably eroded since then. The confusion of their aims over religious education and religious broadcasting is evidence of this. Many of the traditional social functions of the churches have now been taken over by rival state and voluntary organisations and there has also been a growth of rival philosophies, both religious and secular, to challenge Christianity itself in Britain. But the Christian religion itself has changed, perhaps not in its essence (though that is open to argument) but certainly in its whole ethos and way of appealing to people; it is often said that the churches themselves have contributed as much as social change to the decline in their influence. We can expect to see some evidence of this in the statistics.

There are, however, obvious difficulties attached to any study of religion based on statistics. Some of the difficulties were well described by two of Britain's leading sociologists of religion during the sixties, which was the heyday of religious sociology. In *Religion in Secular Society*, Bryan Wilson acknowledged that the use of statistics for gaining a 'true' understanding of the place of religion in people's lives was both limited and controversial. King David had incurred the wrath of God for numbering the children of Israel and the counting of heads has seemed to many Christians to be a denial of the Holy Spirit. From any standpoint, statistics of churchgoing and even opinion polls about people's beliefs are an imperfect measure of what religion really means to them. But Dr Wilson maintained that the use of statistics was a useful index of what he called secularisation—'the process whereby religious thinking, practice and institutions lose social significance.' But, in *A Sociology of English Religion*, David Martin pointed out that the figures of religious activity need to be set in their demographic context and their meaning may derive more from that context than from the apparent precision of the figures themselves. This may seem an obvious point but it is one that is often overlooked by commentators on religious affairs. One cannot, for example, gain an accurate view of the Church of England's poor support in the major conurbations like London, Liverpool and Birmingham (or of the Roman Catholics' strength in these cities), unless one pays some attention to the incidence of foreign immigration. Nor can one understand the resilience of some smaller Protestant churches in certain parts of the country, unless one looks at the proportion of the local population which is over the age of 45. A 1975 Gallup Poll showed that, while 8 per cent of all their respondents claimed to be Free Church, in the age group 45–64 it was 9 per cent and for the over 65s it was 15 per cent.

Another difficulty concerns the different meanings that the churches attach to membership. In former times, both the Anglican and Roman Catholic churches held that membership was conferred by baptism, whether the person baptised was an adult or a six-week-old child being 'done' for traditional social reasons. At the other extreme, the Baptist Church requires a profession of faith before the sacramental immersion which signifies full church membership. In between are most other Free Churches, which practise infant baptism in a limited way and regard it (whatever the theological niceties) as only a form of qualified membership to be completed later by a mature decision. The traditional criteria of membership have lately been modified and there is keen theological debate in most churches about the meaning of Christian initiation. For all practical purposes, the Church of England now disregards its $27\frac{1}{2}$ million baptised 'members' and even its $9\frac{1}{2}$ million confirmed members and uses the more realistic figures of those who actually go to church, particularly for their Easter and Christmas communion. Yet this may be too restricted for, despite the effects of liturgical renewal, the Eucharist clearly does not signify Anglican membership in the same way that attendance at Mass fulfills the obligation of membership for Roman Catholics. In the Church of Scotland and the Free Churches, where the Holy Communion does not enjoy anything like the same frequency within regular worship, the communicant rolls can be quite misleading indicators of membership. On the one hand, they may include people who have not set foot within the church door in years and, on the other, they miss the substantial fringe of occasional or less committed or liturgically old-fashioned churchgoers. The pendulum is now swinging back and attention is again being given to the substantial number of people who from time to time swell the ranks of the congregations but hold back from committed, weekly attendance. The Methodist Church now places considerable emphasis on its 'Community Roll' of men, women and children with whom the Church is 'in touch'; in recent years, this has been growing and is now almost three times as large as the diminishing Methodist membership returns. And the small Episcopal Church in Scotland, which gives the Eucharist first place in its worship, now enumerates twice as many 'definitely attached'

adherents as it does communicants. So concepts of church membership are changing all the time and they vary considerably from one
church to another. This makes it very difficult to attempt any multi-
denominational assessment of the state of religion in Britain today.

However, it is still possible to take a broad look at what David
Martin called the religious constituency—'all those who when asked
their religion by pollster, army corporal or hospital attendant reply
Catholic, Church of England or whatever it may be.' Writing in 1966,
Professor Martin apportioned the religious constituency as follows:
Church of England—two-thirds of the English population (less if
Wales and Scotland were included); Free Church—one in ten of the
whole population and the same for Roman Catholics; Church of
Scotland, although the majority church in Scotland—less than one
in ten for the country as a whole; and the remaining proportion of less
than a tenth—shared by those who had no religious label, by Jews and
members of other non-Christian religions, by Eastern Orthodox and
by the smaller sects (like Pentecostalists, Jehovah's Witnesses, the
Brethren and so on). In the past ten years, on the evidence of opinion
polls and the various church yearbooks, there have been some significant changes in the apportionment of the religious constituency. The
Anglican share of the English population has fallen to about 59 per
cent and in Great Britain to just over half; the Roman Catholic share
is between 10 and 14 per cent for England and Wales and 16 per cent
for Scotland; the Free Church constituency has fallen to less than one
in twelve persons (8 per cent); the Church of Scotland, although
retaining a quarter of the church constituency north of the Border,
represents less than 5 per cent of the total population; while in the
remaining 30 per cent or so there have been significant increases
among those disclaiming any religious label and those who follow a
non-Christian religion (particularly, of course, Asian immigrants).

All of these figures exclude Northern Ireland, which is in fact the
only part of the United Kingdom where the religious constituency
can be assessed with accuracy. The censuses of the province, for
obvious political reasons, include a question about religious affiliation,
something which has happened only once in the rest of the kingdom
and that was in 1851. The 1971 census returns for Northern Ireland,
with 1961 percentages in brackets, were: Roman Catholics 31.4
(34.9); Presbyterians 26.1 (29); Church of Ireland 22 (24.2); Methodists 4.7 (5); other denominations 6.4 (5); and no religion stated 9.4
(1.9). The growth areas were marginally among the Baptists and the

Rev Ian Paisley's Free Presbyterians but, mainly, among those who disowned all religious labels, a group which also grew significantly in the Republic of Ireland in the same decade.

In order to gain a realistic picture of the effects of secularisation, one has to look behind the religious labels that people claim for themselves at the practices and returns of individual churches. We begin with the statistically best documented religious body in the country, the Church of England. During this century all of the Anglican indices have pointed downwards. In 1910, just under 69 in every hundred babies born in England received Anglican baptism, 43 out of every hundred adults were confirmed and just under 10 per cent made their Easter Communion. In 1973, baptisms were down to 47 per hundred, confirmations were under 20 per cent and Easter Communicants were less than 4 per cent. It looks a uniformly depressing pattern, but there have been interesting variations. Baptisms actually rose during the twenties and there was a temporary rally in Easter communicants during the sixties, as there was also in the number of men coming forward for ordination. In fact, only the numbers on the Church's electoral rolls have fallen without any respite, with a particularly steep fall of 21 per cent between 1970 and 1973, but this was largely due to the drastic pruning of the rolls when synodical government was introduced.

It is the geographical rather than the historical variations that are the most revealing. In the dioceses of Birmingham and Sheffield, only 25 people in every thousand were Anglican communicants at Easter 1973, but in the diocese of Carlisle the figure was 96 in every thousand and in Hereford 120. In the same year, baptisms in the diocese of Hereford were 726 per thousand (more than 50 per cent above the national average) while in London they were 252 per thousand (45 per cent below the average). So the decline in the influence of the Church of England, as measured by the use of its two major sacraments, is more of an urban phenomenon than a rural one, which is of course something that the wisest Anglicans have been saying for two hundred years, since the time of the Industrial Revolution. But it is not even as simple as that. In Sheffield, where Easter communicants were among the lowest in the country in 1973, baptisms were among the highest which, among other things, says a lot for the attachment of the South Yorkshire working class for the Church's traditional 'rites of passage'.

The Anglican decline has been matched in this century by a similar drop in the membership of the English Free Churches. This too has been widely recognised. It began much later than the Anglican decline, which was going on steadily throughout the nineteenth century although its effects were obscured by a rise in the birth-rate and the building of many new churches. Until 1910, however, the Non-conformist constituency was a major and growing force in both religious and political life in Britain. The 1851 census revealed that there were as many Nonconformists in church on a typical Sunday as there were Anglicans; and the parliament which was returned at the 1906 General Election had a higher proportion of non-Anglican members than any English parliament since the Civil War. But from 1910, all Nonconformist indices point downwards and in latter years the fall has been much steeper than for the Church of England. From 1910 to 1974, Methodist membership throughout Britain declined from 1,168,415 to 557,249, a drop of 52 per cent. Over the same period, Baptists declined from 400,000 to 187,066, a drop of 53 per cent. But Congregationalists in England and Wales declined from 456,613 in 1910 to 165,331 in 1971, a drop of 63 per cent. In the year following, the Congregationalists joined with the 59,000 members of the Presbyterian Church of England to form the United Reformed Church, but the 1975 membership of the URC was only 181,445. Even including the 20,000 or so Congregationalists who remain outside the Union, the URC figure represents a 10.4 per cent fall in membership within four years, which is hardly a good advertisement for the ecumenical movement. The only section of British Congregationalism to have maintained its former vigour is the Union of Welsh Independents.

But, as with the Church of England, it is the variations in the decline of Free Church membership which are as revealing as the decline itself. David Martin pointed out that from 1910 to 1966, the net losses of the Methodist Church had tended to run at 3,000 a year, with a sharp rise during 1940 to 1943, a respite from 1947 to 1957 and a sharp rise again from 1963 to 1965. He suggested that the decline in the birth rate during the late forties had had the effect of exaggerating the true loss for the early sixties by diminishing the inward flow of young people. This is even more the case in the seventies, when Methodism's membership losses have been running at some 14,000 a year, although the rate of decline is now falling. However, to offset this fall in membership the Methodist 'Community Rolls' of people the Church is 'in touch with' have been rising in the same period by some 15,500 a year. The biggest gains have been in the Midlands, South Yorkshire and Lancashire, but there have been notable losses on the Community Roll in London and Newcastle where the Church has also experienced a sharp drop in membership. In Wales, a traditional stronghold of Methodism, the Community Roll returns are poor, membership has fallen sharply and average Sunday chapel attendance as a proportion of membership is the lowest in Britain. But we are talking here about 'English' Methodism in Wales and not of the more nationalistic form of Methodism found in the Calvinist Methodist Church, which is really Presbyterian in ethos. What one can see in the statistics of the Methodist Church is not only a relentless fall in membership, which is partly accounted for by changes in the birth-rate and in the effects of migration in the major cities, but also a different form of religious adherence which puts less emphasis on regular, committed attendances and more on being in touch with the Church.

Similar factors are no doubt at work behind the depressing statistics of the Baptists. In 1967, the Baptist Union of Great Britain and Ireland received a report from its Ministry Commission which predicted that at the current rate of decline the Baptist Church would be well on the way to extinction by the year 2001—or at least back to its 1867 membership of under 100,000. The Commission hoped that the decline would soon begin to flatten out. But the contrary has happened and the downward curve has become steeper. The expected membership for 1974 of 200,000 was in fact 6 per cent lower at 187,066.

In the other major Protestant denomination—the Church of Scotland and its sister Presbyterian churches—a different picture emerges from the statistics. In place of the steady decline throughout this century which was noticeable in the Anglican and Free Churches, membership of all Presbyterian churches reached a peak within the last two decades. The Church of Scotland's record of 1,319,574 names on its communicants' rolls came in 1956, after which membership fell back by some 23 per cent to just over a million in 1975. Two years earlier, in 1954, the smaller United Free Church of Scotland reached its high point of 24,688, after which it experienced a rapid decline to its present membership of 15,000. For the Presbyterian Church of England the peak arrived in 1960, when it had 71,329 members, and for the Presbyterian Church in Ireland it came in 1966 with 103,182 members. These figures again reflect a combination of demographic and religious change. The Church of Scotland's membership returns for 1956, for example, may have been the Kirk's highest ever but they represented a smaller share of the Scottish population as a whole than in the twenties. The population of Scotland had gone on rising, partly on account of immigration, but the Scottish birth-rate had declined since the twenties. It was the post-Great War bulge that mainly swelled the Kirk rolls in the fifties. At the same time, one can see in the Presbyterian figures the survival of a more assiduous form of religious practice than in other Protestant churches. Thus, during 1974, more than 61 people in every hundred on the Church of Scotland's rolls made their communion at least once, compared with less than 55 per hundred of registered Methodists and only 18 out of every hundred confirmed Anglicans.

A major demographic factor which has contributed to the secularisation of religion in Britain has been migration. Immigration throughout this century has been one reason why the traditional Protestant churches have experienced a sharp decline in their support in the major conurbations, where in any case they had had a poor showing since the Industrial Revolution. But there is another side to the migration question. It is through emigration in the last century and this that the pattern of British church life has reproduced itself throughout the English-speaking world. It is as much the result of emigration as of missionary endeavour that Anglicanism, for example, has been transformed from a national church, based on a 400-year-old compromise between politics and religion, into a world-wide communion in which the Church of England is no longer the largest constituent.

The main beneficiary of immigration in Britain has been the Roman Catholic Church, drawing most strength from Ireland but also from Italy, Poland and other parts of Europe. The period of biggest Catholic immigration since the war was the fifties when the net average gain of Irish direct immigrants (that is excluding those who came by way of Northern Ireland) was 36,000 a year. Since then Irish immigration has fallen away sharply except for a brief resurgence in 1965–67, just before the Northern Ireland troubles and the onset of major unemployment difficulties in the British economy. The places where the Irish settled can be plotted from a map of the major Roman Catholic dioceses—from Liverpool through Birmingham, to Westminster and Southwark, with major outposts at Glasgow and Cardiff, and smaller ones in towns like Leeds, Northampton and Portsmouth.

On the east coast and in the south-west, Roman Catholics are still comparatively thin on the ground. The result of immigration can also be seen in the figures. In 1851, Roman Catholics in England and Wales accounted for some 5 per cent of the population, half of them Irish born; in 1911, the proportion had risen to between 6 and 7 per cent and, according to the Newman Demographic Survey, it rose to 10.7 per cent in 1951 and to 12.2 per cent in 1961. A. E. C. W. Spencer, who ran the Newman Survey until it was closed down by the hierarchy in 1964, estimated that by 1972 the Catholic share of the population of England and Wales had risen to almost 15 per cent ('Demography of Catholicism', *The Month*, April 1975). These figures do not tally with the official parish returns published in the *Catholic Directory*, but we shall return to the discrepancy later. On the basis of any figures, however, it is clear that the high point of Roman Catholic strength in England and Wales was the early sixties. Catholic marriages, which had represented 4.1 per cent of all marriages in 1908, rose to 12.76 per cent in 1961 and fell back to 9.5 per cent by 1972. Baptisms, as a percentage of all live births, were 7.7 in 1911, 16.1 in 1963 and down to less than 13 in 1972. Attendances at Mass on a typical Sunday in May reached their numerical peak in 1966, though as a percentage of the total Catholic population the peak year was 1962.

Apart from immigration, three other factors have helped to augment the Catholic population of Britain: mixed marriages, higher fertility and conversions. Mixed marriages have been one important means by which the largely immigrant growth of the Roman Catholic Church has extended its indigenous base in Britain and they have gone on rising, so that by the seventies mixed marriages accounted for about half of all marriages celebrated in Roman Catholic churches. The proportion would be higher if one included mixed marriages celebrated in non-Catholic churches and in Registrars' offices, but they do not count here for one cannot in these cases assume that the children will be brought up as Roman Catholics. This is still the canonical *quid pro quo* for a Catholic marrying a partner from 'outside the faith', although the promise about the children's religion is now required from the Catholic rather than the non-Catholic partner. Higher fertility among Roman Catholics, although the subject of extensive popular conjecture, has always been difficult to prove: first generation Irish immigrants may marry at a later age than their non-Catholic counterparts and many Catholics, who use birth control methods not sanctioned by the Church, may no longer wish to identify themselves as Catholics. The Royal Commission on Population in 1949 could find little evidence of higher fertility among Catholics than in the population at large. But from his researches, Anthony Spencer suggested that Catholic fertility was of the order of one and two-thirds higher than the population as a whole from 1914 to 1934, had fallen below one and a half by 1952 and was less than one and a third times higher by 1962, since when it has risen slightly.

The other important means by which the Roman Catholic Church has extended its indigenous base in Britain is through conversions. For more than a century after the re-establishment of the Catholic hierarchy in Britain in 1850, converts were an important qualitative and quantitative source of recruitment. The qualitative aspect, the roll-call of famous converts from the intellectual, professional and upper classes—from Newman and Manning to Lord Longford and Alec Guinness—figured prominently in Roman Catholic propaganda. It was for similar propaganda reasons that the Church published its annual tally of converts with a great fanfare of publicity. In 1959 the practice ceased and it was widely assumed that this change of policy was a sign of ecumenical friendliness, a foretaste of the spirit of Vatican II. In fact, 1959 was the peak year for converts (15,794) and there has been a steady fall ever since (the 1975 tally, buried away in the statistics of the *Catholic Directory*, was 5,253). Moreover, since 1959, the publication of figures about converts has come under strong criticism from both Roman Catholic statisticians and theologians. Did the totals, for example, include children and were they tallies of true converts—i.e. those who had no previous Christian allegiances and were therefore in the Vatican II sense converted to Christ—or were they simply transfers from other churches? Father John Coventry, SJ, who was lecturer in Christian Doctrine at Heythrop College, said that all the evidence about converts points overwhelmingly to their not being previously practising Christians. The decline in conversions since 1959 should not therefore be attributed to any thaw in ecumenical relations but to the falling off of interest in institutional religion which has affected all the churches. 'If the Roman Catholic Church is seen as the most institutional, it can expect to suffer most.' (*The Month*, March 1975).

The fall in conversions, along with the falling off in the use of the Church's sacraments, are evidence that secularisation is now affecting the Roman Catholic Church as it has been affecting the other churches for much longer. Further evidence of secularisation is to be found in the discovery of a problem, fairly new to Roman Catholics in Britain, that of 'leakage'. This is not just a question of the drop in attendance at Mass or the use of other sacraments, but of baptised Catholics who have cut themselves off from the Church's ministrations to such an extent that they are not even recognised as Catholics by the clergy. This is, of course, a controversial issue for it calls into question the Church's official estimates of its own flock. But there are, according to Father John Gaine, national secretary of the Secretariat of Non-believers, three distinct estimates of the Catholic population for England and Wales (*Young Adults Today and the Future of the Faith*). One is the figure in the Catholic Directory, based on parish priests' returns—four million or 8 per cent of the total population; the second is that indicated by opinion polls, of people who identify themselves as Catholics—six million or 10 per cent; and the third is Anthony Spencer's figure for all baptised Catholics, which he has taken from the baptismal records and extrapolated in accordance with normal life expectancy, plus conversions and migration—seven million or 14 per cent. On the basis of his figures, Anthony Spencer concluded that the Church was losing about a quarter of a million 'drop-outs' a year and by the end of 1971 about 2.6 million baptised Catholics had been alienated to the extent that they do not use the Church's offices, even at the crucial turning points in their family life like marriage, birth and death. 'The Catholic folklore that "once a Catholic, always a Catholic",' said Mr Spencer, 'that Catholics seldom totally abandoned their religious identity, even if they ceased going to Mass and did not carry out their Easter Duties, was substantially true of England and Wales in the late 1950s; it had altogether ceased to be true by the early 1970s.' (*The Month*, April 1975.) Spencer's methods and conclusions have been roundly challenged by other Roman Catholics but there is some corroboration for his view from another research source. Dr Michael Hornsby-Smith, of Surrey University, conducted a survey in twenty Roman Catholic secondary schools in South London (where children were selected largely on religious grounds) and found that disaffection with the Church and its worship had generally set in by the age of 13 or 14 and extended to almost half the children by the age of 15.

The decline in institutional religion has thus become an established feature of all the churches, although it is not the same for them all. Roman Catholics are still the most assiduous regular churchgoers (according to some polls, three times as assiduous as Anglicans) but it would seem that once a Roman Catholic abandons his religion to become a 'drop-out', the break is far more final than it is for the nominal Anglican. One has to see the decline in regular churchgoing and in church membership against the background of continued, but far less frequent, attendance by a considerable section of the population. Attendance at church twice or more on a Sunday is now out, except for choirboys and other front-of-the-house persons. But the figures for occasional churchgoing have been remarkably stable. In 1966, David Martin estimated that 15 per cent of the population would be in church at least once on a typical Sunday, 25 per cent would be there once a month and 45 per cent at least once a year. The figures for the mid-seventies (from an Opinion Research Centre poll for the BBC TV programme 'Anno Domini') were 14 per cent once a week, 21 per cent once a month and 47 per cent once a year. The respondents to this and similar religious polls may, of course, be exaggerating their appearances in church but, as David Martin pointed out, the fact that they should bother to exaggerate is in itself socially significant. Moreover, all polls about churchgoing indicate that religious factors, such as no longer believing in God, are put forward by only a small minority of non-churchgoers; the majority say they are either 'too busy' or 'you don't have to go to church to be religious'. Yet the fact remains that one in every two members of the population of Britain do appear in church at least once a year or at least wish to give the impression that they do. When one considers the enormity of the social and economic changes that have taken place in the past 25 years, including the recent spate of gloomy predictions about the impending rupture of the whole fabric of British civilisation, then the churchgoing figures are indeed remarkable.

Even so, the statistical evidence of the onward march of secularisation will seem far too negative to many Christians. They may well say, and they would be right, that statistics can be used to answer only the questions that are put to them. And even if church leaders in the past have used statistics about churchgoing as a justification for their own position, they are clearly not the be-all and end-all of religion in Britain today. Secularisation is a word coined by sociologists to describe something which is easily observed and measured by the outsider—the decline in the churches' social standing. It does not provide answers to other, more important questions like the place that religion plays in the everyday lives of people, or whether those who do not go to church derive any spiritual benefit from religious books or religious radio and television broadcasts. Nor can it tell us much about the continuing social and political influence of the churches, whether, for example, their work and study of housing, or family problems, or sexual ethics, or overseas aid has touched the lives of ordinary citizens who are not churchgoers. Secularisation is a very restricted concept which leaves out a great deal of life which is of the first importance to the churches. Moreover, from the Christian point of view, secularisation is sometimes seen as a positive blessing. Though it would be very difficult to quantify it, it could be argued that church-going for the minority who still do it is a more important activity than it was for the Victorian middle classes and their servants who went to church because it was the socially done thing. Secularisation has removed from religion all sorts of social, as well as superstitious and authoritarian connotations. Indeed, some theological writers have suggested that, far from being the modern incarnation of the anti-Christ, secularisation is the child of the Judaeo-Christian tradition for it has released men from the spiritual bondage of paganism and medievalism. This is not a line of argument that one would wish to take very far for, whatever the intellectual accommodation that some writers have made with secularisation, it is clear that this is not a trend that the churches would ever have chosen for themselves and it has often been a spiritually shattering experience.

Religion in Britain is at an interesting stage of transition. Institutional religion is everywhere losing its traditional hold over the population, but religious thought and activity as such is still remark-ably vigorous, very often outside the institutional framework. Despite the relentless decline in church-going, many people are still prepared to tell the opinion-pollsters that they believe in prayer and teach their children to pray. And the study of religious experience, or quasi-religious experience away from the context of orthodox Christian belief, has now become a minor growth industry in British universities. But the churches have not been completely written off, as they have been by the majority of the populations of Scandinavia, for example, or France. Certainly, there is no evidence of an upsurge of virulent atheism or anti-clericalism in Britain. As we shall see in a later chapter, the clergy are still regarded highly among comparable pro-fessional groups. Although 29 per cent of the population say they believe in a personal God (the ORC poll), as compared with 38 per cent in 1963 (Gallup), yet 47 per cent of the population claim that they still go to church at least once a year. Opinion polls going back to the fifties indicate that there is a sizeable proportion of churchgoers who cannot subscribe with complete certainty to many of the churches' traditional teachings about the existence of God, the efficacy of prayer or life after death. Few opinion polls venture into the even more problematical areas like the Trinity or the Virgin Birth, but there it would seem the doubters include many of the leading thinkers within the churches. Even if it does not completely bear out Alasdair MacIntyre's nice observation that 'the creed of the English is that there is no God and that it is wise to pray to him from time to time', yet it does show that agnosticism is no longer the exclusive domain of those outside the churches.

3

The Arrival
of Secular Christianity

Despite the far-reaching nature of the changes described in the last chapter, it can hardly be said that 'secularisation' is a word that is on every Christian's lips. It is too much of a tongue-twister (though not as bad as 'desacralisation', which we shall have to meet later). The concept behind the word also is difficult for most churchgoers to digest. Secularisation is a sociologists' word, describing a process which has a long history in British society. It is not the description of a sudden event as in some communist countries where secularisation has been introduced by government decree. Secularisation in Britain as defined by Bryan Wilson, is 'the process whereby religious thinking, practice and institutions lose social significance'. It is a social trend and it does not necessarily mean that the majority of people in the country have yet exchanged religion for irreligion, or theism for atheism. It is not really a question of the personal beliefs of individuals in supernatural things, but primarily of the social importance they attach to those beliefs. In other words, the often-heard remark that 'you don't have to go to church to be a Christian' fits in very well with the sociologists' definition of secularisation. Or to put it another way, in the words of David Edwards, 'secularisation occurs when supernatural religion becomes private, optional and problematical.' As most churchgoers are neither sociologists nor social historians, they tend to ignore the disquieting implications of this vast process and concentrate instead on their own private religion. They are well aware of the 'optional' nature of their own commitment to religion and this may give them a sense of exclusiveness or conversely a feeling of insecurity among their secular friends and neighbours.

Thus it is difficult for the average churchgoer to comprehend secularisation at work. It is easier to attribute the decline in public religion to other causes. The middle-class population of the parish has moved away to the outer suburbs. The present minister or priest is less dynamic or approachable than his predecessor. As one West

Country vicar put it: 'if the people no longer come to church, then there is something wrong either with Christianity or with me.' That sort of 'either/or' attitude has led to many surrendered vocations. On the other hand, to admit that people no longer come to church because they are caught up in a relentless and perhaps inevitable historical process may seem to many Christians to be almost blasphemous. How can one accept such a view of society without denying the power of the Holy Spirit at work in the churches? That is certainly a problem and one which the sociologists tend to pass across to the theologians and most modern theologians prefer not to answer. Yet the lack of a realistic appraisal of secularisation in British society has led to some rather credulous attempts to identify the work of the Holy Spirit in the churches since the end of the war. In the fifties, it was widely proclaimed by church leaders that the experience of the Coronation Service would turn the nation back to the worship of God. In the fifties and sixties similar faith was pinned in large-scale evangelistic enterprises, like the Billy Graham crusades. The Church of England had published a report on evangelism in 1945 with the ambitious title 'Towards the Conversion of England'. More recently, hopes of turning back the tide of secularisation have been fixed on one or other of the 'movements' at work in the churches—the charismatic movement, the liturgical movement and the ecumenical movement. The latter after all takes as its motto the prayer of Jesus 'that they may be one so that the world will believe'. But if the realism of the seventies has shown anything it is that faith in any panacea for the ills of secularisation is misplaced. What all these post-war developments, these manifestations of a new 'spirit' in the churches, have done is to deepen the inner life of the Christian community in Britain and not to win back any of the lost territories ceded to the secular world over the last century. When Billy Graham last came to Britain in 1973, he came on what his supporters called a 'Spree' (SPiritual RE-Emphasis), a sort of topping up of youthful evangelical spirituality and not a 'campaign' or 'crusade' to convert the pagans he had given so much attention to in the swinging sixties.

The realisation is coming home to more and more Christians that secularisation is not a post-war phenomenon, or a fifties or sixties phenomenon, but a continuing and irresistible process, and this has confirmed the view of an increasing body of churchpeople who actually welcome secularisation as a purification of the Christian faith. If it means that Christian belief and commitment are becoming optional for the majority, then it is becoming all the more important that those who call themselves Christians should make a deliberate and open commitment. The activities of the churches should be differentiated from what goes on in the secular world. The churches ought to cease their pandering to the sentimental, pseudo-religious desires of the mass of the population, for example by baptising the children of unbelievers. They should stop spreading the churches' scarce talents thinly throughout society, for example by espousing wordly good causes which do not necessarily advance 'God's kingdom and his righteousness'. They should aim at quality and depth, not at quantity and breadth. They should concentrate on the needs of the faithful flock, on the spirituality of the churches' 'members'. It is interesting to note, however, that among Anglicans and Roman Catholics, the idea that people can qualify for membership of the church by attending so many services a year or by performing some other obligation, as distinct from being made members by baptism, is a very recent one.

But these sketches of a few Christian responses to secularisation in society are only nibbling at the edges of the problem. It is obvious to anyone with even the most casual acquaintance with the life of the churches that the inroads of secularisation have gone much deeper than the social standing of the churches and the number of their adherents. The inner life of Christianity has been affected, religion itself has not been immune from secularisation. Here we need, if not a new definition of the sort of changes we are talking about, then at least a few examples. For a start, we can take a familiar figure, the 'with it' priest or minister. He puts a coffee bar at the back of his church and the inevitable guitar group out in front, and in the pulpit there may be a variety of showbiz antics going on, from a ventriloquist's dummy to older and less rivetting visual aids. He is a recognisable figure in all the British churches today, but are gimmickry and up-to-date techniques of communication what is meant by the secularisation of religion? Or take three examples from our modern preoccupation with air travel. The present Pope is the first Roman pontiff to have flown in an aeroplane, which he has now done many times always to press comment, but the Archbishop of Canterbury flew to Nairobi for the World Council of Churches' Assembly in 1975 and drew comment only because he travelled first-class and wore a tweed suit and a tie. Another Anglican bishop, however, Dr Hugh Montefiore of Kingston-upon-Thames, flew to Washington to argue the environmental case against the Concorde airliner, and there he used an odd mixture of language. The noise of Concorde, he said, is not like hell for hell goes on forever, but 'more like a secular form of purgatory'. Are these examples of religion being made secular? Or we could take one of the more outrageous examples of the churches' entanglement with contemporary values. The London bookmakers, Ladbrokes, accepted bets on the successors to both Dr Ramsey as Archbishop of Canterbury and Cardinal Heenan as Archbishop of Westminster: about £30,000 was wagered on the Anglican race but only £24,000 on the Roman one, which may surprise some Protestant opponents of betting. Among the more typical Christian experiences of today which one might label 'secularisation' is the fact that almost all Christians in Britain (except for a few unregenerate Anglo-Catholics and Orthodox) can now see and hear everything that takes place during the celebration of the Eucharist, that is if they care to keep their eyes and ears open. The secret mystery of the mass is no longer secret. On another level, secularisation appears to mean that there is no longer a specifically Christian view of life and very little to differentiate the life style of the believer from the good agnostic. Indeed both tend to claim that they are 'humanists'. Moreover, there appears to be no limit now to the questioning of some of the basic tenets of Christian religion—of the Resurrection and Virgin Birth, for example, or of the authority of the Pope or of Scripture, even of the existence of God himself, in any sense that God has been understood in the past. And most of this questioning is being pursued by reputable clergy and theologians whom no one is seriously trying to cast out of the churches as heretics.

If all of these examples are true illustrations of what secularisation has done to the inner life of the churches, then clearly this is a mighty revolution. One might well ask, and many Christians frequently do, where it will all end. Can the churches emerge from this climate of secular change in anything like their present recognisable form, or will they in the end be subsumed in the secularising process which makes all things conform to its worldly, non-supernatural view of existence? To understand better the scope of the changes we are talking about, we ought to make our analysis more systematic than it has been so far.

The religious and the secular views of life are usually seen as opposed to each other, as mutually exclusive and rival attitudes to living. This was the distinction that was implicit in the last chapter, but while it was an adequate one in discussing the outsiders' attitude to religion, it clearly will not do here. If secularisation means the denial of the supernatural—or even giving it a lesser significance as something 'private, optional and problematical'—then the radical theologians who talk about the secularisation of Christianity are traitors to their own cause. This is even more the case if we identify the secular with atheism, as did some of the nineteenth century exponents of the secular view, like Charles Bradlaugh. The National Secular Society, which Bradlaugh founded in 1866, still exists in North London from where its secretary sends argumentative letters to the religious newspapers. But the word 'secular' originally meant 'belonging to its own age' and what the radical theologians have been trying to do is to make the Christian religion into something which belongs to this present age, which can speak to modern man in his own language. In particular, these theologians see a dominant characteristic of this present age to be its material and intellectual self-sufficiency, its rejection of any influences and explanations which are outside our ability to understand or verify them by scientific enquiry or just plain modern common sense. 'Religion' too is a word that reveals more than one layer of meaning. It refers not only to belief in a supernatural being, whether or not it is called 'God', but to a whole gamut of other, subsidiary attitudes and practices. For the Christian, religion will certainly mean trying to live according to God's commandments, however these commandments are understood, and it will mean a life 'in communion' with Christians of similar belief, whether that is the communion of Eucharistic worship, of hymn-singing, of speaking with tongues, or just discussion groups. But religion may also mean all sorts of other things such as a certain attitude towards prayer and piety, a whole culture of worship and life styles. Many of these subsidiary connotations of the Christian religion are now recognised to have been added to Christianity in later ages than the central events described in the Gospels. These historical accretions that Christianity has picked up over two thousand years are seen by the radical theologians as possible candidates for the sort of reassessment which secularisation implies. Since many of these theologians are also engaged in ecumenical dialogue with other Christians, they have an additional motive for discovering an essential Gospel, free from later cultural accretions. But whether motivated by a desire for unity or by a desire to bridge the yawning chasm of understanding between the churches and the secular world, the work of the radical theologians has a common feature. It is to break down some of the exclusiveness of traditional Christianity, to remove the barriers that have separated Christian from Christian and now separate Christian from non-Christian.

All of this can be a very dangerous activity. Once you begin peeling the onion, how do you know when to stop? Can you be sure that you are not tearing into the heart of religion itself? And what may seem inessential and marginal for some people, particularly scholarly people, may be very essential to others. For many ordinary Christians, there may be little left of their religion once the theologians have begun to cast doubts on prayer to the saints, on belief in the infallibility of scripture or the Pope and on the importance of personal salvation. There are church leaders who for their own reasons will use the fears of simple believers to try to silence the theological radicals. 'It is a form of pastoral sadism to disturb simple faith,' wrote Cardinal Heenan in *Council and Clergy* about the controversies following Vatican II. 'Those close to God are untroubled by the winds of academic controversy.' The Cardinal had a point, for there is a tendency in theological controversy to overlook the importance of individual faith and even to blur the difference between the faith of the believer and the lack of it by the agnostic.

So, the radical theologians are exploring two complementary ways in which the Christian religion might be reinterpreted or rediscovered. They are trying to reinterpret it in terms which have meaning for the present age, and they are trying to rediscover its essential, authentic core once the later additions have been peeled away—or at least recognised to be of lesser significance. There are three major aspects of the Christian religion where this process of reinterpretation and rediscovery has produced results, where in other words Christianity itself is being secularised. They are the concepts of 'authority' and of 'sacredness', which Christians share with the followers of most other world religions, and the specifically Christian emphasis on 'individual salvation'. Dietrich Bonhoeffer regarded this last to be so central to the Christian understanding of religion that he described his attempt to rediscover a Gospel without it as 'religionless Christianity'. What a troublesome phrase that has been since it first gained currency in Britain during the fifties!

As we noted in Chapter 1, authority is not a notion which goes down at all well in modern times. As Edward Heath observed, when as Prime Minister he was addressing the General Assembly of the Church of Scotland in 1973: 'we live in a world in which authority is uniquely exposed to scrutiny and criticism'. Authority in this century has too many associations of repression and the right to expect orders to be obeyed without questions, even when they are blatantly unjust or inhumane orders. Authority is out in the modern world but there may still be room for leadership. 'The task of leadership,' said Mr Heath, 'is not to utter rhetoric or mouth high-sounding but empty phrases . . . it is to help people to understand what the difficulties are and how the problems can be solved.' The politician can get round the difficulty by substituting one term for another, but it is not so easy for the Christian to do so. Authority for him is ultimately the authority of God and without that there is no faith. But how can he express the authority of God in practical terms, when authority itself is an unacceptable idea? It is a problem that runs right through the Christian experience from top to bottom as Professor James Barr of Manchester University pointed out in *The Bible and the Modern World*:

> The general crisis of authority affects not only the Bible but also the authority of the church, bishops, Popes and other church leaders, of constitutions, legal systems and governments, of teachers and professors, and last but not least of parents and the older genera-tion, as members of it are painfully aware.

For the Christian, the divine authority has been recognised as coming down to men either through the Bible or through the Church and tradition. Both of these areas of authority have been strongly under attack in the last decade and debates about biblical or church authority have occupied a great deal of the attention of theologians and church leaders. But there has been a more dramatic, perhaps a more funda-mental, retreat from one traditional Christian idea of authority and this has received less attention than it should have done. The reason may well be that the change has been so universal, especially in a sophisticated society like Britain, that it is not really worth arguing about. It is the part that religion plays in moral behaviour. Until a generation or so ago, it was assumed that all reliable moral decisions were based upon religion and the only vocal dissent from this view came from eccentric people who called themselves Freethinkers. The usual argument was that God had implanted in men their knowledge of right and wrong, and right behaviour or goodness was ultimately a matter of following the unchanging laws that God had ordained for all mankind—for example, in the Ten Commandments or in Jesus's summary of the Judaic Law or in something much wider called 'the natural law'. It followed that people who left the religious dimension out of their moral decisions and behaviour tended automatically towards sin and immorality. Thus, Matthew Arnold described God as 'a power not ourselves that makes for righteousness'. The idea that man could still be righteous while rejecting all supernatural authority over his conduct—as Bertrand Russell did when he proclaimed that the agnostic will 'reject all authority' and 'think out questions of conscience for himself'—was regarded as not only shocking nonsense but potentially damaging to the whole basis of civilised society. There are still people who think in these terms. 'Without religion there can be no morality,' said the High Court judge, Lord Denning, 'and without morality there can be no law.' But in the last fifteen years, Lord Denning's view has become the minority attitude in Britain. The majority view has become that of thinkers like Russell who said that 'goodness is logically independent of God's decrees', that man must make up his own mind about his behaviour and that, if he follows the precepts of the Bible or the Church, he is not making a mature moral decision but following orders like a child. It is worth noting that the generally accepted moral priorities of today are much nearer to Bertrand Russell's priorities—for example, in ranking truth-fulness, intellectual integrity and public honesty as more important than sexual purity or fidelity—than those of church leaders before the last war. 'To this day,' said Russell in 1930, 'conventional Christians think an adulterer more wicked than a politician who takes bribes, although the latter probably does a thousand times as much harm.' In this post-Watergate, post-Poulson age one can only blink at his words in astonishment.

For a short while in the sixties, this dramatic change in public attitudes was picked up by the theologians, particularly by Cambridge theologians like Bishop John Robinson and the contributors to the avant-garde work, *Objections to Christian Belief* (1963), and labelled the New Morality. Newspaper columnists commented upon it in a knowing manner and said it was the result of young people maturing earlier and of older people, particularly women, becoming emanci-pated. The word 'permissive' became all the rage, but there was more to it than that. In the same period, sociologist Bryan Wilson could say (without much fear of contradiction) that while people still looked for the approval of others in their moral behaviour, 'the strong subsidiary motivation of "serving God", "doing what is right in the sight of God" and perhaps of winning God's approval or at least conforming to ideals which, however unscrutable he might be, God demanded and which he might not entirely ignore at the day of judgement—all this has gone.' We in the nineteen-seventies may feel that the New Morality of a decade ago was a swindle and that emancipation and permissiveness have not added one jot to the sum total of human happiness. But there is no sign that most western Christians are willing again to sit under the moral direction of religious authority. As evidence of that one can note the criticisms from all quarters that poured down upon the Vatican's condemnation in early 1976 of masturbation, pre-marital sex and homosexuality as being contrary to the 'natural law' ('every genital act must be within the framework of marriage'). The Vatican statement quite ignored much modern Christian thinking about sex as self-fulfillment within relationships where there is no exploitation of one person by another. It was moreover a futile attempt to reassert authority in an area where it is no longer recognised.

Unlike authority over moral conduct, the authority of the Bible over Christian faith and thought has not been abandoned overnight. The Bible is after all one of the main, if not *the* main, arbiter of the Christian's religion. Even for Roman Catholics, who rely upon the primacy of tradition as embodied in the Pope and the Church, the Bible is still seen as a 'reliable witness' to the truth. Indeed, Roman Catholics have been rediscovering the Bible since the Second Vatican Council. But in other churches over this same period, something significant though not dramatic has been happening to the status and influence of the Bible. It has begun to take second place to other guides to modern life, to works of sociology, psychology, politics and even theology. In *The Bible in the Modern World*, Professor Barr observes that this change is all the more surprising because in the years following the war 'the importance attached to the Bible in Christian faith and thought was very high, perhaps as high as it had been for a century or more'. The Bible was seen as the unifying factor between the disunited churches and it was quoted often in the newly-established World Council of Churches, as it was for perhaps similar reasons at Vatican II. The theology of the post-war period emphasised the Bible strongly, notably the 'neo-orthodox' theology of Karl Barth which had a particular appeal in the Church of Scotland. Moreover, a broad consensus seemed to have been reached in the long and bitter debates over 'historical criticism', the attempt to discover whether the various biblical texts were written by the people to whom they have been traditionally attributed and to see whether they contained historical reporting, myths or theological statements. Even the fundamentalists, who took the strongest exception to these critical methods, appeared to have reached a position where they were prepared to accept some parts of the Bible as symbolic, although not of course untrue. In the post-war period, most leaders of Christian opinion seemed to agree that, however you approached it, the Bible taken as a whole was central to the Christian faith. It was the high point of Biblical authority. But, as Professor Barr points out, in the last decade all of the old problems about Biblical authority—and many more—have reappeared. A World Council of Churches study on the subject prepared for a seminar at Louvain in 1971, said that 'authority is no longer conceded *a priori*, but is accepted only where it actually proves itself as such. Accordingly, it has become increasingly difficult to assert biblical authority in a general way.' That is the scholars' view but Professor Barr sees increasing evidence of Christians, other than scholars, becoming impatient with the idea that the Bible is the authority to which they should look:

It is amongst the younger people that uncertainties about the Bible are most felt: felt among the younger clergy, and often among the most progressive members of it; and, as with many other things today, felt among the students. It is asked: Why so much study of the Bible? Can it have much relevance for our needs today? Would not a social study of contemporary society, a discussion of present philosophical trends, a course in psychology, offer us more?

There can be little doubt that Professor Barr is describing a trend which is gaining ground in the churches in Britain. His experience is that of a Presbyterian, but if anything the trend is more pronounced in the Anglican and Roman Catholic churches, despite the reawakening of biblical study among the latter's theologians. Both churches are using the Bible less and less in their everyday affairs. The liturgical revolution has not helped here. The biblical readings that take place during the liturgy of the Eucharist are not intended to teach people what the Bible says: they are part of the ritual and usually accompanied by somebody moving around or people standing up and sitting down. And the short sermon or homily during the liturgy is clearly no place for preaching upon a biblical text. Indeed, as Professor Barr points out, it is becoming common for sermons to be preached without a text or on a phrase drawn from 'Kafka, or Camus, or D.H.Lawrence, or a newspaper article'. The theologians and young clergy who favour this sort of sermon are the people to whom the churches of the future will look for their leaders.

Yet this is not the whole story and, in a parenthesis to our main argument about authority, we might usefully note what has been happening to the Bible in modern Britain. The first thing that strikes the interested inquirer is that, whatever scholars like Professor Barr may say, the Bible is far from losing its popularity. Among Evangelicals, their has been a revival of the Bible's spiritual authority and this applies especially to those influenced by the 'charismatic movement' which has been accompanied by a resurgence of fundamentalism. At the same time, Roman Catholics, encouraged by their bishops and their theologians, are using and studying the Bible in greater numbers than ever. Bibles or extracts from the New Testament are now distributed free by such groups as the Salvation Army, 'Wales for Christ' and some churches hand out the Bible at the church door along with prayer and hymn books. The Bible itself is still a best-seller for the few publishers which specialise in Scripture, although it remains true that most Bibles as such are bought as presentation copies for brides and confirmation candidates and only 20 per cent of sales are believed to be for the use of the purchaser. At least this was the case until the paperback revolution affected Bible-publishing and this has produced a wide variety of versions and translations, not all of which meet with the approval of church people. On the one hand, there are the scholarly versions, like the *New English Bible* which, despite the fanfare with which it was launched in the sixties, has failed to become a popular work: only the *Jerusalem Bible*, the product of French Dominican research, has really become a popular success in this field. On the other hand there are the versions which aim not at scholarly precision but at providing a 'good read'. One of these, *The Good News Bible*, in colloquial modern English, was introduced into Britain in the mid-sixties in its New Testament version, *Good News for Modern Man*, and sold about a million copies a year for the British and Foreign Bible Society. Now the full version is available with the same text, but two different paperback covers—blue for Protestants and red, with an 'Imprimatur', for Catholics. The other Bible in this category is not really the Bible as such, but a paraphrase of it. This is *The Living Bible*, the work of an American Baptist minister who first paraphrased the Pauline epistles for the benefit of his ten children and was encouraged by Billy Graham to do the rest of the 66 books. The overall trend is for the Bible to become directly available to people and especially young people, without the intervention of church teaching and theology. The increased Bible use among the 16–25 year olds has not, for example, led to any notable increased demand for the sort of Bible notes produced by the Scripture Union or the Bible Reading Fellowship whose sales in the United Kingdom have not at all matched their expansion overseas. Significantly though, the Scripture Union now estimates that about four per cent of its scripture notes are used by Roman Catholics, compared with an insignificant proportion five years ago, and the Bible Reading Fellowship is now producing a special issue of its notes for Roman Catholics in conjunction with the Catholic Truth Society.

In discussing the authority of the Bible, there is one significant word that has been left out. It is Rudolf Bultmann's famous word, 'demythologization'. He used it to describe the rediscovery of an essential Gospel, valid for all men in all ages, after stripping away such temporal 'myths' as Jesus's assumption that men lived in a three-tier universe of heaven, earth and hell. However, Bultmann's insights have had little influence on British attitudes towards the Bible as such —unlike the Germans, we do not take myths that seriously. 'Demythologization' has been important here mainly as one of the motley ingredients of the new thinking about religion as a whole, associated with John Robinson's *Honest to God*.

But there are other myths besides the biblical ones that have come under attack, particularly those associated with the authority of the Church. It is in this sense that Hans Küng uses 'demythologization' in *Infallible?* his devastating analysis of the teaching authority of the Roman Catholic Church and in particular of the papacy. If some Protestant Christians are having difficulty in reconciling the Bible with the 'general crisis in authority', then how much more are some Catholics agonising over the authority of the Church? The Bible in itself can never be more than a moral and spiritual authority; the church's authority can be disciplinary as well. Whether or not it is still authoritative for the modern world, the Church can be and often is authoritarian.

For the Protestant churches it is the loss of moral authority that has concerned them most. They were never much concerned, with the exception of the Presbyterians, with the exercise of disciplinary authority: schism was the ready answer to that. Now all of them have lost whatever inclination they had to enforce their moral rules upon their members and upon society at large: indeed, some of them seem to have lost the inclination even to teach those rules. The reason is that the authority of the Protestant churches in Britain depended on a consensus in society which we now call the 'Protestant ethic' and that consensus has disappeared. As recent examples of this, we can cite the failure of the Welsh Independents to prevent the Sunday opening of pubs from spreading throughout the principality; or the failure of the Northern Ireland churches to take the political leaders of their communities along with them in their new efforts at inter-communal reconciliation.

The Church of England has suffered from the same erosion of its moral authority, but in the enforcement of its authority it has a slightly different record. At one time, the State enforced Anglican doctrine and worship upon the nation by means of the Act of Uniformity. On the other hand, the Church of England is not by nature an authoritarian church: under the system of lay patronage and the parson's freehold, its clergy have been immune from interference by high-handed bishops, although that immunity may be removed by reforms which the Church is now trying to get through Parliament. But in general the Church of England has behaved as if it were an association of independent clerics rather than a hierarchical structure. If you explore the index of any contemporary book about the Church of England, even an exhaustively detailed one like Leslie Paul's *A Church by Daylight*, you will find few references to 'authority'. Contemporary books about the Roman Catholic Church on the other hand bristle with references to it.

Traditionally, the Roman Communion has had a strong hierarchical chain of command, coming down from the Pope, step by step through Cardinals and Curial offices, through bishops and priests to the passive laymen. All bishops were appointed by Rome, theologians required the *imprimatur* of their superiors before they could publish, the discipline of the clergy was strictly enforced and the laity were given detailed instructions on what they must believe and do, and even while the Index was in force on what they might or might not read. Hans Küng described it as the 'only absolutist system that survived the French Revolution'. Vatican II was widely expected to change this rigid system into something more flexible, something that left more room for participation from below. The Council did indeed set a new view of authority alongside the old one, which was restated almost in its old form. Freedom of conscience was enshrined in Council texts and the Church was defined afresh, not as a centralised and mystical structure, but as 'the People of God'. Some bishops began to teach a new doctrine of authority. Cardinal Suenens of Brussels, who published a book called *Coresponsibility in the Church* (1968) said: 'Authority, if it is to be effective, must gain consent and consent can only be gained where those involved have been able to take part . . . if not in the final decision, at least in the steps leading up to it.' Archbishop Beck of Liverpool put it even more plainly when speaking to his diocese in 1968: 'The Church's life does not flow down from the Pope through the bishops and clergy to a passive laity; it springs from the grassroots of the People of God; and the function of authority is coordination, authenticiation and, in exceptional cases, control.'

By the end of the 1960s, however these new liberating ideas of Roman authority had a hollow ring to them. The decisive set-back was *Humanae Vitae* (1969) Pope Paul's encyclical condemning all forms of artificial birth control, for it flew in the face of all ideas of participation and of the majority views of the Pontifical Commission of bishops, theologians and lay experts on birth control set up by Pope John. The teaching of Vatican II that the Church is not the Pope answering all possible questions but the People of God formulating them from their own experience was overturned at a stroke. A French theologian, Jean-Marie Paupert told the newspaper *Le Monde*: 'Though it distresses me deeply, I must declare my belief that, in view of the encyclical *Humanae Vitae*, we can regard it as certain that the door that was opened for the first time by the Council has been shut again even before the Church was able to tread the path to which it gave free access.' In Europe and the United States, it was seen as the exercise of naked papal authority, even though Pope Paul had refrained from making it an *ex cathedra* and therefore infallible pronouncement. As an English Roman Catholic bishop told me: 'It was worse than the infallible pronouncement of a new doctrine, for you cannot imagine a more explosive issue than one that combines the authority of the Church delivered by celibate clergy, with sex and the most private decisions of married life.'

The damage to the faith and family life of ordinary Catholics was to some extent minimised by telling them that they must in the last resort follow their consciences, but the damage to the authority and credibility of the Church could not be minimised. Tensions were set up between what priests counselled privately in the confessional and what they were required to teach from the altar steps. The tensions produced rebellion and the rebellion though not widespread, produced a return to full-blooded authoritarianism. About a dozen, mainly young, priests were suspended by the bishops for openly criticising the encyclical and a considerably larger number were allowed to stay in their parishes only on condition that they remained silent. Some of the best of them subsequently left the priesthood. In a later and much more broadly based clash with authority, the entire teaching staff except for one resigned from the respected Corpus Christi catechetical centre in London and it was closed to the great sadness of many Catholics. In an unfortunate sequel the principal, Father Hubert Richards, was prevented by the personal intervention of Cardinal Heenan from getting a Catholic teaching post elsewhere, and went as a layman to teach in an Anglican college of education. Repression of dissidents had become almost a reflex action in the hierarchy and in 1975 it was turned upon those conservative Catholics who held out against the new Mass in English at Downham Market in Norfolk.

The one glimmer of hope was that some non-diocesan clergy like the Farm Street Jesuits in London still felt able to speak out against the abuse of authority. Father John F.X. Harriott, writing in *The Month* of September 1973:

All too often those who are accused by bishops and priests of dishonesty and injustice can turn on their accusers and say *Physician heal thyself*. They can point to officials who attempt to bolster their authority by sacrificing justice and truth to personal or party advantage; to bishops who try to silence theological dissenters by attacking their personal character instead of answering their arguments; to speeches and documents from Church leaders which are based on inadequate research and fallacious arguments, even though they can be checked against other sources of information, and mistakes of fact or weakness in argument quickly noted; to the lack of neutral courts where wrongs can be righted and conflicts resolved; to the automatic defence of those of higher rank against those of lower, no matter what injustice has been committed; to the secretiveness of ecclesiastical dealings. All such practices undermine confidence in the Church as a moral authority.

The authority of the Roman Catholic Church is being undermined from within but one cannot yet describe it as being in danger of imminent collapse, least of all in Britain. The crisis of authority may have driven many laypeople away from the Church and forced priests and nuns to seek other employment, yet what alternative is there for the average Catholic to the Church of the saints, however imperfect it now is? Many may privately agree with the views about infallibility of Hans Küng and other radicals, but they hesitate to express these views openly and precipitate a crisis. Instead they bide their time in difficult obedience, waiting for a new era to dawn perhaps for a new Pope to be elected in Rome and new bishops appointed in Britain. Cardinal Hume's enthronement at Westminster has certainly encouraged them. And all the time the myths upon which the credibility of the Church's authority has depended are steadily crumbling.

One of the most powerful of these 'myths' (the word is not used perjoratively) is the concept of the sacred, the belief that certain things and certain people are set apart by being in a special relationship to God. Thus, the Pope can speak with the authority of infallibility because he is the most sacred member of the Church; he has—as the First Vatican Council in 1870 put it—'a prerogative which the only-begotten Son of God deigned to link with the supreme pastoral office'. You cannot argue with holiness of that order. The concept of sacredness, however, has been changing significantly during the past decade and, as with authority, this is again a question of concern primarily to Roman Catholics. 'Desacralisation', as the process is sometimes called, took place for most Protestants at the time of the Reformation, when the whole medieval edifice of sacredness was demolished. After that only the Bible and, infrequently, certain spirit-filled men and women, were regarded as sacred. The rest of mankind and his works were held by Protestants to be tainted by original sin and no man such as a priest or bishop and no objects such as sacramental bread and wine could be regarded as being in a sacred relationship to God. The only priesthood was the priesthood of all believers. It was an austere and cerebral religion and of course since the Reformation many Protestants have recreated new hierarchies of sacredness. The Church of England did this extensively after the Oxford Movement of the last century and the Free Churches are constantly doing so in revival meetings and pentecostal movements, or simply by recognising 'holiness' in some local preacher.

Within the Roman Catholic Church, on the other hand, the post-Reformation period witnessed a vast extension of sacredness. The whole medieval hotch-potch of genuine faith mixed up with vulgar superstition and power politics, was refashioned by the Council of Trent into a disciplined institution, for all parts of which sacredness was claimed. Even the civil servants of the Vatican became known as Sacred Congregations and one group as the Holy Office. The Kingdom of God, in which Protestants put their faith for the future, had come already in the Roman Catholic Church. It was Triumphalism triumphant.

But again, as with authority, the Second Vatican Council introduced new ideas alongside the old. In the Council, as Peter Hebblethwaite observes in *The Runaway Church*, 'the real quarrel was between two conflicting notions of the "sacred" or "holy" which struggled with each other and still do in a conflict that remains unresolved. One view stresses the "vertical" element in faith, the relationship to God; and it selects certain persons, institutions, objects, which in a privileged way are held to give access to the divine clearly and unmistakeably ... the other view of the sacred refuses to localise it in persons, places and things. Its favourite text is John 4, where Christ says that worship in the future will not take place in temples but will be "worship in spirit and truth".'

The conflict goes on to the bafflement of non-Catholics, who see their separated brethren at times moving towards Protestant ideas of spirituality and at others retreating hastily into the old Roman habits. For the ordinary Catholic, of course, it is much more than a question of interpretation, it is one that goes to the heart of his own religion. The new ideas of the sacred may either seem an invitation to a new invigorating life of faith, or yet another cynical blow by the 'progressives' at the foundations of religion itself. A Londoner, who thought in those terms, told the *Catholic Herald* that he had visited the new cathedral at Clifton in Bristol and found that he could not even pray in the building, because of its bareness and absence of images. The same bare decor strikes one in many Roman Catholic parish churches. And yet no one has banned the old visual aids to devotion; indeed, the statuettes of the Virgin and the technicolor pictures of the Sacred Heart are still in plentiful supply in religious shops and Archbishop Dwyer of Birmingham has exhorted his flock not to neglect the Holy Rosary. In Rome, too the old and the new notions of the sacred co-exist rather uneasily. The trappings of Triumphalism—the three-tier papal tiara, the plumed helmets of the Swiss Guard—have been banished to the Vatican storerooms, but Pope Paul still recognises miracles, creates saints, confers pontifical knighthoods and granted indulgences to those who passed through the Holy Door in St Peter's during Holy Year. Was that year really 1975 and not 1875 or 1575?

For ordinary Catholics, what goes on in Rome is of less interest than the new notions of the sacred which have invaded the Mass. With the priest now facing the people in the midst of the church, with his actions visible to all and the words spoken in English it is not surprising that the doctrine of transubstantiation—the ultimate in Roman Catholic teaching about the sacred—is no longer given great emphasis. The doctrine has not been denied, but priests and teachers are told to turn people's thoughts towards Christ's redemptive action and away from the sort of mechanical question, for which transubstantiation provided the quasi-magical answer. It is no longer possible for the cynic to say, as Bertrand Russell did, that 'the Roman Catholic Church holds that a priest can turn a piece of bread into the Body and Blood of Christ by talking Latin to it'. No whispering in Latin, therefore for some no transubstantiation. The radical reassessment that has taken place in this most sacred area of Catholic life can be judged from the way that theologians now speak of the 'sacrifice of the Mass'. 'The Mass is a sacrifice not in the way in which Christ offered himself,' wrote Father Thomas Corbishley sj in the *Catholic Herald*, 'Christ's death on Calvary is the unrepeated, unrepeatable sacrifice of our redemption.' The respected Jesuit could well have been quoting from the Anglican Thirty-Nine Articles as far as many of his traditionalist readers were concerned. And yet, alongside this revolution quite incidental liturgical changes that have become commonplace in America and Western Europe—communion in both kinds (receiving the chalice as well as the host), communion in the hand rather than directly into the mouth, ordinary bread instead of special wafers, experimental and houses Masses—all originally met at least with disapproval and often with outright condemnation from bishops in Britain. When communion in the hand, for example was at last approved in 1976 as an optional practice in some English and Welsh churches, it was converts from Anglicanism who most welcomed the change and ironically took it upon themselves to teach their fellow-Catholics how to present hold their hands out at the altar. As for receiving the Mass in both kinds, two correspondents for the *Catholic Herald* indicated how great a diversity existed in Britain. The Labour MP, Kevin McNamara, reported that he had had to travel to the West Indies before first receiving both parts of the Mass while, in another edition of the paper, Patrick O'Donovan reported that in his Hampshire parish the chalice stood upon the end of the altar waiting for any communicant who had the temerity to go up and drink from it. The 'desacralisation' of the Catholic Mass—ridding it of its popular 'magical' attributes while retaining the theological 'mystery'—is clearly a complex affair.

Yet, as seen from the frontiers between the life of the churches and the secular world outside, these debates about authority and 'desacralisation' appear to be of marginal importance or worse. Among young people, reported Fr John Gaine, secretary of the RC Secretariat for Non-Believers, 'the Church is seen as an organisation primarily concerned to perpetuate itself. Its debates on matters such as celibacy, the employment of laicised priests and communion in the hand, are regarded as internal squabbles, magnifying minutiae in a pharisaical fashion.' Kenneth Leech in *Youthquake*, referring to attitudes towards the churches among the youthful Underground culture, quotes an article by the Dominican Fr Paulinus Milner: 'most of the people in the Underground experienced Christianity as a negative system breeding guilt and fear, denying spontaneity in the name of a facile otherworldliness.' As both of these writers point out, many of today's young people believe that by their institutional pettiness and their negative attitude to living, the churches have in fact betrayed the Jesus Christ of the Gospels. The churches' insistence on putting questions of morality and ritual above the pressing needs of social revolution bears little relationship to the dynamic Jesus, who said he had come to save the world. 'Generally, the institutional Church appears parochial, concerned primarily with individual morality and not dealing effectively with wider issues. The Church is not seen as dynamically involved in the major questions of the day such as justice, peace, the needs of the poor and deprived, social, racial and sexual equality . . .' (J.J. Gaine, *Young Adults Today and the Future of the Faith* 1975). It is ironic that British society has had to undergo the social traumas and moral confusion among young people about which Frs Gaine and Leech were writing, before a popular vindication could be found here for Bonhoeffer's radical perception: 'Christ is no longer an object of religion, but something quite different, indeed and in truth the Lord of the world.'

This brings us to the third major area in which religion itself has become secularised. The now famous letters which Bonhoeffer wrote from the Tegel Prison in Berlin in 1944, the year before his death, are the foundation of most subsequent attempts to interpret the Gospel for a world that has 'come of age', that has grown out of religion. The letters were translated into English in 1953 as *Letters and Papers from Prison*, with a paperback version in 1959 and a revised translation in 1971. They reached an even wider audience through other writers' works, particularly three controversial books of the sixties: John Robinson's *Honest to God*, Paul van Buren's *The Secular Meaning of the Gospels* (1963), one of the books involved in 'the death of God' row, and Harvey Cox's *The Secular City* (1965), a thorough-going attempt to relate the Gospel to the 'liberated' culture of urban America. The controversies surrounding these books of the sixties are now largely forgotten but the Bonhoeffer ingredient in each of them contrasts strongly with other sources which now look very passé. Does anyone now really try to think of God in the Tillich and Robinson terms of 'ground of our being' or 'deepest springs of our social and historical existence'? The freshness of Bonhoeffer's attraction for the modern age remains. Part of the attraction, admittedly, lies in the very elusiveness of Bonhoeffer's ideas. They were written in an urgent, fragmented shorthand and are full of promises to expand or explore particular points. But Bonhoeffer was executed before he could fully work out his 'religionless Christianity' and, like the Dead Sea Scrolls, his letters were discovered by posterity after being buried in the ruins of a conquered civilisation. Moreover the appeal of his ideas is bound up with the attraction of Bonhoeffer as a man. He was a prototype of the Christian 'for our time': a martyr, a convert from pietism to political action (even the necessity for assassination had the opportunity arisen), but also a man of great personal charm, of intellectual and cultural accomplishment (his piano, his tennis, his appreciation of a good cigar), someone familiar with the scientific mind through his own family, as well as being a theologian, an ecumenicist long before ecumenicism became fashionable and also the founder of a small religious brotherhood.

How he would have developed his interpretation of a Christianity which dispensed with what he called the 'religious premise', the resort to metaphysical language and the concern for personal salvation and inwardness—is a matter of unending debate among theologians. But there is no doubting the lasting appeal of some of his ideas. 'I should like to speak of God not on the borders of life but at its centre, not in weakness but in strength, not, therefore in man's suffering and death but in his life and prosperity.' '... I am so anxious that God should not be relegated to some last secret place, but that we should frankly recognise that the world and men have come of age, that we should not speak ill of man in his worldliness, but confront him with God at his strongest point.' Or when he writes of an experience common to Christian activists, the experience of being drawn in 'brotherhood' more to religionless people, than to the religious: 'While I often shrink with religious people from speaking of God by name—because that Name somehow seems to me here not to ring true . . . with people who have no religion I am able on occasion to speak of God quite openly and as it were naturally.' There is an echo of that thought near the beginning of John Robinson's *Honest to God*: 'Not infrequently, as I watch or listen to a broadcast discussion between a humanist and a Christian, I catch myself realising that most of my sympathies are on the humanist's side.'

This is the essential point about the secularisation of religion to which radicals are turning. It is not just that religion and religious authority, from whatever source, are having to prove themselves relevant as never before. Nor is it just an attempt to release the Gospel of Jesus Christ from the traditional restrictions of personal piety and personal morality. However hard those changes may be for Christians to swallow, the secularising movement has gone further. It turns the whole ecclesiastical view of life upside down. It says that if a dividing line has to be drawn between the religious and the religionless, between the churches and the world, between the righteous believers and the sinful pagans, then the radicals would rather be on the pagan side of the line—for that is where they would expect to encounter Christ. 'It is only by living completely in the world that one learns to believe.' Of course, it is a theology that is open to attack. It is argued that too much concentration on the thought and language of this age rather than on God's work through Christians in history is likely to produce an adulterated Gospel, one that is palatable for this age, but probably incomprehensible for the next. It is argued that the secularists are really crypto-atheists, they want to have their cake and eat it, they want to pick and choose the bits to be retained as 'the Gospel' and the bits to be discarded as 'religion'. It is argued that it is all in fact an attempt to sanctify Marxism and libertarianism. It is argued that the world may well have rejected the 'religious premise' but what hope is there of it embracing a Gospel that has no roots in traditional Western values or religious thought? It is argued that, far from being self-reliant and having 'come of age', modern man is in fact irresponsible and afraid, unable to control the technology he has created, a lonely and dehumanised creature in a denaturalised world.

The reactions to secular Christianity have become as much a part of the theological heritage of the seventies as were Bonhoeffer and his disciples for the sixties. But secular Christianity has taken on something of the irresistibility of the secularisation outside the churches, which of course it reflects. The openness of religion, the dispelling of older ideas of sacredness, the endless questioning of authority of all types and above all the taking up of secular causes by churchmen—all of these are now common features of all the churches. Churchmen today are as likely to make their mark in Amnesty International, Shelter, the Samaritans, the Committee of 100, in housing associations and social work of all types as they are in parish work. But it would be useless to pretend that the new style of secularised Christianity has worked any miracles for the churches' influence among the people to whom the radicals hope to appeal. Far from it. For an informed judgement on the impact of this modern style of Christianity on the young, we must continue a quotation made earlier in this chapter, from Fr Paulinus Milner, the Dominican who has worked among the 'drop outs' of the Underground in Oxford:

> Most of the people of the Underground experienced Christianity as a negative system breeding guilt and fear, denying spontaneity in the name of facile otherworldliness. The more modern style Christianity with its emphasis on human relationships, political involvement and social work, its greater permissiveness and its respect for human values, does not impress them any better because of its timidity with respect to spiritual values and the supernatural. The Christianity of the secular city has even less to offer them than that of the ecclesiastical city. In both these forms Christianity with its voluminous intellectualism and activist preoccupations seems to be bound up with what they diagnose as the diseases of western culture.

4

Religion Makes a Comeback

But 'religion' in the nineteen-seventies was by no means dead. In June 1971, *Time* magazine, which keeps an ear carefully tuned to the latest religious trends in America, gave some indication of the changes its British readers might expect in the year ahead. Under the headline *The New Rebel Cry: 'Jesus Is Coming'*, it devoted twelve pages to an anatomy of the so-called Jesus movement that was sweeping the youth culture of America's 'alternative society' and reaching wider audiences through pop music. In 1966, it said, John Lennon had claimed that the Beatles were more popular than Jesus but now the famous quartet, whom Timothy Leary had described as the four modern evangelists, had split up and George Harrison was singing 'My Sweet Lord'. Moreover, two bright new rock shows, *Jesus Christ Superstar* and *Godspell*, had arrived in New York. And throughout the whole United States, young people were turning to Jesus and feeling the power of the Holy Spirit, in revolt not only against American materialism but also against American theology: 'Christianity—or at least the brand of it preached in prestige seminaries, pulpits and church offices over recent decades—has emphasized an immanent God of nature and social movement, not the new movement's transcendental personal God who comes to earth in the person of Jesus, in the lives of individuals, in miracles. The Jesus revolution, in short, is one that denies the virtues of the Secular City and heaps scorn on the message that God was ever dead.'

Time referred to a recent book by Edward E. Plowman whom it dubbed the historian of the movement (*The Underground Church*, published in Britain in 1972 as *The Jesus Movement*) and he gave 1967 as the year of the movement's birth. In San Francisco in the hippy summer of that year, the disillusioned quest of the 'street people' from violent and non-violent protest over race and Vietnam, through sublimation into drugs, love-ins, mysticism and the occult, was nearing its end. 'Most of the street people *knew* that the supernatural was a real realm and that they were soulish beings somehow related to

59

it. How and where did they fit in? From 1967 on, ever increasing numbers of them turned to Christ for the answer.' Much of Plowman's book consists of the testimonies of the converts who formed 'the sparkplugs at the beginning of the Jesus movement'. They had been hippies, acid trippers, witches, prostitutes, high school gangsters, Krishna disciples, drop-outs, revolutionaries and communards: 'It's the story of how God broke into a seemingly impossible human scene.' Their religion was simple and spontaneous (hence the 'sparkplugs'), centred upon the Jesus portrayed in the Gospels. It was often remarked how many of the men resembled the Jesus painted by Holman Hunt. Their appearance, their itinerant and communal life-style, their continued use of drug language in phrases like 'having a high on Jesus' or 'freaking out on the Jesus thing' earned them the equivocal nickname of 'Jesus freaks'. There was also condemnation from some parts of the established churches. They were a new extrem-ism, wrote one Presbyterian minister, who worshipped 'a hip Jesus of the cheap grace quick-fix'. But they also shook the complacency of the churches. 'One can accuse them of naïveté, theological ignorance, political ignorance, yet they stand in judgement on the organised churches,' wrote a correspondent in *New Fire*, the Anglican Cowley Fathers' quarterly. And as Edward Plowman remarked, the new Jesus people were being joined throughout America by thousands of 'straight establishment-type people' who were still to be found in their usual church pews on Sundays but worshipped 'with kindred spirits in cell-like meetings later in the week'.

In Britain, it did not happen at all like that. The Jesus scene here was not a spontaneous eruption from the Underground, nor did it really belong to the street people or the drop-outs. Indeed, the non-conformists of the Underground culture were deeply suspicious of the links that existed from the beginning between the British Jesus scene and the 'moral pollution' crusaders of the Festival of Light. 'To the youth culture the Festival was like a red rag to a bull,' wrote Michael Jacob in *Pop Goes Jesus*, largely because of the Festival's timing. Authority in Britain with the backing of the churches had recently moved against *Oz* magazine, the *Little Red School Book* and Dr Martin Cole's sex education film, *Growing Up*. The Jesus move-ment in Britain bore the evidence of being a well-planned import programme, carefully marketed by the far from youthful evangelical establishment of the existing churches. 'In Britain, it is probably true to say that, with the exception of the Children of God (a fundamentalist commune based in Bromley), the Jesus people are drawn mainly from within the established churches,' wrote Kenneth Leech in *Youthquake*. 'Some would claim that the British Jesus movements are not indigenous growths from the youth culture at all, but have been manufactured by the churches as ways of communicating with youth.'

Most chroniclers of the British Jesus scene agree that a significant event was the arrival of the American evangelist, Arthur Blessitt. By background, he was a typical Southern Baptist evengelist-showman, from the same mould as Billy Graham, but there was an extra quality of nervous daring about Blessitt. He had proclaimed the Gospel in Nevada casinos, Hell's Angel camps and love-ins, and had opened a counselling bar for teenagers, called His Place, in the thick of the topless go-go clubs on Hollywood's Sunset Strip. Blessitt once carried a cross for twenty-eight days on a 3,500 mile walk of national repentance to Washington DC. 'In his heart, Arthur Blessitt is a street Christian,' wrote Edward Plowman. Blessitt arrived in London in August 1971, six weeks after the first Festival of Light rally which had been disrupted by Underground demonstrators, but in time for the following month's Hyde Park Pop concert, to be preceded by a big rally in Trafalgar Square. It was this Trafalgar Square rally which brought the Festival of Light to national attention through television, and Arthur Blessitt's presence transformed it. In marked contrast to the square talk of 'moral pollution' and the 'contraceptive society', here was a trendy American with long hair and bright clothes, doing the 'one-way' sign (the index finger pointing towards heaven) and leading the Jesus cheer (Gimme a J, gimme an E . . . J–E–S–U–S, *JESUS!*). Britain would experience a spiritual awakening greater than anything previously known, he said, and a revival in Northern Ireland would alter the province's history. The crucial factor in that awakening would be love and he told the Trafalgar Square crowds to turn to the person next to them and say 'I love you'.

This was the authentic Jesus scene and just what the majority of the young people had come to experience. But the young audience was not all it seemed. 'It would not be accurate to suggest that the Trafalgar Square crowd truly represented a cross-section of British society,' wrote John Capon in the Festival's official history, . . . *and there was light*. 'They were obviously almost all committed Christians—mainly drawn from the evangelical tradition.' The Festival's secretary, Steve Stevens, later explained to Clifford Longley, religious correspondent of *The Times* that, in sending out invitations to the 1971 rallies, it had seemed natural to use the existing range of contacts and so the young people in Trafalgar Square were almost entirely coach parties from Baptist, Pentecostal, Plymouth Brethren and Independent Evangelical youth groups. The organisers of the rallies later regretted that they had not tried to broaden the base of the Festival.

Looking back over the well-publicised events of 1971–72, Michael Jacob concluded that there had not really been a Jesus movement at all in Britain. 'What does exist are a selection of evangelists who look like the people they preach to, a collection of sects all believing that theirs is the one true way, thousands of kids who belong to no particular grouping, and thousands more, the vast majority in fact, who attend their local churches and who have adopted the slogans and outlook of the "Jesus movement" they're always hearing about.' Jacob believed that already in 1972 the movement was going the way of all trends imported from America and that little more would be heard about it. If that judgement was a little premature, it was proved correct within a year. It was therefore ironical that the first that many of Britain's top churchmen knew of the Jesus scene was in 1973 when it was already on the wane. At the Church Leaders' Conference in September of that year, the archbishops and archimandrites, the monsignors and moderators were mobbed as they entered Selly Oak College, Birmingham, by young people who put 'Jesus is alive today' stickers on their lapels. By 1976, Michael Jacob's prediction has indeed come true. *Jesus Christ Superstar* was admittedly still playing to the out-of-town coach trade in London's West End, but *Godspell* had gone and will be chiefly remembered as the vehicle that brought David Essex to fame. Cliff Richard, one of the leading lights of the Jesus scene has returned to secular pop and what became known as 'God rock' was a fading feature of the pop scene, which itself has faded in popular appeal. Few other survivals of the Jesus scene remain, except perhaps for a handful of rather aged Jesus people like Malcolm Muggeridge and Lord Longford, both of whom have written recent biographies of their rediscovered hero. Consideration of these and other luminaries of the Festival of Light, however, belongs to a later chapter concerned with Christian attitudes to contemporary morality.

In 1971, many people were under the impression that the Festival of Light was a spontaneous gathering of young people and that these young people, like the Jesus freaks in America, were turning to Jesus partly from their own revulsion with the 'moral pollution' of secular society. That view was wide of the mark. The Festival was a skilfully managed revivalist campaign with strong puritanical overtones, in the mainstream of Billy Graham, Tom Rees and the evangelical tradition. There was nothing wrong with that, of course. It brought great joy to thousands of ordinary young churchpeople and a little of the flavour of the American Jesus movement. What it did not do was in any sense to bridge the gap between the churches and the alternative youth culture. This was a great opportunity missed, not only in mission or outreach but also in self-awareness. Despite the antagonism of the demonstrators at the first Festival of Light rally, for a month or so afterwards there was a chance, perhaps a very slim one, that establishment Christianity and the youth culture might enter into a fruitful dialogue. It was not completely out of the question, for both were bodies ostensibly in revolt against secular society and its materialist values, both upheld the spiritual life and distrusted the media, both were in a sense 'alternative societies'. Indeed, after the initial Westminster Central Hall Rally, the Festival's founder, Peter Hill, did attempt to organise a meal for the 'leaders of the underground' to meet Festival of Light people, but the offer was rejected with the suggestion that the money be donated to relief in Bangladesh. A bigger obstacle was the evangelicals' conviction that the way of life of the underground—its radicalism, its nonconformist life-style and most of all its drug usage—was totally sinful and that the member of it who chose Christ had to give up every feature of his earlier life. The Festival's leadership was even a little unhappy about Arthur Blessitt's flowing locks—they preferred the Cliff Richard look—and they never countenanced the 'tripping on Jesus' drug language of the American Jesus Freaks.

The real contact between the churches and the youth culture was left to the less conspicuous efforts of other, individual Christians. At the 1970 Isle of Wight pop festival, for example, which was attended by 250,000 young people and by widespread fears of a drug-induced orgy, the Christian presence was organised by the local Rural Dean and included Anglicans, Methodists, Roman Catholics and the Church Army. The more evangelical Free Churches were not in evidence. A significant presence was a party of workers from St Anne's, Soho, in London's West End, led by a young Anglo-Catholic priest experienced in working among drug-users. This was Kenneth Leech and he brought with him some helpers from Release, the underground's own welfare organisation, with whom Fr Leech had established contacts in the Piccadilly Circus area.

Kenneth Leech is one of the small handful of churchmen from all denominations (others names which spring to mind are Paulinus Milner of the Oxford Dominicans and David Collyer who in 1970 became the Bishop of Birmingham's 'Chaplain to the Unattached') who have made a serious effort to minister to the alternative youth culture on its own ground. His experience of the drugs scene in Soho from 1967–71 is distilled in two remarkable books (*Keep the Faith Baby* and *A Practical Guide to the Drug Scene*) and he has taken a wider look at the search for spirituality in what he calls the 'counter-culture' in *Youthquake* (1973). His approach is a two-fold one, of trying to find the most suitable form of pastoral care for casualties of the counterculture, at the same time respecting the inherent values of this form of anti-social behaviour and indeed learning from it. His books are so important that they should be read from cover to cover and not dipped into for the odd tasty quotation. But for our purpose, in examining the missed opportunities of the 1971 Jesus scene, Kenneth Leech has some pertinent observations. On drug addiction, for example, he rejects the Billy Graham attitude that only a complete religious conversion can cure the addict and he quotes the conclusion of three young Salvationists that 'our evangelistic ardour could be in danger of denying the individuality of the person we are confronting'. Kenneth Leech's own attitude is that 'too much emphasis has been placed, within the current "pastoral care" movements, on a clinical model, which sees "sickness" as a private disturbance, and shows little understanding of the social forces and the community structure . . . the Church's role is not to rescue and isolate individual members (though it should be emphasized that this is often a necessary stage of healing) but to build within the subcultural groups the structure of spiritual renewal.' That was from *A Practical Guide to the Drug Scene*, where he points out that no Christian ought to regard drug-taking as in itself sinful without regard to the personal circumstances, even the spiritual hunger of the drop-out in search of 'new scenes, new experiences, new dimensions'. In *Youthquake*, Kenneth Leech takes this point further by inquiring into the counter-culture's exploration of eastern mysticism, particularly Zen Buddhism and Krishna consciousness, and of the magical and the occult. 'It is in fact significant that the mystical revival among young people has occurred at a time of spiritual confusion in the institutional churches. At exactly the time that liturgical reform was leading to simpler forms of worship and the casting out of unnecessary garments, the colourful psychedelic youth of 1967 began to wear chasuble-like vestments in Portobello Road.' He sees the hope for the future in the churches establishing lines of communication and dialogue with the spiritual movements of the youth culture but also, as a prerequisite of that, rediscovering their own Christian spiritual tradition.

Both of these things are now happening. Throughout the churches there are clear signs of spiritual renewal, with a re-emphasis on the value (indeed the necessity) of spiritual prayer and meditation. This is not necessarily seen as a denial of the more pervasive secularising movements within the churches (though sometimes it is) but more as a counterpoint to them. The approach is in any case different. The troublesome antithesis between God and the supernatural on the one hand and man in his material self-sufficiency, on the other, has been by-passed. In these movements, the Christian's attention is fixed on God-made-man, on Jesus. Even the Holy Spirit-filled 'charismatics' are not trying to direct attention to the third person in the Trinity, for they in particular are Jesus-centred. The rediscovery of Jesus as a person for today, rather than as an unapproachable part of the deity or as a theological and historical problem, is one of the great changes in the contemporary church. It may certainly at times be a naive and contentious phenomenon, but surprisingly enough it is not a return to other-worldliness or quietism. We can see this Jesus-centred spiritual renewal at work in three areas; in the renewed search for union with God through mysticism, in the new sense of Christian community and in the charismatics' proclamation that the gifts of the Holy Spirit are not a first century AD peculiarity but the inheritance of today's Christians.

The interest of British intellectuals in the mystics of Asia predates by many years, of course, the hippy generation's discovery of the road to Kathmandu and back. And so do the foundations laid by scholars and missionaries for the new openness of the main Christian churches towards Eastern religions. Two influential and prolific writers in the field of comparative religion were Professor Geoffrey Parrinder, of King's College London, who had been a Methodist missionary in West Africa, and the late Professor R. C. Zaehner, of All Soul's College, Oxford, who had been received into the Roman Catholic Church while serving with the British Embassy in Teheran. They were trailblazers and it took time for the official churches to follow their lead, but follow it they have done. 'When we approach the man of another faith than our own,' wrote Canon Max Warren, former General Secretary of the Church Missionary Society, 'it will be in a spirit of expectancy to find how God has been speaking to him and what new understandings of the grace and love of God we may ourselves discover in this encounter.' That sums up the new attitude.

More cautiously but with more authority, Vatican II declared that the Roman Catholic Church 'looks with sincere respect upon those ways of conduct and life, those rules and teachings which though differing in many particulars from what she holds and sets forth, nevertheless reflect a ray of that Truth which enlightens all men.' The teachers of the new spirituality have followed this lead. Dom Bede Griffiths in *The Christian Ashram* (1966) subtitled 'Essays towards a Hindu-Christian Dialogue', opened up the religious thinking of India to Western Christians, and another Benedictine, Aelred Graham has done the same for Zen Buddhism, in his *Zen Catholicism* (1963). It is primarily the techniques and insights of these Eastern mystical systems that are being adapted to Christian use, not their philosophy of withdrawal from ordinary life. In contrast, to the popular Transcendental Meditation, taught by the Beatles' guru Maharishi Mahesh Yogi (which some American researchers have deduced is not very different from having forty winks), Father Herbert Slade of the Cowley Fathers has this to say about the Christian adaptation of Hindu meditative techniques: 'Loving Communion with the living Lord requires the use of all the faculties in actions which often leave us exhausted. Contemplation is not primarily about relaxation but about love. That is why the symbol of this prayer is not a man relaxed in the corpse posture but a king reigning from the tree.' (*Exploration into Contemplative Prayer*, 1975.) Attempts have even been made to understand and use popular dabbling into the occult activities of witchcraft, spiritism and psychic powers. In a book that was serialised in the *Church Times*, the Rev Anthony Duncan wrote that blanket condemnations of these practices miss the basic truth that 'psychic gifts are a burden to those upon whom they are bestowed; they only attain fulfilment and joy when they are consciously given back to the Almighty' and transformed into gifts of the Holy Spirit (*The Fourth Dimension*: 'A Christian Approach to the Occult', 1975). Anthony Duncan tells of his 'favourite witch' whom he describes as a devout Anglican and a member of her local diocesan synod, using her psychic powers to heal a muscle he had pulled in his neck. That sort of 'discerning between the spirits' can be contrasted with the blanket condemnation by many evangelical charismatics. 'Far from being harmless, witchcraft and other forms of the occult are harming, yea, wrecking and ruining lives today to an alarming degree . . . the occult has spread over the world like a malignant cancer.' That is the view of Doreen Irvine, in *From Witchcraft to Christ* (1973), a book whose title speaks for itself.

Greater contact with the mystical techniques of the East and with the more faddish mysticisms of the Western underground culture have sent many Christians back to their own traditions, which over the past decade have become more widely known. Half a century ago, the ordinary Christian who wished to tap the wisdom of the great con-templatives like St John of the Cross, Meister Eckhart, Dame Julian of Norwich or the unnamed writer of *The Cloud of Unknowing* would have been sent to dusty library shelves or to searching for Victorian editions in second-hand book shops. Now they are readily available in paperback, along with a host of modern guides to the contemplative way of prayer like Teilhard de Chardin's *Prayer of the Universe*, Thomas Merton's *Seeds of Contemplation*, and Monica Furlong's *Contemplating Now*. Many people have learned about mystical prayer through television from Archbishop Anthony Bloom, who has opened up a whole field of Orthodox spirituality to British viewers who thought that it had perished in the Russian revolution. Similarly, 'retreats' and 'quiet days' are not at all what they were in the days when a lay man or woman entered a religious community very much on sufferance and could not avoid feeling that in the contemplative life he or she was a worldly amateur or a 'plastic' religious (to use a word from the Underground). Now an increasing number of retreats are specifically designed for people who have not the slightest intention of withdrawing from the world into an exclusive spiritual realm. Nor is this regenerative movement confined to the Catholic tradition. It is significant that when the Roman Catholics were engaged in ecumenical dialogue with the Methodists, one of the more socially active of the British churches, it was the spirituality of Methodism that was most strongly stressed.

This movement of spiritual regeneration is often linked with the rediscovery of a deeper communal life in the churches. That does not mean that English, Irish, Welsh and Scottish Christians have had any more significant success with the establishment of 'Jesus communes' than did the California Jesus people of half a decade ago. Separation from the world, exclusivity and rigid discipline are not distinguishing marks of the new communal movement. Indeed, those older religious communities within the Roman Catholic and Anglican churches which are based on the monastic rules of poverty, chastity and obedience have experienced a sharp fall in vocations (an exception is the Franciscans who through their lay 'third order' have bridged the ecumenical and secular gaps more successfully than most). The new communities, however, are not recreations of past structures. They are largely ad hoc, loosely-knit, predominantly lay communities, which do not discriminate between denominational ties, between the sexes or between married families and single members. The emphasis of most of them is on sharing—sharing income and talents, as well as responsibilities within the community—and some of them see this in the context of 'sharing in the life of Jesus in the world'. It is a remarkable movement of mission and experiment, though perhaps it should not be called a movement as such since the new communities cover a very broad spectrum of aims and achievements. Some have a clear bias towards contemplation, some towards social and political action, while others have adopted a 'therapeutic' role, not always as their first priority. In London in the early seventies, for example, the Kingsway Community became a Christian centre for former drug addicts; across the river, the Blackheath Commune was also of Christian origin but more politically oriented. The Manchester Slant Group, a Roman-Catholic based commune which in 1972 took over publication of the Underground journal *Roadrunner* (formerly the *Cantonsville Roadrunner*) from its left-wing Anglican founders, strove so hard towards a political gospel that its many critics concluded that Christianity had been left far behind. These are very different from the London communities of Folcolare, an international network of lay communes founded in Italy at the end of the war by a group of girls; or from the Othona Community, on the banks of the Blackwater Estuary in Essex, which is closely associated with the Protestant Taizé Community in France and has a similar orientation towards youth and ecumenical activity. In Northern Ireland, the Corrymeela Community, founded in 1966 on the beautiful North Antrim coast, was also inspired by Taizé and quickly established itself as an ecumenical refuge where the social casualties of the province's violence, particularly children, could be given back a sense of their individual humanity. But Corrymeela was not originally intended as a 'therapeutic' community and it has still managed to become an international network, whose members and supporters are dedicated to healing the communal divisions of Northern Ireland itself. As its historian, Alf McCreary, has said: 'it is a community of people, a concept in reconciliation, a way of life.' (*Corrymeela—The Search for Peace*.) Groups of Christians have felt a similar need to move nearer to the sea in order to reorder their spiritual values away from the urban turmoil and many have sought to do this along the Celtic coasts and islands. Here of course they are following in the steps of the pioneer community of them all, the Iona Community founded in 1938 by the Rev George Macleod and his fellow-workers in the slums of Glasgow. In 1962, the Findhorn Trust established a commune in Moray for contemplation in 'the Western occult tradition', which included Christian mysticism alongside other lines of possible spiritual development. A more orthodox group of Christians, the Community of Celebration, settled on the isle of Cumbrae in the Firth of Forth in 1975. This interesting community, part charismatic, part communist (though in a completely non-political sense for they have always placed themselves under the authority of their local bishop) was founded in 1964 at the Church of the Redeemer, in Houston, Texas. In search of an answer to the problems of a hostile, inner city parish, the Anglican Rector, Graham Pulkingham, and five laymen decided to live with their families in a corporate community centred on the Eucharist. They were committed to renewal of the structures of the church and looking for a new style in Christian leadership. The proof that they found it can be seen in their growth in the United States and Britain and in the demand for their missionaries, or Fisherfolk, in many parishes. They settled at Yeldall Manor, at Wargrave in Berkshire, in 1974, which has now become both a therapeutic centre and the base for Celebration Services (International) Ltd, which markets Christian records, cassettes, books and graphics. Their missionary and 'research' base is now at the tiny Cathedral of the Holy Spirit on Cumbrae.

One could add many more communities to the list. Side by side with them, however, there has been a reawakening of the sense of Christian community in many parishes. The mushroom growth of 'house churches' is one sign of this, another is the spread of team ministries and informal ecumenical associations of local clergy throughout the country. The new feeling of togetherness may partly come from the realisation that Christians are now a small minority in the population and must move closer together to survive. But it is also a realisation of Bonhoeffer's evocative definition of the Church as 'Christ existing as a community'.

5

The Charismatics

The last of the three movements of spiritual regeneration in the British churches already mentioned—the charismatic movement—deserves a chapter to itself. It is by far the most publicised, certainly the most controversial and arguably the most important for the future of Christianity in this country. The charismatic or pentecostal movement is again not so much a movement as a large and growing number of Christians from all denominations, including significantly the Roman Catholics, who have experienced what the Bible calls 'charismata—the gifts of the Holy Spirit'. In particular, they are recognised by the gift of tongues (glossolalia). They are the spiritual heirs of the first Pentecost when the apostles 'were all filled with the Holy Spirit and began to speak in other tongues as the Spirit gave them utterance'. (Acts ii 4).

Traditionally, the churches have regarded the happenings described in Acts as a once and for all experience, as the seal of the Holy Spirit's presence with the post-resurrection church, in accordance with Jesus's promises (John xiv 16, but Jesus's promise of the actual gift of tongues in Mark xvi 17 is not found in the earliest texts of the second gospel). The periodic attempts throughout the ages by groups of uneducated Christians to relive the pentecostal experience have been condemned, and often harshly suppressed, as evidence of 'enthusiasm' (i.e. fanaticism) or possession by other spirits. In this century, suppression has become less successful and the orthodox churches more tolerant—undoubtedly, because they have seen their main enemy as despiritualised materialism rather than spiritual deviation.

The modern pentecostal movement is usually said to have begun in 1900 at Topeka, Kansas, from where it quickly spread throughout the southern United States among the urban poor who were members of fundamentalist churches. It also spread to Europe, particularly Scandinavia, and arrived in England in 1907 in an Anglican parish in Sunderland. Later it led to the foundation of new denominations, like the Assemblies of God and the Elim Four-Square Gospel Alliance, which was particularly strong in Northern Ireland. But its greatest success occurred later in less developed countries, where it spread rapidly during the forties and fifties in Africa, South America and Java (in the social turmoil following the overthrow of the Sukarno regime in Indonesia). It was from these countries that pentecostalism as a mass movement of positive Christianity first came to the attention of Western Christians, like missionaries and delegates to the World Council of Churches. There are now said to be about 30 million members of pentecostal churches throughout the world, some of them represented in the World Council. Then, in the early sixties in the United States, the direction of the movement changed again and it became what Frederick Dale Bruner has described as 'the major grass-roots religious revolution of our time. Born in this century, raised largely among the poor, at mid-century entering the middle class, it is reputedly growing faster than any other modern Christian movement and is increasingly pressing its existence upon the attention of the church and the world.' (*A Theology of the Holy Spirit*.)

The new pentecostalism is not a religion of reason, nor even pre-eminently of faith or decision, but of experience. Its adherents speak of 'being seized by the Spirit', of being 'filled with the Lord' and of receiving the 'Baptism of the Spirit' as a separate experience from conversion. The times and places where this often unexpected phenomenon has occurred are part of the history of the movement. Michael Harper, who was the founder of the Fountain Trust which has tried to inform and guide the movement in Britain, has written about his own first experience of glossolalia. As an Anglican curate at All Soul's, Langham Place, in London in September 1962 he attended a weekend conference where he was required to preach on a text from Ephesians. He was filled with an elating sense of what Paul was really saying. During the following year he heard about the gift of speaking in tongues, and after some months of inquiry into it, he was urged by a friend to try to speak in tongues:

So I tried. Maybe for a split second there were some man-made sounds. I forget. But almost instantly I was speaking a new language. As I did so, two wonderful things happened all at once. The Lord seemed to take two steps forward. He had seemed a little out of touch. Now He was really close. And secondly, those worries and fears evaporated. And here I was, not in any state of ecstasy (I defy anyone to feel ecstatic lying on a hard floor!) but speaking to God with a freedom and joy I had always wanted to and never quite found possible. My mind was unclouded, and fully aware of what was going on. It was a most glorious sensation of perfect communication between God and man. (*None Can Guess*, 1971)

Michael Harper has always maintained that being possessed by the Spirit has nothing to do with ecstatic or trance-like states.

The charismatic movement had already become strong in the United States before its full force was felt in Britain. Harper cites a significant event on Passion Sunday, 1960, at St Mark's Episcopal Church, Van Nuys, outside Los Angeles, where the Rector told the congregation that through the influence of some church members he had been filled with the Spirit and spoken with tongues. Because of strong opposition from some quarters in the church, the Rector later felt it right to resign and to move to a new appointment in Seattle, but the movement was already spreading rapidly through the Episcopal (Anglican) Church. Another significant event in the United States occurred in March 1967, among a group of young, progressive Roman Catholics at Notre Dame University, Indiana. 'For six weeks we were kicking and screaming against it (the Holy Spirit), no doubt out of fear of being changed,' said Kevin Ranaghan, a lecturer in liturgical studies, 'but then we prayed and during that prayer my wife and I enjoyed the almost tangible experience of Jesus in the room.' The movement again spread rapidly among young Catholics on a number of Mid-West campuses and Kevin and Dorothy Ranaghan later formed a commune, with twenty-seven other Catholic charismatics, called 'The People of Praise'. There were recently estimated to be more than 200,000 Roman Catholic charismatics in the United States and at Whitsun, 1975, 10,000 of them visited Rome where they received the Pope's blessing. In no part of the Roman Catholic Church has the movement brought about such radical change as in Ireland, a country not noted for either its ecumenical fervour or the active participation of its lay people. In Dublin, the breakthrough is dated 4 January 1972, when twelve people met for prayer in the front parlour of Kimmage Manor, the seminary of the Holy Ghost Fathers, and some 'received the Spirit'. But there had already been charismatic experiences among Protestants in Northern Ireland and soon Catholic and Protestant charismatics were meeting together at mid-week prayer sessions on both sides of the border. They later formed a single organisation to promote charismatic renewal throughout Ireland.

The movement is clearly no respecter of ecumenical or political divisions, or of divisions of education, class or churchmanship either. In the Church of England, for example, there are a significant number of adherents from the Catholic tradition. The ecumenical nature of the renewal was strongly promoted from the beginning. At an international conference held at the University of Surrey and in Guildford Cathedral in 1971 under the auspices of the Fountain Trust, more than forty Lutherans and thirty Roman Catholics played a full part and for Catholics this is generally regarded as the starting point for their charismatic renewal in Britain. When the Second National Conference for Charismatic Renewal met in Dublin in the summer of 1975, bringing together 5,000 people from all parts of Ireland, the workshops and prayer meetings had already been arranged on an inter-denominational basis, with for example a Presbyterian deaconess and a Carmelite friar taking turns to lead the proceedings. The keynote address of that weekend conference was given by the world's best-known charismatic Cardinal Suenens, the progressive Primate of Belgium, who said that the disunity of the churches would be healed, not by their mutual dialogue but by each of them entering into dialogue with 'the living Jesus'. At a similar conference in London, in the same summer, the Anglican Archbishop of Capetown, Dr Bill Burnett, confessed that until he had known the Lord through the Holy Spirit he had been quite unable to 'communicate the power of the Gospel' to the racial divisions of South Africa.

The conferences and the festivals are only the tip of the iceberg for as F.D.Bruner said this is essentially a grass roots movement. Almost without exception its clerical adherents have been drawn to 'seek the gifts of the Spirit' by contact with charismatic lay men and women—Cardinal Suenens, for example, became involved by attending prayer meetings incognito—and it is the mid-week meetings of prayer and spiritual manifestations, usually held in private houses, that are the heart of the movement. Charismatic parishes are few and far between, but where they do exist religion has been transformed. The churches are full, particularly with young people, strangers are welcomed, the Bible is proclaimed eagerly, the worship is informal, uninhibited and often quite protracted, congregational participation is total, and everyone appears to be standing on tip-toe to see some new manifestation of the Holy Spirit, for example, in the curing of the sick. Near miraculous cures are often claimed, though few of them have been medically authenticated. David Watson the vicar of one such church, St Michael-le-Belfry, York (which was once declared redundant) has said: 'I believe that unless this spiritual renewal is allowed to continue and unless we are willing to have our lives really turned upside down, we're going to end up playing religious games in a little corner, while the rest of the world is plunging to violence and despair.'

But the charismatics have as many critics as they have supporters. They are frequently accused of being irrational and against any form of learning which does not come from their own experience. They are accused of lacking theology and of being literalist in their use of the Bible. They are accused of proclaiming a one-sided, emotional form of Christianity with more emphasis on the first Pentecost than on the Crucifixion. In any case, it is said, there is a high fall-off rate among young charismatics. They are accused of jeopardising the cause of Christian unity by a naive dismissal of the genuine theological and historical differences between the churches. They are invariably accused of lacking interest in politics and social action, a charge which has split the Anglican Church in South Africa. In the Roman Catholic Church, charismatics are particularly accused of down-grading the importance of the Eucharist and of making their mid-week prayer meetings the central act of their Christian worship. They are also accused of playing fast and loose with traditional Catholic piety, of putting the Holy Spirit in the place of the Virgin Mary—a criticism which Cardinal Suenens partly admits in his book *A New Pentecost?* Above all, charismatics are accused of over-emphasising their exhilarating experience of the Spirit, particularly the gift of tongues, and of tending towards an élitist view of Christianity, in which those who do not share their experience are relegated to a second-class status. This last accusation has been made most strongly by some British evangelicals who see the conversion experience, of 'making a decision for Christ', as in danger of being regarded as only a preliminary step to a state of grace.

The church in Britain which has investigated most fully these aspects of the charismatic movement is the Methodists, although others, like the Church of Scotland, have called for reports. The Methodist Conference in 1974 fully endorsed a report which praised the charismatics for proclaiming 'a patient acceptance of the Spirit's influence' instead of 'a grim striving to achieve' and for enabling many 'to discover hope and liberation' in Christian living. But the report also offered some clear words of warning:

We wish to encourage those involved in the charismatic movement as, they continue to explore the theological and biblical—as well as the psychological and sociological—bases of their experience and teaching. We would presume to advise, however, that they avoid the snare of stultifying the joyful experience they know in the interests of a watertight apologia for their position.

Some Methodist leaders are particularly concerned at what they see as the possibility of a charismatic 'take-over'—not only of geographical areas like the West Riding of Yorkshire and Essex, where Methodism's traditional strength has gone into decline, but also in the church's theological and Bible colleges. It is now felt that charismatics entering these colleges are out of all proportion to the movement's following the church as a whole and that there is the danger of corporate life being disrupted much as it was during the hey-day of Moral Rearmament a generation ago. This danger is also present in the Church of England, but the bishops appear to be less concerned about it than the Methodist Church.

Two major dangers, at least, have been widely recognised in the movement of charismatic renewal—schism and the use of exorcism. In the United States, where the movement is already some fifteen years old, there are warning signs that some charismatics are striving towards a new, exclusive denominationalism. One reason for this is undoubtedly the greater hostility shown by the official churches. Another reason lies with the large number of adherents to the movement who have no traditional links or loyalties to the official churches. Thus, while the majority of American charismatic groups (with the exception of 'uplift' groups like the Full Gospel Businessmen's Fellowship International) are dedicated to a new form of Christian leadership, many of them are looking for this within their own ranks rather than in the older churches. Additionally, there has been the emergence among these unaffiliated charismatics of an authoritarian hierarchy, led by those who are recognised as having had a fuller or earlier 'visitation by the Spirit'. 'With so many spiritual tramps around, as it were, there is clearly a need to bring order into chaos,' one leading British charismatic told me, 'but in the United States at the moment there is the danger that anarchy will be replaced by tyranny.' So far, this is a danger that has not become so apparent in Britain, where the official churches have been more tolerant. But the spread of 'house churches' which often have no contact with the local non-charismatic Christian churches, and the emergence of federal links between them, are ominous signs. The more prominent charismatics in Europe are fully aware of these dangers. In *A New Pentecost?* Cardinal Suenens says that the charismatic movement should aim to do its work within the churches and then to disappear, like a river which loses its identity when it reaches the sea. Michael Harper, the founder of the Fountain Trust, takes a similar view and points out that the movement is essentially a move to correct the headlong swing of modern christianity towards materialism and secularisation and that the corrective should not come to be regarded as the norm. On the other hand, some students of church history, having regard to the large number of denominations and sects which were thrown up by the Evangelical Revival at the end of the eighteenth century, would be surprised if the charismatic movement did not also produce some schismatic offshoots in Britain.

The other danger, that associated with the practice of exorcism, became tragically all too apparent in March 1975. Public attention had already been directed towards the practice by the widespread interest in witchcraft and the release of the Hollywood film 'The Exorcist' in 1974, but it was a Yorkshire murder case which really shook the churches. The killer was a young man who had apparently shown no interest in religion until he and his wife joined a house meeting, called the Christian Fellowship Group, in which glossolalia and exorcism were practised. In this company, he began to behave erratically and violently, in particular towards a young woman who had some authority within the group (she was reported to have celebrated Holy Communion). After one incident, the man was taken to a church at Gawber, near Barnsley, where he was laid on the vestry floor and exorcised. Throughout the night seven people, including the Anglican vicar and a Methodist minister, took it in turns to 'deliver' him of 'about fifty devils' which named themselves as 'incest, bestiality, blasphemy, heresy, lewdness, masochism and many others', although the exorcists were aware that the spirits of 'insanity, violence and murder' were still left. In the early hours of the morning, the man was driven to his home where within an hour he tore his wife to death 'with unspeakable brutality'. At his trial, he was found not guilty of murder on the grounds of insanity.

The case horrified the whole nation and there were immediate demands in the Press, in Parliament and from some quarters of the churches that exorcism should be banned completely. But the Church of England—and, among the major churches, this was primarily an Anglican problem—was in no position to make up its mind on the matter. The historical view of exorcism was quite clear, but the pastoral view complex. Exorcism had been extensively practised in the Middle Ages and had indeed formed part of the rite of Baptism (a relic of this survives in the popular belief that if a child cries at its christening that is the devil escaping). Under the Anglican Canon Law of 1604, as in current Roman Catholic Canon Law, exorcism was expressly forbidden without the permission of the diocesan bishop and for centuries, permission had been neither sought nor given. Within the past twenty years, however, exorcism had again been practised in the church in two distinct forms. On the one hand, there was a small number of priests, normally one to a diocese, who were recognised as official advisers on exorcism and who in a few cases were prepared, after extensive medical and psychiatric consultation, to perform a brief liturgical service of exorcism. On the other hand, there was a large and growing number of charismatics, both clerical and lay, who were practising exorcism as a gift of the Holy Spirit; they claimed their authority to do so not from bishops or Canon Law but from the example of the Gospels and from Jesus's express commission to exorcise (in Mark xvi 17, the disputed coda to the second gospel). The differences between the two practices were very wide. On a BBC radio programme, an official Anglican exorcist, Dom Robert Petitpierre, said that the 'picture of possessions as the form of demonic attack is quite hopelessly overdrawn—if there are a dozen cases in England at the present time, that is the maximum.' Dom Robert added that in most cases of alleged demonic possession, the saying of the Lord's Prayer would suffice and even in more extreme cases, exorcism could be completed by a simple formula within ten minutes. On the other hand, there was the all-night exorcism at Gawber and the claim of an Anglican vicar in Hampstead that he had cast out a thousand devils within a year. That sounds incredible, until one recalls that each time the person being exorcised grunts, sighs, mutters or even vomits, it is believed that a devil is leaving him. And far from being a simple liturgical formula, like 'in the name of Jesus I command you to leave this man', the charismatic exorcism could well involve physical force to hold the person down, and even reactions which resembled epileptic fits.

The Anglican bishops were in a quandary. Although psychiatrists had unanimously condemned the inexperienced dabbling in the practice in the case of an obviously sick man at Gawber, even they were not prepared to dismiss all claims of demonic possession as 'hysterical disassociation'. In a few cases, exorcism had clearly worked where psychiatric treatment had failed. There was, however, the need for safeguards and this was something on which the more responsible charismatic clergy were agreed. But as the bishops deliberated, a new dimension was introduced into the debate. Sixty-five theologians, representing the cream of the Anglican intellectual establishment, warned the church that it was in danger of making a serious error of judgement by attempting to regulate exorcism and thus giving it some form of official status. The core of their letter, circulated to all bishops and members of the General Synod, was the statement that:

> the liberation of mankind from demonological and similar beliefs since the Reformation and the rise of modern science has been a great blessing. The Christian concept of the supernatural is quite distinct from that implied by occultist beliefs and it would be quite wrong for the Church to suggest that her beliefs are in any way on the same level as those.

The theologians conceded that, according to the gospels, Jesus performed exorcisms but 'the Church has never expected that her members must necessarily share all Jesus's beliefs'. This introduced a rather different argument into the debate and was seen as highly tendentious by a number of churchmen. Pens were taken up and letters sent off to *The Times*, pointing out that while exorcism might be a problem for the Church, to go to the other extreme and equate belief in devils and personal forces of evil in the cosmos with pre-scientific superstition and occultism was something else It smacked too much of a secularised gospel. As a Jesuit writer put it, 'it lets a very large and active cat out of a theological bag already giving at the seams'.

The intervention of the theologians notwithstanding, the Archbishop of Canterbury in July 1975 issued a set of five guidelines for the practice of exorcism. It must be carried out in collaboration with the resources of medicine; in the context of prayer and sacrament; with a minimum of publicity; by experienced persons, authorised by diocesan bishops; and followed by continuing pastoral care Taken together with the widespread shock caused by the Yorkshire killing, no doubt the Archbishop's guidelines did have some effect on limiting exorcism. But of course, the guidelines were ultimately unenforceable.

The Church of England does not have the central moral authority to enforce such rules and it is scarcely conceivable that any English bishop would haul a clergyman before the ecclesiastical courts to charge him on pain of deprivation from his living with an offence against the Canon Law of 1604. Exorcism continues to be practised, not only by authorised exorcists, but fairly widely in charismatic communities. It is now done more discreetly, so as not to cause scandal, and as far as one can ascertain with a high degree of responsibility and pastoral care by exorcising clergy and laymen. Perhaps it is as well that this is the case for the demand for some form of spiritual shock therapy, as shown by Scientology and the EST group therapy that has been sweeping America at $250 a head, is clearly much greater than secularised Christians are prepared to admit. But exorcism is something which is no longer within the control of the Anglican bishops. In 1975, an Essex clergyman, the Rev Trevor Dearing, resigned his living in order to become an itinerant charismatic preacher and exorcist and there was nothing the church could do about it.

The exorcism debate is important mainly because it revealed the total unpreparedness and in some cases the ignorance of the official churches in the face of one dangerous excess of the charismatic movement. As we have seen, there are other less conspicuous dangers in the movement, which could have a more far-reaching effect than providing copy for national and local newspapers hungry for sensation. The danger of schism and discord is one. But perhaps the greatest danger is the threat that this form of instant Christianity poses to the whole concept of institutional religion, which appears to the charismatics to be characterised by complacency, worldliness and an overbearing intellectualism. Reading the signs of the times, one could well conclude that unless church leaders give urgent and sympathetic attention to the reasons why the charismatic renewal movement has the appeal that it obviously does, then there could well be more rude awakenings like that caused by the Gawber exorcism.

6

Unity: The Elusive Quest

One area of 'official' church activity in which the Holy Spirit is acknowledged to be at work is the search for Christian unity. For those who proclaim this as the work of the Spirit, it is no routine doctrinal formulation. In their own lifetime, the present generation of British church leaders have seen the whole gamut of inter-church relations transformed. Dr Kenneth Greet, secretary of the Methodist Conference, says that as a boy he used to cross the road rather than walk past the local Roman Catholic church but now 'the unaffected warmth of the welcome extended in Roman Catholic pulpits and among groups of priests and laymen of that church is a frequent experience which never fails to evoke a sense of gratitude for the way the barriers have been going down.' (*When the Spirit Moves.*) The whole atmosphere has indeed changed. The defensive denominational tensions of even thirty years ago which could still flare into offensive rivalry, for example over 'converts', have given place on all sides to courtesy and cooperation. When, in 1975, a Roman Catholic archbishop made history by addressing the General Assembly of the Church of Scotland, he was received not just with courtesy but with loud applause. Six months before, a Roman Catholic bishop had received two standing ovations in the General Synod of the Church of England—one before he spoke and another afterwards. The 'warmth of the welcome' has been matched by increasing contact, especially at local level, and by joint social action across a broad front, stretching from demonstrations against pornography and abortion on the right to demands for social justice for the Third World on the left.

'There is abundant evidence,' wrote Dr Greet, 'that the turning of the tide of history in the direction of closer unity between the scattered members of Christ's flock is the work of the Holy Spirit.' Archbishop William Temple had said something similar in 1941 and at Vatican II, the bishops of the Roman Catholic Church had reaffirmed it in the *Decree on Ecumenism*, which was no routine dogma either. As an experienced Rome-watcher, Peter Hebblethwaite, has pointed out: 'against the background of previous utterances, to say that ecumenism was the work of the Holy Spirit was no mere pious cliché: it was a dramatic reversal.' Perhaps the biggest reversal of all was the Council's recognition of other Christian bodies not as groups of individuals separated from the 'one, true Church', but in their own right as churches or 'ecclesial communions'.

It is useful at this stage to put these commonly used words like 'ecumenism' and 'unity' in their proper context. By its origin, the ecumenical movement was a move towards international Christian cooperation rather than organic, theological unity (the word 'ecumenical' and its pre-war form 'oecumenical' come from the Greek word, *oikoumene* meaning 'the whole inhabited world'). The movement was born at the World Missionary Conference in Edinburgh in 1910 and in the inter-war years it developed three strands—the continuation movement which became the International Missionary Council (IMC); the 'Life and Work' movement, concerned with social, economic and political questions; and 'Faith and Order', concerned with the more theological questions of disunity. The latter two came together in the World Council of Churches, established at Amsterdam in 1948 (with which the IMC merged in 1961). As most people are now aware, the dominant element of the World Council became the 'Life and Work' strand of socio-political concern and this was nowhere more clear than in the discussions about Third World problems at the World Assembly at Nairobi in 1975. 'Faith and Order' has taken such a second place that it was recently described in a Church of Scotland report as 'the theological counterpart of Christian Aid', which is really putting the cart before the horse.

Between the wars, the ecumenical movement had a strong influence in Britain—in the 'Call to All Christian People' from the 1920 Lambeth Conference, in the Anglican-Roman Catholic talks at Malines in Belgium in the twenties and in the opening of formal talks between Anglicans and Presbyterians in 1932. But its fullest fruits were seen in the unity achieved within certain confessions—in the reunion of Scottish Presbyterians in 1929 and in the reunion of the three main branches of Methodism in 1932.

After the war, spurred on by the example of the wartime coalition led by Archbishop Temple (and to a lesser extent by Cardinal Hinsley, though his successors were concerned less with leading than restraining ecumenical contacts), there was a renewed drive towards inter-church dialogue. After a brief attempt at a federation of the Free Churches, the main thrust was put into exploration of possible union between the two established churches—the Church of England and the Church of Scotland. These talks, however, came to grief in 1957 when in the so-called 'Bishops Report' the Anglicans proposed that Presbyterians should 'take episcopacy into their system', which stirred up many historic resentments north of the Border. Talks between the Church of England and the Methodist Church opened in 1956, were taken up in earnest in 1965 and resulted in a two-state Union Scheme, incorporating a Service of Reconciliation to unite the two churches' ministries. But although the scheme received the necessary approval at all levels in the Methodist Church, it failed to gain the required 75 per cent majority vote of the Anglican Convocations in 1969 and the General Synod in 1972. With the failure of these two schemes, the only major scheme for church unity to be successful in Britain has been between the Congregational Church and the Presbyterian Church of England which in 1972 came together to form the United Reformed Church.

It is a chequered history. If one pins one's eyes on the present, rather than on the impressive gains in the churches' neighbourly relations during the last fifty years, then one gets a very different impression from the grateful optimism of ecumenically minded church leaders. Among the younger generation, there is impatience with the lack of progress and there is despondency too among some older men. After the 1972 Synod debate, in which Dr Michael Ramsey had described Methodists as 'our brothers in faith and cousins in church history', the Archbishop was quoted as saying: 'we are in darkness, we must become more humble.' And the Church of England's inability to consummate its union with the Methodists has been followed by the breakdown of talks between Anglicans and other churches in Australia, Canada and Scotland.

One explanation that is often given for these setbacks involving Anglicans is the new situation that has been created by the revolution in Roman Catholic attitudes since Vatican II. But here too there have been setbacks. After careful preparation by members of the Catholic Ecumenical Commission, who sensed that there was a 'rising tide' of cooperation, it seemed possible in 1973 that the English and Welsh hierarchy might agree to membership of the British Council of Churches. 'It very, very nearly came off. The sad thing is that "Yes, but not just yet" in 1973, followed by "Not just yet" in 1974, sounds more like "No," and is bound to retard local development and provide an alibi for the already reluctant.' (John Coventry SJ, *The Month*, March 1975.)

The 'rising tide' of cooperation and understanding between Catholics and non-Catholics has also to be seen in the light of recent storms over Rome's policy on canonisations. Having pruned the Church's calendar during the sixties of many popular but historically dubious saints, the Vatican in the seventies was coincidentally embarked on a policy of giving each English-speaking church its own modern saints. 'Modern' in this context meant post-Tridentine or post-Reformation and this inevitably roused the suspicions of some non-Catholics. The first sign of trouble came with the announcement of the 25 October 1970 as the date for the canonisation of forty English and Welsh martyrs of the Tudor period, a 'cause' which had lain dormant for centuries and in the opinion of many British Christians was best left that way if the embers of a particularly nasty period of British religious history were not to be rekindled. The British Council of Churches, putting on a brave face, issued a statement to the effect that the canonisations would not necessarily harm ecumenical relations if they were carried out in a mood of common penitence for the past rather than Catholic triumphalism. In the event, it was Pope Paul who saved the day, with a late addition to his address at the canonisation. 'May the blood of these martyrs,' he said, 'be able to heal the great wound inflicted on God's Church by reason of the separation of the Anglican Church from the Catholic Church.' And he went on to speak of the time when Rome might be able to embrace 'her beloved sister' in one communion which would still preserve the distinctive Anglican contribution to Christendom. It could not have been what the English Catholic proponents of the 'cause' had in mind. Other canonisations followed in 1975—of Mother Elizabeth Seaton, the former Anglican who pioneered the indigenous religious orders in the United States, and of Oliver Plunkett, the Irish Archbishop who was hanged by the British at Tyburn in the seventeenth century. The sanctification of an eminent Irish victim of the British seemed the height of irresponsibility at a time when Anglo-Irish tension was at one of its worst pitches since the seventeenth century, but this time it was popular apathy which saved the day. In Northern Ireland, there were reports of resentment among the urban Catholic population at the pressure put upon them and their children to collect signatures for a saint who in any case attracted little popular devotion. In the

Irish Republic, an embarrassed government in Dublin preferred to play down the whole affair. 'No Flags for St Oliver,' said a headline in the *Catholic Herald*. But the final canonisation of the series did cause real damage to inter-church relations; this was the canonisation on the 17 October 1976 of John Ogilvie, a Scottish Jesuit who had been hanged in 1615 for his defence of the Roman faith. Offence here was taken not so much at the raking over of the hostilities of the past so much as at the Catholic doctrine of saints in the present. The 'proof' of John Ogilvie's sainthood was the miraculous recovery in 1967 from terminal stomach cancer of a Glaswegian whose wife had placed an Ogilvie medal upon his chest. 'The mediatory role and veneration accorded to saints are unacceptable to Protestant Christians,' declared the Church of Scotland journal, *Life and Work*, and it called for a cessation of church unity talks in Scotland if the canonisation went ahead. The ceremony in Rome did take place and, although there was no dramatic rupture of ecumenical contacts in Scotland, the atmosphere was noticeably cooled.

As a result of these and other setbacks, much of the psychological 'spirit' has gone out of the ecumenical movement in Britain. But perhaps the setbacks only deepened a gloom that was already gathering on the horizon of the seventies. Writing in 1971, Barry Till in *The Churches Search for Unity* saw a number of factors already at work:

Partly it is a running-out of steam after the promising-looking progress of the fifties and sixties and the brief general feeling of optimism in the churches at that time. Partly it is a resultant loss of confidence, which is coupled with profound questioning about the validity of institutional religion itself. Partly, it is the fact that at the beginning of the seventies in the churches, as in politics and indeed over the whole world scene, there seems to be a decline in the consensus of western liberal opinion and an increasing polarization of opinion. Inevitably, this affects the ecumenical outlook and means that many premises which would have been taken for granted ten years ago are now being questioned—the necessity of the visible organic unity of the church among them.

Not all church leaders share the despondency of Barry Till and Lord Ramsey. There are after all considerable consolations to be seized and exploited in the present situation, particularly in the large measure of inter-church cooperation and friendliness that now exists. In London, for example, all the churches are joined together in the extremely useful but ponderously tilted Greater London Churches Consultative Group, which has been effective in putting church affairs and problems firmly before the attention of the government, the GLC, the BBC, the IBA and similar bodies. Westminster Abbey and Westminster Cathedral work so closely together these days (and with the Methodist Westminster Central Hall), that it seemed only natural that the new Archbishop of Westminster, Dom Basil Hume, should sing the Latin Benedictine Vespers in the Abbey a few hours after his enthronement in the Cathedral. After all, Dr Coggan heads the list of sponsors to the Westminster Cathedral appeal and the (Anglican) Church Commissioners played an important part in opening up the attractive 'piazza' in front of the nineteenth-century Cathedral. You have only to walk a few hundred yards down Victoria Street with these cooperative ventures in mind to know exactly what Cardinal Hume meant when he spoke of the two communions as formerly estranged sisters. With cooperation of this order, still amazing and even perplexing the older men in both churches, is it so desperately important that there have been setbacks on the road to organic unity? Perhaps too much time, it is now argued, has been spent on ecumenical conversations and on the detail of unity schemes to the neglect of other areas where cooperation is easier and more fruitful. Besides there are far more pressing issues altogether, like mission. Perhaps the enthusiasts for church unity have been too impatient in expecting the divisions of centuries to be healed within a decade or two. Let's give it time. Let us wait until a new generation of church leaders has taken over, with a fresh outlook on unity. Perhaps by then the grass-roots movements will have grown into something that demands a national drive for unity and we can then have unity by acclamation, rather than unity as the result of argument and negotiation.

It is of course a cliché to say that church unity has reached a cross-roads. If the right road forward can be clearly identified (and there are doubts about the unmarked paths of local ecumenicism), even so the way ahead is bound to be more difficult than that travelled up to now. The weakness of the analogy, however, is that many people clearly wish to remain at this present cross-roads, savouring the better atmosphere of Christian cooperation and courtesy, rather than attempting to press on towards organic unity. Lack of progress is a dangerous state: there is always the possibility of falling backwards once the forward momentum has been lost. It is to try to maintain this momentum that the multilateral Churches' Unity Commission was formed in 1972 in the wake of the failure of Anglicans and Methodists to implement bilateral unity. The CUC includes members from seven churches in England (the Church of England, the Roman Catholic, Methodist and United Reformed Churches, the Baptist Union of Great Britain and Ireland and the Moravians and Churches of Christ) and it has now put forward ten 'propositions' on what have been described as the 'crunch ecumenical questions', like intercommunion and mutual recognition of ministries. Member churches are asked to consider these propositions seriously with a view to covenanting to achieve unity at some future date. Multilateral rather than bilateral dialogue is also being tried in Wales and Scotland, although with fewer participants and conspicuously without the Roman Catholics. The idea of covenanting to achieve union however is a difficult one for many churches to swallow. In any case, there has been a resounding lack of popular interest so far in the multilateral approach; to many people it seems like talks for the sake of talks.

Nevertheless, it shows the determination of those inspired by the ecumenical ideal not to let things stand still. As the CUC put it in their first proposition: 'We reaffirm our belief that the visible unity in life and mission of all Christ's people is the will of God.' It was a timely restatement of the conviction that has always been central to the ecumenical movement, that only by achieving the visible and organic unity of the Church, will Christians then be able without equivocation to proclaim to an unbelieving world the one body of their incarnate Lord. The motto of the movement is Jesus's prayer 'that they may all be one, even as thou Father art in me and I in thee, that they also may be in us, so that the world may believe that thou has sent me.' (John xvii 21.) While there is division, the world will go on disbelieving.

Seen in these terms, not only the ecumenical movement but the whole mission of the Church in Britain has reached an impasse. Having grasped the truth of Jesus's prayer for unity, the Churches—or at least the ecumenically-minded leaders in their ranks—cannot now settle for anything less. There can be no provisional solution which stresses the present climate of good relations or joint ventures in social action. They see unity not as a desirable long-term goal, which might have many spin-off benefits in other areas of church life, but as the immediate priority, the *sine qua non* of the future. And yet he would be a rash man who proposed reopening in the near future even the unity talks between Anglicans and Methodists. So it is to the local scene that the leaders look for a way around the impasse, for a way forward from the dangerous crossroads.

The various manifestations of unity in local churches have all grown out of closer personal relations. Describing this as 'the most potent force for unity', Fr Coventry wrote in *The Month*: 'You do not discover the Christianity of Baptists by reading official statements or even by going to Baptists' services. It is when you meet them in an effort to cooperate, and are therefore led to talk about your faith, that you discover their love for Christ, their dedication to his Good News. In personal discovery you come up against the truth of a person rather than the truth of an institution.' The 'discovery of Christian persons' behind unfamiliar denominational labels and attitudes is an experience that has long been familiar to the ecumenical activists, particularly in the student generation, who have freely communicated across the confessional boundaries at seminars, conferences and camps in Britain and abroad. Somehow it has always seemed easier on foreign soil, at Taizé, for example, or at the Ecumenical Centre at Bossey beside Lake Geneva. The limitation of that experience was that it could not often be communicated to parish Christians in Britain, whether clergy or laypeople, and it did not long survive exposure to parish life. This was especially true of the Roman Catholic Church in Britain. But its extension into precisely those areas of church life is what Fr Coventry calls 'by far the most important thing that has happened' since Vatican II.

> You meet the people, you make friends, you may soon discover that they share your theological taste and sense of priorities more than some fellow-Catholics do. It is happening in small house groups all over the country, where laity have just decided to get on with it in their own homes, with or without favour of clergy. It happens in a few parishes as such ... This unitive personal encounter is also a profoundly important aspect of the charismatic prayer movement, which of its nature is undenominational and accepting.

Fr Coventry sees a special value in the ecumenical dimension of mixed marriages—an extremely touchy subject for many Catholics—and cites the pioneering work of the Association of Interchurch Families, 'originating from the local effort of the Rev Martin (CofE) and Ruth (RC) Reardon'. The ecumenical potential of inter-church marriages, as well as their great social value particularly in a divided society, like Northern Ireland, is a point made forcefully by another Roman Catholic writer, Adrian Hastings: 'The traditional Catholic concentration upon the importance of avoiding a religiously mixed marriage . . . implies a restrictive and inadequate understanding of the very nature of marriage, both socially and theologically . . . Instead of excommunicating the mixer, it is surely the role of the Church to bless the pioneer who thus steps out to extend the frontiers of fellowship.' (*The Faces of God.*) That eventuality is still some way off though it is a mark of the new atmosphere that such a (for Catholics) controversial point of view is now increasingly heard.

Another area in which remarkable progress has been made is theology. In the new ecumenical climate, the energy that is generated by personal encounters is able to move theological obstacles that a few years ago looked eternally immovable. An outstanding example of this has been the 'Agreed Statements' on the Eucharist, the Ministry and Authority in the Church produced by the Anglican/Roman Catholic International Commission, set up in 1970. The Eucharist and the Ministry were among the most contentious areas of division between the two churches. To appreciate just how contentious, one has only to look at the Church of England's Thirty-Nine Articles which described the Roman 'sacrifice of Masses' as embodying 'blasphemous fables and dangerous deceits' (Article XXXI) or at the swingeing condemnation of Anglican orders as 'absolutely null and utterly void' by Pope Leo XIII in 1896. The causes and implications of these historical confrontations were left on one side by the Commission's theologians, who concentrated instead on the common faith and experience of today's Christians. In the words of an Anglican member, Dr Henry Chadwick of Oxford, they aimed 'to outflank the Maginot Line of sterile controversy'. And indeed they did. In September 1971, the theologians reached 'substantial agreement' on the Eucharist, reflecting both the Reformation insistence that the Crucifixion was a once-and-for-all and perfect redemption for the sins of all mankind, while preserving the Catholic emphasis on the 'Real Presence' of Christ in the Eucharist—'the sacramental body and blood of the Saviour are present as an offering to the believer awaiting his welcome.' The importance of this statement was that, unlike earlier talks in America between Roman Catholics and either Methodists or Lutherans, there was no need to register points of agreement and disagreement. Although the statement did not pretend to be a comprehensive treatment of the subject, it reached agreement on all 'essential points of Eucharistic doctrine'. The statement on the Ministry, published in December 1973, went one better for it recorded 'full agreement' on the meaning of ordination and the ministry's place within the Church. However, the theologians were careful to point out that their statement did not commit either church to the mutual recognition of ministries (Pope Leo's Bull *Apostolicae Curae* remains in force), yet it did put the issue of recognition in a new context. The statements were, by any criteria, a breakthrough and they gave a new dimension of openness to other ecumenical conversations—for example, to the Scottish Multilateral Church Conversation which in its 1974 report on Worship and the Sacraments referred extensively to the Anglican/Roman Catholic statement on the Eucharist.

In January 1977, after two years of consultation, the theologians produced their final statement, on Authority in the Church. This was by far the hardest test of their endeavour to outflank 'entrenched positions of past controversies', for it was rejection of the primatial authority of the Pope that had been the main plank in the English Reformation ('The Bishop of Rome hath no jurisdiction in this Realm of England,' said Article XXXVII). Moreover, the First Vatican Council had widened the gulf with the doctrine of infallibility. On this issue, there could be no full or substantial agreement which ignored points of disagreement. And they constituted a formidable list: infallibility and the 'divine right' of St Peter's successors, the universal jurisdiction of Rome and also the recent Marian doctrines of the Immaculate Conception and the Assumption. And yet these formed only the coda to what was by any standards a remarkable theological statement. 'The agreement is broad, categoric and massive,' wrote Bishop Butler, the Roman Catholic vice-chairman in the *Guardian*; it had not tried to prove anything but instead to evaluate the lessons of history. Thus the report tried to show how papal primacy had evolved from the Christian community (koinonia), through bishops (episcope) to the conciliarity of the universal Church. 'Primacy fulfils its purpose by helping the churches to listen to one another . . . it does not seek uniformity where diversity is legitimate or centralize administration to the detriment of local churches.' It was remarkable indeed that nine eminent Roman Catholic theologians could view the papacy in that way and no less so that nine eminent Anglicans could contemplate re-submission to Rome, even on those terms. But Archbishop Ramsey had previously said that he could envisage the Pope as 'presiding bishop among the bishops of the world'.

These theological agreements, however, are some considerable distance removed from the personal encounters and ecumenical experiments on the local church scene. Indeed, the evidence points to a substantial lack of popular understanding of the breakthroughs that have been achieved by the Anglican/Roman Catholic Commission. But the theologians have been able to teach other Christians two very important lessons, which deserve wider recognition. The first is that by meeting together rather than separately, they were able to see substantial areas of agreement in even the most intractable differences of doctrine; and secondly, whatever the churchmen of the past might have thought, they have shown that it is not really doctrinal differences that separate the churches of today. This last point was well illustrated by a book published in Britain in 1975 under the title *The Common Catechism*, in which Roman Catholic and Protestant scholars from the Continent were able to devote 550 pages to their common understanding of the Christian faith, and only 116 pages to questions still in dispute. These are valuable exercises in constructive ecumenism, but perhaps even they have already been superceded. It is now the opinion of some theologians, and of many untheological laymen who have arrived at the same conclusion intuitively, that a complete unity of belief need not be a pre-condition of the unity of Christians together. The working hypothesis of many grass-roots experiments in unity could be said to be: 'We live in communion with each other not as a sign that we all believe the same things but in order that we can learn to share in each other's beliefs.'

Unity on the local scene, which is far more evident in England than in Wales, Scotland or Northern Ireland, has taken two forms. The first is essentially a matter of cooperation, which leaves the structures of the local churches—their staff, finances, buildings and organisations—intact. Cooperation may take the form of Local Councils of Churches, now quite widespread with Roman Catholics as full members in up to three-quarters of them. It may take the form of specific ventures in evangelism, for example on new housing estates, in social care, like the 'Fish' scheme for helping the aged and infirm, in youth work, discussion groups, indeed in a whole range of activities which are more effectively done together than along separate denominational lines. Often, local cooperation takes the form of one church offering another the hospitality of its building during a time of reconstruction or retrenchment. An increasingly common development is for clergy from different churches to meet together on a regular or even a daily basis for prayer, Bible study and cross-fertilisation of ideas. Many of these ventures in local cooperation, however, are hedged about with limitations. They may depend heavily on the personalities of the clergy involved, so that the depart-ure of one or two of them leads to collapse or apathy They may not get through to the ordinary churchpeople for whom local ecumenism may appear an optional extra to Sunday worship. There are legal difficulties, too, particularly for the non-Anglican use of the buildings of the Established Church. And there is the constant friction of the local group with the rules and attitudes of the wider church institu-tions, which do not always deal imaginatively with local opportunities and problems as they arise. The British Council of Churches, which has a watchdog committee for 'local ecumenical projects', points out that the main difficulty is the absence of any national framework into which local initiatives can fit. The BCC has also reported that many of the Local Councils of Churches fall between two stools: they are either too big in terms of their committee structures for the limited aims they have set themselves, or they are too small effectively to cope with major challenges or to relate to local authorities in their area. It is all too easy, as many local ecumenicists know, for these limitations to stop local cooperation dead in its tracks or to turn it into something formal and superficial.

On the other hand, when the wider church does give its full blessing and assistance to local ventures, remarkable things can be achieved. For example, the 'proposition' of the Churches' Unity Council that member churches should share their services of initiation, like baptism, confirmation and reception into membership, is already a significant feature of many ventures in local cooperation. At Andover, in Hampshire, a joint reception service was first held in 1974 by the Methodists and Anglicans. In 1975 it was expanded so that the chair-man of the Southampton Methodist District and the local United Reformed Church minister both received members into their churches at the same time as the Bishop of Winchester confirmed ten young Anglicans. The occasion was completed by a Communion Service, at which the president was the URC minister with the bishop and other clergy assisting. It was by no means a typical example of local ecu-menical cooperation, but nor was it an isolated example. Indeed, the Bishop, Dr John Taylor, has said that there is no point in the churches making such services possible and offering the possibility of inter-communion, unless people are prepared to take up these opportunities.

It is in the second field of local ecumenism, in the sharing of parishes and churches, that this sort of joint sacramental experience is really being explored. These are exceptional and largely experimental examples of cooperation. They include inter-denominational parishes served by team ministries drawn from a number of churches and in some cases the joint use of church buildings on a permanent and shared basis. Thus they are very different from the extension of hospitality by one church to another. In a booklet, *Adventures in Unity*, the former head of the BCC's ecumenical relations department, David Blatherwick, gave details of fifty places in England where these pioneering schemes operated in 1975 and in twelve of them Roman Catholics are participants. Many of these experiments are in New Towns or development areas, where the absence of inherited buildings and established congregations gives the local ecumenists virgin territory on which to build. And they have not only built church buildings, but new ways of sharing administration, money, governing bodies and pastoral responsibilities. The constitution of a shared church like the one at Desborough in Northamptonshire is a document of much more than local interest. Indeed, the one example of this form of cooperation in Scotland, in the joint venture by four churches at Livingston New Town, West Lothian, has become such an object of interest for both sympathetic and critical observers that the local Ecumenical Council is now begging to be regarded as no longer experimental, but as normal and permanent.

In Scotland, there is as yet no involvement by Roman Catholics in the sharing of churches. This is in line with the Vatican's insistence that 'Catholic churches are reserved for Catholic worship' except in special cases like chapels at airports or military camps. But in England, ecumenical experiments have already stretched this rule considerably. At Pin Green, in the New Town of Stevenage, Herts, a church built within the community centre is shared by Anglicans, Roman Catholics and Methodists, and there is an Anglican/Roman Catholic church at Cippenham, Slough. Similar projects are also planned for Hemel Hempstead and Telford New Town in Salop. At Pin Green, as at Cippenham, the Sacrament is reserved by both Anglicans and Catholics in a common tabernacle, divided by a glass partition. The clergy say that it ought to carry a notice saying: 'In the event of unity, please break the glass.'

One particularly vexed problem that these experimental churches have thrust upon the attention of their parent bodies is intercommunion. Here the demand for full participation in the Eucharistic celebrations of their partners in the local experiment is often way ahead of the practice or rules of the national churches. For the non-episcopal churches, this presents less of a problem for they have traditionally 'welcomed to the Lord's table any Christians who can conscientiously accept the invitation'. But the Methodist Church has found it necessary, largely for legal reasons, to commission a small number of Church of England clergymen into a dual ministry. The official Anglican practice on intercommunion has changed dramatically in the last few years. In 1968, the Church undertook a lengthy process of consultation to produce the report *Intercommunion Today*, which even then was guarded in its majority recommendations about the occasions on which intercommunion should be allowed; now Canon Law admits to the Eucharist any 'baptised persons who are communicant members of other churches which subscribe to the doctrine of the Holy Trinity'. The official line has changed, but Anglican practice is moving only slowly in the same direction.

For Roman Catholics, however, intercommunion is forbidden except in cases of 'urgent necessity', like imminent death or travel abroad. When asked in 1972 what he would give as the special circumstances in which intercommunion could be practised, the late Cardinal Heenan replied 'maybe in a concentration camp'. The Vatican's rule is clear, but the practice is certainly not. There have been spectacular transgressions of the rule at ecumenical gatherings in Europe and America since the Second Vatican Council and on a less noticeable level intercommunion by individuals and small groups, especially of charismatic Christians, is going on despite the rule. As Fr Coventry observed: 'Even five years ago, this was something we associated with wild Dutchmen and obviously disintegrated Americans. Now it, or at any rate the admission of others to our Communion, is increasingly common at home.' But when Fr David Woodward, the Catholic priest at the shared church in Cippenham, announced his proposal in early 1976 that 'the distinction between Anglicans and Catholics at the respective Eucharists should not be observed after Maundy Thursday for anyone in the two communities who so wished', there was uproar. It was forcefully pointed out to Fr Woodward by his diocesan bishop and by members of the Catholic Ecumenical Commission that he was not only acting without authority, but jeopardising wider ecumenical progress and really declaring a sort of parish UDI on the larger question of the validity of Anglican orders. Fr Woodward withdrew his proposal, but whether intercommunion is unofficially practised at Cippenham who can tell.

Intercommunion is seen as the major barrier through which the churches must break if there is to be any substantial progress towards unity. As Adrian Hastings observed: 'today intercommunion is without doubt the most important internal issue facing the ecumenical movement . . . it cannot and must not be by-passed anymore.' Yet intercommunion is a many-sided issue, both between the churches and within them. The strict Roman Catholic regulation of intercommunion, for example, reflects an obvious determination to maintain the discipline of all local churches in communion with Rome and it is claimed that the rule protects the feelings of the many Catholics who are psychologically and culturally unable to accept the practice. Local UDI's on intercommunion, unless restrained by the bishops, could lead to rebellion on the conservative, anti-ecumenical wing. That at least is what those close to the Roman Catholic hierarchy would have people believe. But a more substantial objection to intercommunion is that it pre-empts the solution of the theological issues which separate the churches. For Roman Catholics, the Eucharist is the communion of those who share the same faith, particularly the faith in the special presence of Christ in the Eucharist itself. But, surely, ecumenists ask, the Anglican/Roman Catholic International Commission has proved that on all essential points of faith the two churches do share that faith: even if the Vatican's embargo on Anglican orders rules out Catholic participation in the Church of England Eucharist, there is no theological reason why Anglicans should not be welcomed at the Catholic altar. In the last resort, however, the objections to intercommunion are not theological so much as psychological. The fact that many lay people are daily breaking through this barrier and are quietly practising intercommunion is something that church leaders as yet prefer not to discuss too openly. And it does not apply only to the Roman Catholic leaders. The Scottish Episcopal Church (Anglican) which has a very 'High' view of the Eucharist, has so far been unable to agree to intercommunion with the Church of Scotland 'as a necessary step towards reunion', but it has been forced to recognise that many of its people do communicate at the Presbyterian Lord's Table without a qualm. It is said that few things displeased Queen Victoria during her stays at Balmoral so much as Mr Gladstone's insistence on walking off on a Sunday morning to the nearest Episcopal Church. Nowadays, he would probably not have felt he had to be so scrupulously Anglican.

So the movement towards church unity in Britain has entered a diverse problematical phase. Those who still have faith in the ecumenical ideal are pressing ahead with multilateral discussions and with trying to nurture the delicate plant of local unity. Many more are just getting on with it, with or without the blessing of their parent churches. There is still a considerable body of resisters, who see the ecumenical movement as yet another treacherous blow at the faith 'as delivered to the saints' on the part of the secularising and syncretising *avant garde*. And the majority are probably fed up with the whole thing, preferring to leave this aspect of internal ecclesiastical debate to those who have a penchant for it while they press on with the more urgent task of Christian witness to a non-Christian world. But there is a final group, whom we have not so far taken note of. They are by no means disinterested in progress towards Christian unity, but they would rather stand back from the present difficulties in order to evaluate the weaknesses which have perhaps been inherent in the ecumenical movement from its beginnings. Not surprisingly, these critics take as much of a sociological as a theological view of these weaknesses.

First, they see the inability of the enthusiasts for church unity to provide ordinary church people with a picture of what unity would be like for them. It is now an axiom of all planning in the secular field that participation by citizens and workers is only possible if they can visualise the end result and see in some detail the practical application of the planned development to their own lives. In the planning of church unity this has seldom been attempted. The reasons against it are that unity is regarded as an open-ended affair in which the end picture is known only to the Holy Spirit. Some models for *achieving* unity have been put forward, notably the pioneer schemes of the Church of South India and the 'Lanka scheme' in what used to be Ceylon where episcopal and non-episcopal churches have come together. But these can hardly serve as illustrations of how unity can be lived in Britain. A cluster of Asian villages with at the most two or three churches from different Christian traditions widely spaced out among other religious communities bears little comparison with the British town in which rival churches face each other across the High Street. Would all of this ecclesiastical plant continue to operate in a united church or would some be closed, perhaps in order to economise on heating bills and ministers' salaries? And if some close, then will it be the Victorian Methodist chapel or the Perpendicular parish church? It may seem an awfully loaded question to the churchpeople concerned. And yet it is a question that has seldom been faced. But perhaps, unity would not be anywhere so visible or organic as is proclaimed, and there would be a long period in which the parallel worshipping communities continued to co-exist with a greater or lesser degree of contact and intercommunion depending on the local circumstances. That is an end picture which would clearly command more commitment from ordinary Christians.

A *second* and related issue is the question of institutional size. It may be more by coincidence than design but the fifties and sixties which were the decades of most activity in national ecumenical ventures were also the period in which industrial mergers and the construction of huge business conglomerates were a national fashion. Now bigness in industry is no longer seen as necessarily in the interests of the consumer, of worker loyalty and initiative, or even of economic efficiency. The new fashion is that small is beautiful. As in some parts of government, in industry and commerce, so also in the churches, it is to the small, intimate community that people are looking for new ideas and for evidence of new growth. But alongside the attention now being paid to the grass roots and the attempts at devolution, there has been a steady growth of power and bureaucracy at the centre. One can see this in the churches in the proliferation of Synods, conferences, commissions and committees. The Roman Catholic Church, which since Vatican II has been committed to devolution of some of its power down to the national and diocesan levels, is now awash with committees and commissions. The growth of bureaucracy has also become a feature of the ecumenical movement, which is one element in the disenchantment that many people feel for it. The prospects of church unity being built around a simpler, less institutionalised form of Christian community are not good. If any major scheme for church unity does come about in Britain in the coming decade, it will almost inevitably swell the ranks of the committee men and women.

A *third* cause of alienation between the ecumenical movement and ordinary church people is the former's inability to explain how much diversity would be compatible with unity. It is now widely said that unity does not mean uniformity, but this is a concept that was introduced into the ecumenical dialogue at a late stage. It was still being noted as something significant from Roman Catholic speakers as recently as 1972, when Cardinal Willebrands, president of the

97

Vatican's Secretariat for Chrisitan Unity, spoke in a lecture at Lambeth about 'union without absorption'. Similarly, in an enthusiastic comment on *Christian Unity and Christian Diversity* by Professor John Macquarrie in *The Tablet*, Bishop Christopher Butler formulated the vital question for the future as 'How much diversity is compatible with the continuing historical identity of the *ecclesia catholica* that is the mother of us all ?' Yet, for many Roman Catholics and Anglicans, diversity is understood mainly to refer to liturgical diversity—as, for example, in the Uniate churches which use various Eastern liturgical rites but nonetheless are in communion with Rome, the church of the Western rite. But why should diversity stop at liturgy? Could there be in a united church a genuine diversity of teaching and practice over such issues as divorce, the ordination of women, or social questions like abortion and contraception. This is indeed the vital question for the future of ecumenical dialogue. Lay confidence in that question being fairly answered is not necessarily helped by the creeping uniformity of the churches in liturgical matters. The English rite for the Roman Catholic Mass is similar to the experimental 'Series 3' liturgy in use in the Church of England, and neither of them is significantly different from the 'High Church' liturgies currently used in some Free Churches, like the Methodist Church.

Fourthly, if the ecumenical movement threatens viable diversity within the churches, it also creates division where none existed before. It is often said by ecumenical leaders that church unity is not to be compared with diplomatic alliances formed between nations, where entering into one alliance inevitably means the loosening of ties in another direction. It ought not to be like that in church affairs but in practice it becomes so—if for no other reason than the fact that the conclusion of a unity scheme inevitably turns the participating churches inwards upon the problems of consolidating their union, thus making them less receptive for a time to other unity options. On another level, talks of church unity can turn a mission-minded, unselfconscious local church into a body which is forced to study and justify its denominational identity. This may have been the main reason why the Anglican/Presbyterian talks in the fifties were so deeply resented in Scotland where many rural parishes regarded themselves as 'the Church', and not primarily as Presbyterians, until they were forced into doing so.

A *fifth* cause of dissatisfaction with the ecumenical movement is that it seems to appeal to only one side of human nature, and a side which has not always been traditionally given the most value in British history. As Barry Till observed, the movement towards church unity has been linked with the consensus of Western liberal opinion. One could go on to characterise it as embracing the virtues of moderation, compromise, gradualism and the submission of the individual's religious scruples to the will of the community. It is not far-fetched to link it with the Butskillism which sought the middle ground of politics in the early sixties, rather than with the more abrasive politics of the seventies; or with the support of British membership of the EEC rather than the stubbornly nationalist case for Britain staying out and going it alone. But the alternative tradition in British society which places value on individualism, competition, argument and a certain abrasiveness, is one that has served the churches well in the past. What after all were the martyrs and dissenters but representatives of this tradition? This is a major topic, which there is not space to go into here, but the point can be made simply by reference to the style of religious debate in Britain today. It is often remarked that our church leaders, who are largely on the side of ecumenism, lack fire and passion in their utterances. One has only to read most ecumenical documents to see that the desire of their authors to win wide acceptance robs them of their cutting edge, their challenge. By comparison, there is no lack of a cutting edge to the utterances of the opponents of unity schemes. The late Professor Ian Henderson of Glasgow, who had been active in the Scottish resistance to the 1957 'Bishops Report', followed this a decade later with a book entitled *Power Without Glory*, in which he pursued the theme that the Anglican insistence on episcopacy in united churches was a form of imperialism. The professor belonged to a venerable controversialist tradition stretching back to Dean Swift and beyond. And it would not be unfair to them to see the Anglican opponents to the Methodist unity scheme as belonging to the same tradition. They numbered eminent Anglo-Catholics alongside conservative evangelicals (which led one Free Churchman to comment that it was the strangest alliance since Pontius Pilate and Herod) and they singled out for attack the deliberate ambiguities of the Anglican/Methodist service for reconciling the two ministries, which they saw as a throughly dishonest foundation on which to build a united church. 'Scripture records a man who built his house upon the sand. The removal of the foundations of his house led inevitably to the building's collapse. Or was it inevitable? Perhaps the man could have learned from the architects of the rite under review. They built on sand, watched the sand wash away in a storm, and, behold, their house still stood' (*Growing Into Union*, 1969). It may not have been a constructive or positive view of the difficulties of achieving church unity (although elsewhere in the book, the four authors did make positive proposals for the sort of piece-meal, grass-roots unity which is now in fact happening), but the positive view may not always be the most effective or the most persuasive. As Jonathan Swift remarked, 'positive men are the most credulous.'

The *sixth* and final criticism of the ecumenical movement which is worth noting is that, to many people, unity seems to proceed not from strength but from weakness. Adrian Hastings has shown that the ecumenical movement coincided with a slackening of the missionary impetus among Western churches, first by the Protestants and then since 1960 by the Roman Catholics. 'Not only in Britain but also in the young churches it is often noticeable that it is the relatively static groups which are most interested in systematic ecumenism. The strongly missionary ones are really too busy growing and evangelising to bother.' In the words of a sociologist who has made his research in Africa, 'sects proliferate where people are enthusiastic about religion and reunion is often a token of decline.' (*The Faces of God*). Fr Hastings cites an example which is distressingly typical of some ecumenical ventures. At the inauguration of an ecumenical theological college, which joined together two denominational ones, all of the speeches concentrated on the progress signified by the merger and none mentioned the point which had been decisive, that the main college had been half empty for years and was therefore in a critical financial situation. There is of course no reason why the Holy Spirit should not operate through economic stringency as much as through the best ideals of the unity enthusiasts, but it does illustrate the lack of clear, critical thinking that often accompanies ecumenical enthusiasm. If unity is born of weakness, then it is to be expected that it will lead to further weakening or even paralysis of whatever missionary zeal exists. One has only to compare the proselytising zeal of nineteenth-century Methodism in Britain, or of the Roman Catholic Church in this country even twenty years ago, with the present state of introspection in both churches since they have become more ecumenically conscious, to see the force of this criticism. It becomes even more evident if one compares the zeal for evangelism among the main churches with that of the Jehovah's Witnesses, who are totally opposed to any accommodation with other religious bodies.

None of the six criticisms summarised above is a reason for abandoning the quest for church unity. The churches have progressed too far down the unity road for them to turn back. But these observations do indicate that the ecumenical movement has not always been as self-critical as it might have been. It has been swept along by its own momentum, regarding resistance to unity as evidence of human weakness or even sin. It has often been Utopian and has seen unity as the promised land in which all of the other problems of the churches would somehow become solvable. Worst of all, perhaps, it has failed so far to get its priorities right on the crucial questions of mission and diversity. There are now signs that these priorities are being reordered as a result of the problems which the movement towards church unity has encountered in the seventies.

7

Liturgical Revolution

In clear contrast to the ecumenical movement, the movement of liturgical renewal and reform in the churches has completed its main work. In the Church of England, the original Liturgical Commission set up by the archbishops in 1955, held its final meeting at the end of 1975, having drafted new services for almost all occasions in the life of the Church, including no less than three experimental orders of Holy Communion. In most other churches, liturgical commissions and committees have transformed themselves from bands of pioneering draughtsmen into consultancies, promoting and facilitating change at the local level. But the air of work completed does not mean that liturgical change has been universally effective or universally acceptable. In some places, quite the contrary.

Forms of worship (for that is all that the technical word 'liturgy' really means) are one of the most sensitive areas of religion. They are the point at which the official churches of the episcopal hierarchies, the assemblies, conferences and so on, come into close and constant contact with the people. And church people are at heart conservative. Resistance to change in the forms of worship is, therefore, in part resistance to the new and the unfamiliar. After all, one of the chief attractions of Christian worship through the ages has been its unchanging, rock-like character in a world of bewildering intellectual and social change. It is comforting for people who hold on to the 'faith as given to the saints' to know that they are worshipping in the same way that the saints did. Indeed, the two churches most affected by recent liturgical change, the Anglican and Roman Catholic Churches, had maintained their liturgies virtually unchanged for 400 years.

But for laymen, worship is not just a set form of words or a familiar sequence of actions. It is the context and often the necessary stimulus for personal piety as well as the embodiment of the doctrine of the church to which they are content to belong. This has particularly been the case in the Church of England, where the ambiguous, if not actually contradictory, language of the 1662 Book of Common Prayer has enabled people with a wide range of doctrinal beliefs to find a home in Anglican worship. But the conservatism of the laity in the face of liturgical change is a feature of all churches. And the most conservative groups, apart from the elderly, are the lay élite, whether they are the elders of a rural Scottish Kirk, or leading Catholics like the late Duke of Norfolk, who is reported to have told the Pope at a private audience that liturgical change was 'unwelcome' in England and there should be no more of it.

Like most of the movements for change described in this book, the liturgical movement did not originate in Britain. It began in nine-teenth-century France, growing slowly at first within the Benedictine Order and then spreading outwards from abbeys like Solesmes in France, Maria Laach in Germany and Maredsous in Belgium. It received its greatest fillip in Rome when in 1903 Pope Pius X issued a *motu proprio*, encouraging more frequent Communion and better use of music, particularly the Gregorian chant. The phrase of Pius X that best summed up the aims of the liturgical movement was the 'active participation' of the people. It is also worth noting that in the pope's pronouncement, and explicit in much of the early writings of the liturgical reformers, was the theme of a uniform liturgy. Having estab-lished the Eucharist as a participatory event for the people, there was to be no back-sliding by means of local variations and ancient customs. The chief architect of the Anglican liturgy, Archbishop Cranmer, took precisely the same view.

The focus of the reformers' attention then was the Eucharist, the only act of corporate worship that Jesus himself had instituted. In the gospels, Jesus told his disciples not just to attend the Eucharist but to 'do this in remembrance of me'. And that applied to all of them. How-ever, in all of the churches of Western Europe, the doing aspect of the Eucharist had been severely neglected since the sixteenth century. In the Roman Catholic Church, the main emphasis was on attending Mass, which was muttered in Latin by a priest who for most of the time kept his back to the people. They, for their part, watched eagle-eyed for one action, the elevation of the Host, and then returned to their private devotions. Some Catholics did take Communion but, unless they were specially devout, not more frequently than twice a year and even then only after careful preparation, fasting and personal confession. In the Protestant churches, the Eucharist was even more remote from ordinary worship. Despite the intentions of their found-ing fathers—Luther, Calvin, Cranmer and Wesley—they neglected the Lord's Supper and put in its place as the high point of Sunday worship a service of scriptural edification, prayer and song. It was in effect the old Eucharistic rite, cut short at the sermon. There had of course been earlier reform movements before this century's liturgical revival. The Anglican Tractarians had taught the importance of the Holy Communion, but most of them put as much emphasis on the subjective faith of the inactive individual communicant as did their Evangelical rivals.

So, before the Second World War, a clear pattern of denominational worship was established in Britain, with no church putting much emphasis on participation in the Eucharist as the norm of Christian worship. In the Anglican churches, the big event was Morning Prayer, with its protracted chanting of canticles and psalms, after which on one Sunday in four a few, usually aged, members of the congregation would stay behind for Communion if they had not been able to attend 'the early'—the sparsely-attended, music-less 8 a.m. service. The Eucharist only became a big event at Easter and other major festivals. In Roman Catholic and Anglo-Catholic churches, the main Sunday worship was High Mass or Sung Eucharist, which provided the congregation with a distant spectacle of ritual, brightly-coloured vestments and often superb music, but little opportunity for 'active participation'. In the Church of Scotland and the Free Churches, Sunday worship was intended to be less formal, although the pattern had become as set as elsewhere. It consisted of hymns, extempore prayer and sermon, conducted by a black-gowned minister or lay preacher, who seldom moved from the pulpit which towered above the flower-decked Communion table. The latter was put to its proper use no more than once a month, sometimes even once a quarter or less frequently. It was said that infrequent Communion was not a sign that Free Churchmen undervalued the Eucharist, but that they valued it too highly to let it become a weekly routine. One Church of Scotland writer of the forties, describing the 'extraordinary awe' with which the Sacrament was regarded, said that 'people, conscious of their unworthiness, would often wait until old age before becoming communicants'. Even today in many parts of Scotland, communicant members of the Kirk are a minority of regular worshippers and the same is true of other 'Reformed' churches, like Irish Presbyterians and Welsh Independents (Congregationalists).

This then was the arid eucharistic landscape in which from the end of the war onwards the liturgical movement began to take root. The

Roman Catholic Church, with its Irish tradition of a passive laity, was to remain largely unreceptive to the change until the late sixties. It was in the Church of England that the new movement first flourished. The seminal event was a conference in Birmingham in 1949, at which the Parish and People movement was born. Its inspiration was only indirectly continental, coming mainly through the writings of liturgically-conscious Anglican monks, like Gabriel Hebert SSM, editor of *The Parish Communion* (1937) and Dom Gregory Dix, author of the massive and influential *Shape of the Liturgy* (1945). The aim of Parish and People was to establish the people's Eucharist as the central act of Anglican worship, in which the congregation would play an active part in the ritual, the singing and even the prayers. A noted feature of the new service was the Offertory, when a group of men and women would proceed from the back of the church to the chancel bearing, not only money, but bread and wine and on occasion the fruits or symbols of their work, in emulation of the French Young Worker Masses of the period. There were also (for that time) adventurous experiments in music, particularly in the use of Folk Masses and accompanying guitar groups. The symbolism was fine but the Parish and People movement was anxious that the people should also appreciate the deeper significance of the liturgy. Roving monks and friars would go around parishes introducing the new services to lead seminars and teaching courses. At the same time, the traditional Anglican sermon based on scripture began its long decline into a shorter, Catholic homily based on some aspect of the liturgy or of the Church's calendar.

If the growth of the Parish Communion was a revolutionary movement within the Church of England—and by the early sixties, it had made Mattins redundant in many parishes—then this was a revolution whose leaders were kept away from the real levers of change. The problem was the Church's written liturgy. The only legal form of Anglican worship in England remained the Book of Common Prayer of 1662, with the legally dubious amendments approved by the bishops in 1928 (following the abortive attempt to get Parliament to sanction Prayer Book revision in 1927). However, neither the 1662 nor the 1928 version of the Holy Communion, even with the wealth of minor variations which many clergy were making independently, was a suitable vehicle for the new mood of participation. It was like trying to contain an active young wine in old wineskins. The Church had to have the freedom to revise its liturgy, to meet both the popular demand for experiment and the criticisms of the liturgical scholars, who thought that the pedigree of Anglican liturgy should be straightened out with the mongrel elements, deriving from obscure 16th-century controversies, removed.

Freedom of worship has not always been a congenial battle-cry for Anglican leaders. But it was under this theme that the Prayer Book (Alternate and Other Services) Measures, 1965, was steered through the Synod and then through Parliament. The Measure gave the Church freedom to introduce experimental forms of worship for a period of fifteen years, under certain restrictions relating to doctrine and majority voting. The restrictions were there partly in the expectation that by 1980 the Church of England would have acquired sufficient unanimity to embark on a formal revision of its worship, and partly to defuse the conservative opposition within the Church which clung to the legal formularies of 1662. However, in 1975 the Church gained something that it had not had since the Reformation, namely the freedom to re-order its worship without any parliamentary restriction.

So, in 1965, the way was clear for the first major revision of Anglican worship since 1549—fifteen years before the birth of Shakespeare—but finding a viable alternative to the English of the first Elizabethan age was only one problem among many for the reformers. In 1965, the Liturgical Commission, founded in 1955, was given a wider remit and set about its work in two stages. The first was a modest up-dating of the old services, to remove some of the more glaring anachronisms and to give a greater range of choice in prayers. This had already been done in the earlier work of the Commission for Morning and Evening Prayer and for the Litany. The second stage was the drafting of virtually new services in accordance with recent scholarship. This was controversial for it often raised in a new form doctrinal issues which had been dormant for years. Thus, when in 1966, the Commission produced two versions of the Holy Communion, called Series 1 and Series 2, there was no need to debate the former for it was a modest adaptation of the old liturgy. But Series 2, apart from being for all intents and practices a new service, raised issues like prayers for the dead and the question of the sense in which the Eucharist could be said to be a sacrifice. The old Church Assembly spent two days debating the sacrificial language of Series 2. But Series 2 was not pressed upon any parish which did not desire it and it was in any case intended only for five years' experimental use. In 1971, a further version of the Eucharist was published incorporating a number of changes put forward by parishes using Series 2, but more significantly this Series 3 version addressed God for the first time not as 'Thou' but as 'You'. The Liturgical Commission hoped that Series 3 would become the definitive Anglican liturgy for some time to come. But already there were legal alternatives to it in 1662 and in Series 1, and moreover a certain attachment for Series 2 had grown up as a consequence of which its lifespan was extended from 1971 to 1976.

This has been described as 'liturgical chaos'. It was certainly liturgical diversity of a wide variety. And whereas the old diversity of Anglican worship was a set of variations on the original theme of 1662, the new pluralism was polarised between 1662 and Series 3—two fundamentally different forms of worship. They were so different that it is doubtful if a young confirmation candidate brought up on one would recognise the other as being part of the worship of the same church. It is only recently that older members of a few congregations have prevailed upon their church councils to provide a range of alternative liturgies. There have also been suggestions that a 'Prayer Book Sunday' should be held to rescue the 1662 services from oblivion, at least once a year. There is a group called the Prayer Book Society which aims to do just that and particularly to revive the disused Canticles of Morning and Evening Prayer, like the *Te Deum* and *Magnificat*.

It is often said that the deepest divisions of the Church are no longer between denominations but within them. This is certainly true of liturgy. In the Methodist Church, for example, there had grown up since the war a group of liturgical enthusiasts who practised frequent Communion and used rites and vestments similar to those of the Church of England. In 1975, this group was given the official blessing of the Methodist Conference which approved a new order of Holy Communion, very similar to the Anglican Series 3. But the Methodist Church still retains the old Wesleyan liturgy and indeed there is no obligation on ministers to use either, or indeed any set form of service. There is a similar though less marked diversity in the Reformed churches, particularly in respect of the frequency of Communion. When the Church of Scotland's Committee on Public Worship in 1973 proposed that there should be more frequent celebration of the Sacrament, the replies as reported to the 1975 General Assembly were polite but non-committal: 'Only a few presbyteries thought that weekly Communion was, in the present climate of opinion within the Church, practicable. [Most] felt that the Church should rather work towards encouraging monthly Communion, or at least more Communion occasions than the traditional half-yearly or quarterly Communion.'

In the Roman Catholic Church, the arrival of liturgical change differed from both the extreme gradualism of the Presbyterians and the Anglicans' leap into diversity. For Roman Catholics, the change was quick, imposed from above and uniform. The lack of opportunity for any real diversity (though some experimentation was allowed) was partly derived from the old uniformity of the liturgical movement, partly a necessity to get the changes accepted by conservative parishes, and partly the product of the disciplinarianism of Rome. It is said that in the Vatican everything is forbidden until it is actually ordered. For British Catholics, liturgical change was not an indigenous growth but the first really significant change that reached them from the Vatican Council. The Council had taken up in earnest Pius X's phrase, 'active participation', and applied it both to the form of the liturgy and to the language. At first, the Vatican's reformers moved with caution. The Mass was regarded as being in two parts—the priest's part (which remained in Latin) and that which belonged to the people (translated into the vernacular). But that distinction did not last for long under the barrage of changes which emanated from the liturgical draughtsmen in the five years following the end of the Council in 1965. In any case, the Council itself had put a new premium on simpler and understandable rites. Ritual should be 'short, clear and unencumbered by useless repetitions' and 'within the people's powers of comprehension'. Ritual had therefore to be less slapdash, but it also had to be seen.

The most effective change of all was the bringing of the Mass out of the inner sanctuary, where it had been the province of priests and acolytes dressed in white, into the midst of the people. New altars, often of unadorned wood, were set up in the body of the church and the priest turned to face the people, no longer appearing to be their mediator at a remote sacrificial offering but now their president at the corporate act of thanksgiving and dedication. This move, taken together with the use of English and the greater lay participation, was truly revolutionary. It was also powerfully ecumenical. Apart from some variation in the language, there was little that was now distinctively different in the Roman Mass from the Eucharist that was being celebrated in many Anglican, Methodist and Reformed churches.

The ecumenical aspect of the new liturgy was of course double-edged. Its opponents saw it as evidence of a conspiracy by a few traitorous theologians who had somehow infiltrated the Vatican Council (perhaps inside a wooden horse) and opened the gates to the Reformation. After all, the Mass in the vernacular was one of Luther's demands and so was Communion for the laity under both kinds—the chalice as well as the Host. This had been envisaged by the Council but resisted for some years afterwards. In fact, the bishops of Britain often tried to put the brake on the changes, largely out of regard for the more conservative members of their flock. Cardinal Heenan had tried to stop the practice of Communion being received into the hand and Archbishop Cowderoy of Southwark banned as 'unseemly' any physical contact, even shaking hands, at the Kiss of Peace. (Except among charismatics and experimentalists, this liturgical sign of brotherly love was slow to catch on: many Anglicans found it rather 'un-English.') 'Unseemliness', however, was a minor fault compared with some that were detected in the new Mass by a vociferous group of conservatives whose campaign against it reached its peak in the autumn of 1975. The words they used were 'heretical', 'invalid' and even 'un-Catholic'. Conspiracy charges began to fly on both sides. The official Church found clear evidence of conspiracy in the way that the traditionalists had captured the attention of the world's press and television, when they mounted their resistance in a small town in Norfolk.

The Downham Market episode was the sort of dispute that Roman Catholics understandably try to keep from the eyes of non-Catholics. None of the participants, who included two bishops, emerged from it with much credit. But it may have served a useful purpose in bringing into the light a number of skeletons which had been rattling away in the Catholic cupboard for some years. What was at stake was the deep personal attachment of many Catholics in Britain for the old Latin Mass, or to be precise for the 'Tridentine Mass' which had been promulgated at the Council of Trent in 1570. In many respects, the traditionalists were being hoisted with their own petard. They had identified the truth of their religion with the claim that the Mass could never change and that the same Mass was used with precisely the same words in every corner of the Catholic world. It was also the Mass which the recusants had celebrated in England in the dark days of Elizabeth I's rule and for which many of them had given their lives. So, when the new 'Normative' Mass in English was introduced in 1969, and even more when it was made obligatory at Christmas 1970, the traditionalists saw this as the most heinous of betrayals. Such a head of steam had built up against the change that the bishops were prepared to turn a blind eye to the continued celebration of the old Mass in a few parishes. They even sought an 'indult' from Rome, so that the Tridentine Mass could be used on appropriate special occasions, like annual gatherings of the traditionalist Latin Mass Society (and in fact the modern Mass is often said in Latin). But implicit in these indulgences was the understanding that change could not be resisted for long and that the Mass must not be used for public displays of disunity.

It is probably true to say that the vast majority of Catholics in Britain, particularly those of Irish ancestry, accepted the change as a necessary reform, sanctioned by the authority of their church. Undoubtedly many of them did so with regret, but others displayed a determination to re-discover the meaning of worship in the new liturgy. In any case, by 1975 the new Mass was past history for most parishes. The problem for the bishops was how to overcome the resistance of the minority, who were often middle-class and certainly not submissive Irish, without causing any public scandal.

At Downham Market, in west Norfolk on the edge of the Fens, the episcopal solution was to be a merger with the parish of the nearby town of Swaffham. And as the parish priest, Fr Oswald Baker, showed a stubborn attachment to the Latin Tridentine Mass he had been celebrating at Downham Market for the past twenty-four years, he was to lose his job in the merger. What the bishops did not foresee, was that Downham Market would become the field for a last-ditch battle against the new liturgy, and attract resisters from many parts of Britain and from abroad. On a Saturday in August, before television cameras from Britain and the United States, four hundred people (twice the Catholic population of the town) processed to High Mass defiantly singing a Latin hymn. This was the weekend before Fr Baker was due to have his final interview with his diocesan, Bishop Grant of Northampton. The bishop in any case had been bombarded with protest letters including some which he described as 'very antagonistic, and quite vicious'. Reporting the Saturday's events in the following day's *Observer*, Patrick O'Donovan described them as 'triumphant in the old manner, tragic in the new ... the sixteenth-century protesting against the present'.

But it appeared that there might be a more damaging dimension to Downham Market than simple resistance. It was revealed that the preacher at the protest Mass was an itinerant priest, who had been trained and ordained at a privately-sponsored seminary at Écône in

Switzerland. Écône, set up by a retired missionary archbishop, Mgr Marcel Lefebvre, had become the European centre of resistance to the changes of Vatican II. The archbishop had said in Rome the previous year that the reform of Vatican II 'issuing from Liberalism and Modernism, is poisoned in its entirety; it springs from heresy and finishes in heresy, even if not all its acts are formally heretical.' After protracted negotiations, both Rome and the Swiss hierarchy had withdrawn recognition from Écône (and in 1976 indeed Pope Paul suspended Mgr Lefebvre from his priestly duties). But Écône continued to flourish and there were in 1975 at least five Écône-trained priests, touring southern England and setting up 'Mass centres' usually in the front parlours of traditionalist Catholics' homes. In the event there was no schism and not too much of a scandal at Downham Market. Fr Baker, threatened with removal from his parish by process of Canon Law, quietly gave up his church to a new priest who began saying the new Mass in English, while the older man set up a rival Latin Mass centre in the town hall.

At the time, Downham Market was dismissed by the hierarchy as a storm in a teacup, but it did throw light on two significant attitudes among Roman Catholics in Britain. One was the deep and at times strident reaction of some priests and many laity towards a wide variety of the changes emanating from Vatican II, and the defence of the Tridentine Mass was but one symptom of this. In many ways, the traditionalists are as much political reactionaries as they are religious ones. When, in defiance of the Pope's ruling, Archbishop Lefebvre celebrated Mass in the Lille football stadium in Northern France, he preached as much against Communism in French politics as against 'Protestantism' in the Vatican. At meetings in Britain of the Latin Mass Society or the equally traditionalist Pro Fide movement (chaired by Patrick Wall, the right-wing Conservative MP), one is as likely to hear rousing attacks on the Marxists, secularisers and trendy social workers who are alleged to have taken over the Church, as one is to hear restatements of traditional doctrine. At the same time, not all the fault lay with the resisters to change. The Roman Catholic bishops showed that they had few weapons for combatting dissent other than the use of their hierarchical authority. By its nature the Catholic hierarchy has seemed incapable of accommodating dissent and diversity, whether from the Left in the sixties or from the Right in the seventies. But would it have been so terrible if the old Latin Mass had continued to be celebrated in a few parishes? It would certainly have calmed the tempers of some of the 'lost generation' who were socially and psychologically unprepared to change from one form of religion to another overnight. Would it not have been possible, as is now being demanded in the Church of England, for the old liturgy to be kept in being alongside the new? It was a question that was asked by many non-Catholics, who had not the slightest sympathy with the ideology of Downham Market, but were interested to know how much diversity was compatible with the traditional uniformity of Rome. An opinion poll published by the *Catholic Herald* in 1976 showed that 46 per cent believed there should be a choice between English and Latin in the Mass.

The liturgical movement has brought great changes into the life of the churches in Britain. On the whole, these changes have been welcomed and have proved invigorating for the laity. Whether they will achieve all that their most ardent devotees have claimed for them—for example in curing the disenchantment with institutional religion of many young people—is open to argument. But liturgical changes are certainly a sign of new life. The difficulties brought in their wake are obvious. One is the latent discontent of the traditionalists, to which is linked the need for the churches to give their people clearer doctrinal teaching now that some of the liturgical props to unfashionable dogmas have been knocked away. It is a complaint among conservatives in all churches, for example, that the new services of Baptism do not allow much room for belief in Original Sin. Another difficulty concerns the language of the new rites. It is widely recognised that modern English is not as suitable a vehicle for worship as was Tudor English or medieval Latin. The contemporary form of the Lord's Prayer, which has been recommended for use in most churches, is widely disliked, particularly the phrase 'Do not bring us to the time of trial but deliver us from evil.' The delegates of the Church of Scotland used the new form throughout their General Assembly in 1975 and then overwhelmingly rejected it. Often the language is just clumsy as in the Roman Catholic response to the priest's 'The Lord be with you—And with you also'. Sometimes it is ambiguous and risibly coy, as in the draft of an Anglican marriage service which sought God's blessing on the couple 'that they may know each other with delight and tenderness in acts of love.' And linked with the difficulties of language are those of music. Now that the words and often the whole form of the liturgy has changed, the old music—whether it is plain-chant, Merbecke's Anglican Folk Mass, or even Mozart—is no longer suitable. It is not surprising that many of the modern composers concerned about liturgy are turning their talents to something quite different, like settings of the psalms or new types of hymns like Sidney Carter's popular 'Lord of the Dance'.

Indeed, liturgical dance is logically the next step in the renewal of the people's 'active participation' in worship. It is already practised in a few parishes, notably at Morden in Surrey and at Reigate, but there it is more of a liturgical spectacle than a participatory act. Indeed, the whole field of liturgical experiment, though interesting in itself, is so far removed from the experience of most congregations that it does not really merit the attention often given to it by liturgical writers. But there is no doubt that the liturgical changes so far achieved, which have now arrived in such force in Britain, cannot now be fossilised for another 400 years.

8

Ministerial Malaise

At the heart of many of the churches' difficulties today is the sense of doom, of creeping obsolescence and irrelevance which afflicts a growing number of the clergy. It is a well-documented phenomenon in all denominations and goes under a variety of labels, such as the 'crisis of the priesthood' or the 'malaise of the ministry'. It is not, however, a single problem but a whole predatory flock of them which has descended upon institutional religion in the modern world at the weakest point—the churches' professional, full-time ministry.

Any study of the clergy must, at the outset, take account of the effects of secularisation, as described in chapter two, upon the clergy's traditional activities. It challenges their status in the community, their moral leadership, their ability to exercise pastoral care and their role as communicators. There is also the new climate of intellectual opinion which has eroded the former theological and moral certainties upon which the clergy built their lives. There is the steady decline in the recruitment of all ministries and the increasing proportion of priests and ministers who are now within ten years of retirement age, a problem aggravated by the recent expedient of ordaining older men as second-career or part-time ministers. There are special problems of inflation, which have turned parish clergy into underpaid managers of scarcely viable businesses. There is friction with ecclesiastical authority and the widespread feeling that clergy have become the whipping boys of autocratic prelates and of reforming bureaucracies. There are the demands of clergy that they should enjoy at least the professional security and career prospects—if not the incomes—of their professional peers. As a result of these and other tensions, there is a steady haemorrhage of some of the brightest and best of the younger men both from parish work into specialised ministries and from the ordained ministry altogether. And hovering over the whole problematic brood is the realisation that churches everywhere are now paying the price for centuries of clericalism, in which the vigour of the Church was identified with the success or failure of the professional clergy and the 'people of God' were relegated to a passive, 'lay' status.

No wonder that the malaise of the ministry has become a by-word in modern literature. Newspapers, of course, still give prominence to revelations about erring clergy but the editorial tone has now changed perceptibly from outrage to pity. In the reporting of a case in which a Church in Wales bishop was convicted of gross indecency, the newspapers almost without exception stressed the tragic as distinct from the scandalous aspects of the case. It is now not only the curate whose very name, in Sydney Smith's words, excites compassion. In the contemporary novel, the portrayal of the ministerial malaise has gone much further. The whisky priest, the failed or apostate minister, the lonely, oppressed, perhaps unbelieving man in the cassock are all seen as paradigms of our rootless age in much the same way that the Mr Collinses and the Archdeacon Grantleys were symbols of well-ordered life in the nineteenth century. No one would pretend that the Gothic happenings of Iris Murdoch's novels are a picture of actual life, but in *The Time of the Angels* she does encompass most of the elements of the clergy sickness which appeal to the lay imagination. The Rector is an atheist and a recluse. He is surrounded by an assortment of women in assorted emotional entanglements. Thus there is the makings of scandal and tragedy, but the Bishop is impotent to intervene for all he can offer are platitudes and the solace of a secularised 'God of the gaps'. So, the plot moves relentlessly towards nihilism (with incest) and the Rector's suicide: 'The death of God has set the angels free and they are terrible.'

It is of course a lurid caricature and like most caricatures it directs sympathetic attention towards the original. What all caricatures and generalisations about the clergy miss is the infinite variety of this still anomalous profession. There are, after all, more than 50,000 ordained men (and women) in Britain and they cover every conceivable theological, social and emotional response to modern life. They certainly have their common problems and these are daily becoming more acute. But what may drive one minister to despair and to the contemplation of suicide may seem to another to be the most invigorating challenge. One cannot ignore the many priests and ministers who rejoice in their new freedom from traditional attitudes and restrictions and have built thriving church communities in cooperation with lay men and women. The strength of the clergy in Britain, particularly of the non-Roman Catholic clergy, has always been their individualism and despite many pressures from within and outside the churches to curb this individualism, it is still remarkably strong. The clergy enjoy a freedom of action and thought which is unrivalled by other professional groups. They may, if they wish, drop everything and take part in political campaigns, or write poetry, scholarly treatises or newspaper columns. Whether they neglect their flocks, or lord it over them like spiritual tyrants, or serve them as saints, depends almost entirely on the clergy themselves. The clergy's individualism may often be confused with eccentricity—and there are enough examples of that still around, like the curate who pushed a handcart across the Sahara or the Methodist minister who regularly wrestles with Jacky Pallo—but this is not to be wondered at. Professional religion is not far removed from show business. But there are plenty of more constructive and less conspicuous individualists—the East London vicar who pulled down his church and built a housing estate in its place; the workers among addicts and drop-outs; the industrial chaplains and worker-priests, including the Anglican in Oxford who is chairman of his local trade union branch and the Catholic in Bradford who drives a coach. In what other profession could one find such variety and such a premium on individual initiative?

The counterpart of this individualism is that the corporate image of the clergy, their traditional niche in society, has been eroded almost to extinction. All clergy have experienced what Archbishop Grégoire of Quebec, at the 1971 Synod of Bishops in Rome, described as the 'gradual stripping away of fields of activity and competence'. In addition, there has been the churches' own reassessment of the ministry against the role of the laity. As a result, clergy have had to find for themselves new justifying roles, both in society at large and in relation to their own church people. Most have done this by investing a greater emphasis in personal relationships and in rather vague ideas of service. A South Coast priest wrote: 'The job is justified by being useful to people as far as one is able. There are still many ways in which we can be serviceable. Theology is poetry about the human condition.' A similar view emerged from a survey carried out in 1968 by Dr S. H. Mayor, of Mansfield College, Oxford, among 957 Anglican and Free Church ministers in five Midland counties. Dr Mayor found that all denominations saw themselves primarily in the roles of pastor, example of the Christian life or man of devotion—'all responsibilities which depend largely on the individual rather than on the office and may be carried on behind the scenes'—and much less in their official roles as preacher, evangelist, leader of worship or spokesman (quoted in Leslie Paul *A Church by Daylight*). As revealing was a pilot study among twenty young Roman Catholic priests carried out by Father Robert Bogan, of Surrey University. His subjects were a 'cross-section' of the Church's post-Vatican Council recruits, who had all set out in their teens upon the path to ordination as traditional priests. They were to be sacred figures within the Church's structures and obedient priests who would keep the system going. But parish life changed their views and many found their seminary training quite irrelevant. 'Reflecting on all this,' wrote Father Bogan, 'I had the impression that most of these priests were not very clear about their role or function. Nevertheless, they were beginning to see their priest-hood more and more in terms of deeper relationships between them-selves and other people, and through their ministry, between others.' ('Priests, Alienation and Hope' *The Month*, June 1973.)

But there are many constraints on the ability of the clergy to relate to the people and even to each other. There always have been. The old adage that the best way of getting a railway compartment to oneself is to wear a dog collar is still valid, although British Rail now provides fewer railway carriages. People do not know what to expect of a clergy-man: he may be holy and easily shockable or he may be the jolly sort of modern fellow who is more inclined to be a shocker himself, but either way he is a source of discomfort. Even the faithful, or perhaps espe-cially the faithful, find it difficult to relate to their ministers and the clergy feel this acutely. There is often an element of 'culture-shock' in the despair and anxiety that feelings of alienation from ordinary people produce. As one vicar wrote to Leslie Paul: 'In a totally working-class parish (i.e. no resident teachers, doctors or graduates at all and no executives) to deal with one's congregation would give hope . . . but to care for the whole parish sets problems which can hardly be stated.' This often leads to an introverted, sectarian approach by the Anglican clergy which throws the burden for the wider cure of souls upon their Methodist or Roman Catholic colleagues. But they too share the sense of isolation and alienation and for Roman Catholics this is most frequently expressed in demands for changes in the celibacy rule. 'Celibacy does bother a lot of priests,' said one of Fr Bogan's curates, 'not lack of a sexual outlet but lack of companionship which is not supplied by deep relationships with other people. I was so lonely I got a canary—but put not your trust in canaries.'

It is presumably this yearning for companionship which leads many men who have left the ministry (some 25–30 a year in the Roman

Catholic Church in England and Wales) to marry very soon after their 'laicisation'—a fact which is taken by the Church authorities as evidence of the human frailty which led them to quit the ministry in the first place.

A new factor in the alienation of the clergy is inflation. The revolutionary implications of the recent world economic crisis for the churches will be explored in a later chapter, but for the moment we can concentrate on its effects upon the clergy. In almost all churches, the burden of raising the cash to keep the parochial plant running and its minister clothed, fed and housed—costs which have almost doubled since 1973—falls upon the minister himself. In the Church of England, this sort of fund-raising is a new and distasteful part of a priest's work. Traditionally, clergy stipends and housing have been provided from the beneficence of Anglicans long since dead, their funds being administered since 1947 by the Church Commissioners, an efficient but faceless body with offices at Millbank, opposite the House of Lords. But inflation has shifted a heavy share of this burden back to the living Church. In order to provide a basic stipend of £2,400 a year (plus a house), the parishes in 1976 were required to find 67 per cent of the money, an extra £20 million in all or, as the archbishops' advisers rather misleadingly put it, 'an extra 20p a week for every person on the Church's electoral rolls'. It was the clergy of course who had to explain this new quota to the people and also that they must make up the deficit left by people on the electoral rolls who never came to church.

Many clergy find this preoccupation with money-raising, and particularly with money for themselves and their families, too shameful to do well. They have in any case other financial entanglements with their congregations like the annual 'tips' in the Easter offering and the questions of expenses. Thus many clergy prefer to make ends meet by means of their wives' earnings, by cemetery duty and other extras, by gifts from relatives and by the state's Family Income Supplement (which, incidentally, was at one time forbidden to Methodist ministers by their Church). Anglican clergy and their families subsidise their ministry to a degree which few laymen realise, particularly in finding much of their own working and travelling expenses from their meagre stipends or other income. And yet, the biggest cause of clerical discontent appears to be not money but authority. In September 1976, thirty-five clergy in Manchester, most of them Anglicans, joined a trade union—the Association of Scientific, Technical and

Managerial Staffs (ASTMS) whose General Secretary is the left-wing Clive Jenkins. The reasons for this historic departure from the tradition of clerical independence were given by the union's Manchester divisional officer: 'their main contention at the moment seems to be inadequate representation and the lack of consultation with clergymen at a lower level on major church decisions, but there are also problems resulting from their low wages and self-employed status.' Not surprisingly, the bishops took a dim view of the unionisation of their clergy and one said he thought that there was adequate machinery for consultation in the Church's synods and committees! We shall return to that issue later.

With no families to support, the Roman Catholic clergy do not experience the same degree of tension over money but they are certainly under a form of financial pressure. Quite apart from the questions of maintenance of the clergy, the presbytery, missions and so on, there are the parish contributions to the diocesan schools funds. In the Archdiocese of Westminster, for example, the school building fund shows an annual deficit of about £1 million a year out of a total deficit of £3 million, and each man, woman and child who attends Mass is expected to contribute about £1 a year just to meet the schools deficit. The sort of pressure that this can put on the parish clergy was described by a 'special correspondent', writing in *The Tablet* about the other major Roman Catholic archdiocese, Liverpool:

> In those parts of the archdiocese where Mass attendance is low, priests are forced to finance their schools through beer and bingo, fruit machines and club entertainers. It can be very big business indeed and it comes as a sick shock to the young curate who for the first time visits the unoccupied parish club out of hours and sees row upon row of trestle tables topped with hundreds of beer mats, all positioned midway between bar and toilets. This manner of raising money may be an unfortunate necessity but one is forced to wonder just how much money is 'lost' on its journey from the club to the presbytery. (*The Tablet*, 21 February 1976).

It is scarcely surprising that young priests soon find their seminary training irrelevant and begin to wonder just what a parish curate is supposed to be doing.

It is clear that the malaise of the clergy is so many-sided, so deep-rooted, that no package of ecclesiastical reforms can offer a guaranteed cure. But structural reform is really the only remedy that the churches have at their disposal. They cannot hope to initiate social change which might give back to the clergy some measure of their lost status and support, and they appear incapable of restoring the morale of the parish ministry when the parish system itself is everywhere creaking at the joints. Yet institutional reforms, aimed at the redeployment of clergy and the betterment of their conditions of service, have brought some hope to the isolated and poorer-paid rural ministers. In the Church of England, the modest-sounding Pastoral Measure (1968) has enabled the bishops and their diocesan pastoral committees to begin the enormous task of closing redundant churches and amalgamating parishes. The philosophy behind this and many other Anglican reforms has been that the clergy are no longer situated where the people are and that this can only be changed by giving the Church stronger central powers of direction. The Church has acquired a Central Stipends Authority which guarantees all parish clergy a basic income, while promising that no parson will actually suffer a fall in income. There has also been the establishment throughout England of team and group ministries, modelled upon the group practices of the medical profession, and these have given clergy a sense of wider fellowship and professional purpose. But the more radical changes proposed by the Paul and Morley reports in the sixties, which would have abolished all local church endowments and lay patronage of livings and replaced the parson's freehold by a leasehold system, have been strenuously resisted. The opponents of these changes maintain that they would place too much power in the hands of the bishops and committeemen, that they would radically alter the character of the Anglican ministry and that, in any case, they have no more chance of reversing the decline of the church than does the present, familiar system. Indeed, there is much evidence to show that amalgamation of parishes has led to an immediate fall in Anglican church attendances: with a structure as ancient and delicate as the Church, all minor repair work carries the risk of bringing the whole edifice tumbling down.

Other churches in Britain, faced with the same twin problems of declining congregations and soaring running costs, have progressed much faster down the reforming road than the Church of England. Its Scottish sister church, the Episcopal Church, has proposed that its full-time clergy should be reduced by a third over the next four to five years and that more reliance should be put on local lay leaders. The Episcopal Church believes that the reduction in its ministry, which would ensure that those clergy who remained had a decent standard of living, can be achieved through natural wastage and retirement, rather than redundancy, but it is prepared to retrain some of its priests in secular skills.

The same problems of inflation and declining support have also inspired proposals for radical change within the larger Church of Scotland. These have come from the Kirk's impressive watchdog, the Committee of Forty. But in proposing moves towards 'a Church less dependent on expensive buildings and on whole-time salaried workers, closer to the people in their homes and places of work', the Committee had to face institutional structures as conservative and as immovable as any faced by Anglican reformers. The Kirk tradition has been of 'one parish, one minister, one church', which has made it as difficult to launch team ministries in the Church as to amalgamate parishes. Indeed, the Kirk is still closing down churches made redundant by the reunion of Scottish Presbyterians in 1929 and in each case the ex-perience of amalgamation has been a sharp drop in local membership. In view of this, the Committee of Forty framed its proposals in what one commentator described as 'in effect a White Paper on the future of the Church'. It argued both from economic necessity—it warned that the Church could expect to have a third fewer parish ministers within the next ten years; and also from the power of the Holy Spirit—'our plans are put forward in the conviction that if the life of the Church is to be stripped of some of its familiar features, it is God who is stripping us down to make us into a Church more conformed to his purpose.' And the model of the 'stripped down' Church was one that was much looser in organisation, with more vital decisions taken by bodies under lay control, and the difference between the ordained and unordained workers of the Church considerably reduced. The Committee of Forty saw no theological or practical reasons why lay ministers of the Word, for example, should not be ordained as part-time ministers of the sacraments. The reason why this will not in fact happen, at least not until the shortages of the professional ministry have become very much more acute than they are now, is the conservatism of the laity. Even though the Church of Scotland, in common with all other Reformed churches has never made a great theological distinction between ministers and laymen, yet the practical, social and psycho-logical distinctions have been considerable. It is the great irony of the Kirk's situation that it is at the same time one of the most conservative churches in its reliance upon a professional ministry, and also the richest church in the number of its lay office-bearers. It has, in fact, some 50,000 elders and 30,000 other lay officers, as against less than 2,000 clergy.

The fact that it has to be the clergy who come forward with proposals for the greater use of laymen as non-professional ministers is not something that is unique to the Church of Scotland. Lay resistance is the main barrier to change in most churches. The two exceptions, at different extremes, are the Methodist Church, which sees the lay stewardship as akin to the full-time ministry, and the Roman Catholic Church, where there are clerical and theological reasons why the laity cannot take a fuller part in ministerial duties. In England and Wales, there are only some 23 full time Catholic deacons, though in some parts of the developing world, especially Africa, the Church is virtually run by its lay deacons and catechists.

Institutional reforms will not by themselves cure the malaise of the ministry; initially, they could make matters worse by further alienating the clergy from all but the most committed, inner core of lay men and women who are prepared to persevere with their corporate religion in the absence of vicar, priest or minister. But if reform of the churches' structures can alleviate some of the more oppressive features of the ministerial malaise that will be an important step forward. The mission of the British churches, especially what Dr Coggan called their 'entry into the socio-political arena', is considerably weakened by their abject treatment of their own servants.

Ultimately, however, real change in the spirit and competence of Christian leadership will not be prescribed from above by hierarchies, committees and reports, but will grow from below. This is already happening in many of the grassroots 'movements' described earlier in this book—in the house churches, particularly the pentecostal house churches, in the Christian revival of communal living and in industry, where church missions have stimulated groups of trades unionists and others to consider the spiritual and social dimensions of their economic activity. In many of these instances, it is laymen rather than professional clergy who have become the leaders: indeed these largely experimental groups may be quite antipathetic to the professional leadership of the local churches. This is especially the case with some pentecostal house churches. There are a few of the grassroots movements which are not set upon creating a rival, parallel structure alongside the official churches, but are dedicated to a revival of institutional religion: the Community of Celebration, mentioned in chapter four, is one. But the danger remains of traditional parish Christianity being

by-passed by the grassroots movements. Indeed, there is talk in theological circles of the parish system, based on the local church and the
resident minister, as having outlived its social usefulness and being ripe
for replacement by something much more like the system which preceded it in Britain 1,200 years ago—a galaxy of small, informal Christian
groups, with their own local leaders, but served by an itinerant
priesthood. Enthusiasts for such a radical change have not, however,
been able to say how they would redeploy the thousands of redundant
parish clergy, not to mention all their redundant church buildings.

There are, however, some signs of new growth amid the decaying
vegetation of the parish system and they point in the direction of
greater lay participation in church leadership or at least of the 'laicisation' of the professional clergy. One of these is the growing practice in
the non-Roman Catholic churches of ordaining older men as part-time
ministers, while still retaining their secular employment. At first sight,
this is a rather desperate lowering of the standards of the churches'
ministry, prompted by the decline in younger men now offering themselves for ordination to the full-time ministry; (there has been no such
innovation yet in the Roman Catholic Church which until recently has
been able to draw upon the seemingly inexhaustible supply of priests
from Ireland). In fact, there is nothing intrinsically new about part-
time ministers. There has always been a significant number of clergy
who have been employed not in parish work but in education, administration, publishing and so on. And, as Adrian Hastings (a Roman
Catholic) points out, all priests are in some sense part-time: 'a great
deal of time is spent in sleeping, eating, praying, writing letters, playing
golf and so forth.' (*The Faces of God*). Indeed, the lives of the modern
priest and the modern layman overlap in ways that would have seemed
strange to Victorian churchmen. Defending his own work among drug
addicts against the charge that he has been merely a 'social worker in a
dog collar', Kenneth Leech writes: 'it is an odd mentality which sees
activities such as these as "social work" but looks upon the multitude
of unpriestly activities such as running fetes and bazaars, organising
parties, youth clubs, Bingo and the like, as in some sense *not* "social
work".' (*A Practical Guide to the Drug Scene.*) Seen in these terms, a
good deal of a minister's traditional activities would be better done by
laymen and many of the activities he now finds vital to his pastoral care
are in fact done by laymen. This overlapping of roles makes the part-
time ministry not just possible and desirable, but the next essential step
to be taken in breaking down the alienation of the clerical 'caste' from

the 'people of God'. When laymen are used as extensively as they now are in the Church of England to baptise children, visit the sick, bury the dead, preach and administer the chalice at the Eucharist, it is not in fact a major departure to ordain them to perform the few responsibilities still reserved for the ordained ministry, like the celebration of the Eucharist and the pronouncing of blessing and absolution. Moreover, a part-time ministry has great advantages for a Church afflicted with economic and alienation difficulties; priests in secular employment are financially self-supporting and are in more intimate contact with the life of their parishioners than is possible for the professional clergy. Yet the part-time ministry in the Church of England is still regarded as an auxiliary arm of the professional priesthood. The Anglican authorities have yet to grasp the truth, already appreciated by Methodists and other Free Churches, that in the future the majority of their local churches may be run by working men (and women) able to give only their weekends and evenings to traditional ministerial work. This reluctance derives partly from doubts about the laity's readiness to take up its share of the local church leadership and also from doubts about the educational and social standing of these 'priest-workers'. But the ideal of an elite Oxbridge-educated clergy, able to compete with the Civil Service and the professions for the best talent in the land, has been considerably modified since the First World War.

If changes in the direction of a part-time priesthood are ever to be embraced by the Roman Catholic Church, then there would need to be a revision of the rule of priestly celibacy. Here too there are signs of change, though they are for the present tentative. Although popular demands for some relaxation of the celibacy rule have become a major campaign issue in the radical Catholic movements of the United States and Holland, in Britain they have been much more muted. Scarcely anything on the subject has been heard from the National Conference of Priests, which since its inception in 1970 has been mainly concerned with its thoughts about episcopal authority. Indeed, the only voluble body of opinion on the celibacy issue has been outside the official Church in the Catholic Renewal Movement, an association of ex-priests, many of them already married. Between 1965 and 1975 the Vatican granted 30,000 dispensations for priests to marry and in all but a very small number of cases this automatically excluded them from all parts of the Church's ministry. But within the Church there is some evidence, as in surveys like that carried out by Father Bogan, that celibacy is becoming increasingly difficult for many younger clergy. They see it as a barrier to the personal relationships in which many of them see the future of their ministry and they find it especially complicating in their relations with married Catholics particularly in the period since the *Humanae Vitae* controversy over birth control. Yet, although the demands for change in the celibacy rule may have wide, though muted, support among the younger clergy, they are firmly resisted by the senior clergy and most of the laity, who associate a married clergy with the heinous doctrines of the Reformation. At the moment, even discussion of a possible relaxation is stifled in most parts of the Catholic Church. Pope Paul himself intervened to prevent discussion of it at the Second Vatican Council and although the Swiss bishops have initiated a 'dialogue' on the ordination of married men, they have firmly ruled out the possibility of retaining in the ministry priests who wish to marry subsequent to their ordination. If change does take place in this vital area of Catholic life, it will come not from Europe but most probably from Africa, where the shortage of priests has thrown the burdens of the ministry on to the lay, and predominantly married, catechists.

Yet, the obstacles to change in Europe do not depend on any fundamental Catholic doctrines about the Church or the ministry, so much as on the psychological attachment of the Church to the idea of a priesthood which is set apart from ordinary men. Catholic clergy have come to look with interest and some sympathy at their married cousins in the Anglican and Orthodox churches, and also at the married priests within their own communion in the Uniate churches of the Middle East, but they do so in the spirit of 'Yes, but not for us'. The idea of the clerical caste, modelled in some ways on the monasticism of the Middle Ages, is difficult to shrug off. But while there is little prospect of an early relaxation in the celibacy rule, there has been some important rethinking about the purpose and practice of celibacy. Adrian Hastings is one of a number of writers who have pointed out that for many parish priests celibacy has degenerated into a cosy bachelordom which fails to emphasise the status of the priest as being on the prophetic margins of ordinary life. 'Celibacy should free a man for the kingdom; if it appears to free him for long hours on the golf course or before the tele, long hours on the beach, then it has become not a blessing but a curse.' And Archbishop Hume, before his translation from his Yorkshire monastery to Westminster, conceded a similar point about celibacy in a conversation with Clifford Longley, of *The Times*. 'Traditionally, most priests coped with it by maintaining a certain distance from the rest of mankind, a psycho-logical moat and ditch defence which kept everyone at bay and hence prevented the beginning of close personal relationships with members of the opposite sex . . .' His advice to priests he said, was to behave towards women friends 'as a mature man who was head over heels in love with his own wife would treat them, never wanting to do anything to hurt or betray himself. That draws the line at physical sex, but gives considerable freedom to the emotions.' The degree of saintliness this would demand of the average parish priest may make the archbishop's advice somewhat impracticable, but it does indicate the real concern among Catholics to expand the frontiers of celibacy without actually breaching them.

It is the role of women themselves, however, that opens up the most stimulating perspectives of change for the churches' ministries. Women have always made a vital contribution to the life of the churches but their participation in church activity and leadership has usually been indirect and behind the scenes. Taking their cue from St Paul, most churchmen have been content to regard women as the perpetual Marthas of the churches—as nuns, Sunday School teachers, ladies who do the flowers and make the tea, or as the dutiful wives and mothers of the male hierarchy. Two complementary social forces have challenged this traditional view: one has been the movement in the West for social equality, which of course is more widespread than the virulent Women's Lib expression of it, and the other has been the defection of males from all levels of church life. When the Anglican Church ordained its first woman priest in Hong Kong during the Second World War, it was the lack of suitable male candidates that made this necessary. That ordination was later declared invalid by the Lambeth Conference, and the lady in question went to work in a factory in Canton, but it led in 1971 to the ordination of two more women priests. However, Hong Kong was regarded as an exceptional situation and whenever the English-born Rev Joyce Bennett came to Britain on leave, she was the soul of discretion, consulting the Archbishop of Canterbury before accepting any invitation to celebrate the Eucharist within the Church of England.

In the last few years, however, women have been less prepared to be discreet about their contribution to religion. Nuns have been doffing their habits or leaving the cloister altogether, Anglican deaconesses have emerged from their Victorian twilight world to preach and con-duct services, and in all churches women have been far more evident in the worship and government of the Christian community. The Third Estates Commissioner of the Church of England is a woman and, despite her establishment titles, Dame Betty Ridley is at heart one with the women who seek equality in the Church's ministry. Of course, the Church of England is becoming the exception among the churches in Britain in seriously entertaining proposals for the ordination of women but doing nothing about them. There have long been women ministers in the Free Churches and during 1975 two erstwhile male preserves of United Kingdom religion—the Presbyterian Church in Ireland and the Jewish rabbinate—both admitted women ministers. But the ministry of the Anglican churches (as of the Roman Catholic and Orthodox) remained closed to them.

As far as the Church of England was concerned, progress was impeded by the new ecumenical context. The damage that might be done to the improved relations between Canterbury and Rome became a dominant theme in the Church's debate on the ordination of women in the 1975 General Synod. The Archbishop of Canterbury read a letter he had received from Cardinal Willebrands who diplomatically referred to 'the wisdom of taking common counsel on matters potentially divisive while they are still under our control'. Pope Paul, in a letter read by Dr Coggan to the Synod in the following year, was to put it more strongly: he spoke of 'so grave a new obstacle and threat' on the path to reconciliation between the two churches. At any rate, in 1975, despite the fact that 31 of the 43 English dioceses had declared there were 'no fundamental objections' in theology or otherwise to women priests and that lay opinion in a majority of dioceses was in favour of going ahead actually to ordain women, the Synod voted to leave the matter in abeyance. In the words of the Bishop of Winchester, they decided 'for the sake of unity and an unrocked boat to canonise the *status quo*'.

Meanwhile, the Anglican Church in Canada was pressing ahead with plans to ordain women in 1976, New Zealand and South Africa were likely to follow suit, and there were the notorious happenings in the United States where, against the wishes of the bishops' conference, thirteen deaconesses had been advanced to the priesthood. In 1976, the American Church finally sanctioned the ordination of women and in the same year the Pope's own Biblical Commission decided by 12 votes to 5 that scriptural grounds alone were not enough to exclude the possibility of ordaining women and that the Catholic Church would not be going against Christ's original intentions if it were to do so.

Basically, the ordination of women is not an ecumenical question; it is a psychological and emotional one. The same factors of ministerial intransigence, supported by lay conservatism, which impede more rapid change to a part-time ministry and, within the Roman Catholic Church, to a married one, are those which stand in the way of women priests in the older churches. The ordination of women has become a pitched battle between members of the male priestly caste and the alleged feminists who wish to break into the inner sanctum of the male-regarding Church. This is the area of the debate where the bitterest passions are aroused and where concerned churchpeople see the greatest dangers of discord and schism. In a sermon preached at Cambridge, the Rev Cuthbert Keen, chaplain of the conservative Ecclesia group, called for eternal vigilance and 'fierce and unyielding opposition' to what he called 'the strong forces who seek the creation of priestesses'. In the United States, where conservative Anglicans were faced by a *fait accompli*, though at first an illegal one, reactions have been even more vehement. One priest accompanied by a body of his parishioners left the Episcopal Church to join the Orthodox. There was also the widely quoted incident which occurred at Riverside Church, New York, during the visit of the Archbishop of Canterbury (Dr Ramsey) in 1974: a woman deacon who had announced her intention of seeking priest's orders was administering the Communion chalice to a young male priest at the altar rail, when he dug his finger nails into her hand, drawing blood, and said: 'I hope that you burn in hell.' Not that the women concerned in the American declaration of equality have been entirely blameless. Their use of Women's Lib invective, their association with black churches and the civil rights movement, their extravagant claims for the Femaleness of the God-head ('God the Mother') have all caused considerable offence and made some people suspect that the new women priests were trying to replace the traditionally patriarchal Church with a modern American matriarchy. But there is another side to the campaign for the ordination of women. It is evident in the way in which women 'ministers'—nuns, deaconesses, lay counsellors and so on—have quietly become a part of many parish ministries and already displayed 'priestly gifts'. At the Church of the Ascension at Blackheath, South London, for example, the life of the Anglican community depends very much on the very un-feminist Elsie Baker, who has been in the diaconate for thirty-three years: the vicar, the Rev Paul Oestreicher, who is British chairman of Amnesty International, says that in every practical sense he is Elsie Baker's pastoral assistant rather than she his. The other side of the campaign is also to be found in the view of many women that a doomed, male ministry is not worth their invading. As an American nun said at a conference in Detroit which pressed the national Catholic bishops to take action on the ordination of women: 'I think I understand the reluctance of many women in the Church today to allow the issue of ordination to the presthood to become central in an overall questioning of roles for women in the ministry. That is to say, I understand a concern to challenge the very meaning of ministry in the Church and to reform the pattern of ministry so that women will not be caught up in the structures which continue to fail to liberate either women or men.'

If ever the word 'crisis' was appropriate in church affairs, it is in the matter of the ministry. No other organisation could face such mounting discontent from its line managers combined with such a high level of criticism and disenchantment among its clients and shareholders without instituting drastic reforms. But, as we have seen, change imposed from above is seldom effective in church affairs. The churches' patterns of ministry are the conservative hard-core of their life, more immutable in some ways than the powers of the Pope or the formulations of doctrine or liturgy. The only source from which effective and acceptable change can come is from below, from the people or laity, and here the theologians have been indicating a way in which the churches can go forward. Biblical scholars, who have recently given much attention to the meaning of Christian initiation, agree that in the Church of the first century Baptism was regarded as a form of ordination. Every baptised Christian became an apostle, or missionary of the Good News. Once the Church ceased being a sect in an alien empire and became the mass religion of Mediterranean civilisation, the ministry of all baptised Christians became unworkable and was restricted to a professional priesthood, although in rural areas the tradition of the priest-worker continued for centuries. But the lay ministry did continue in the sects, whether they were the heresies which plagued the Early Church or the Mormons, Witnesses and Adventists of modern times. And much the same pattern of an indigenous lay ministry is beginning to emerge in the pentecostal revival movement, though one would hesitate yet to call the charismatics a sect.

It is from these raw materials that some churchmen are attempting to rebuild the ministry of institutional Christianity, now that it is in danger of becoming once again a sect in an alien environment. There is patently no master plan for this work of reconstruction, no prescribed architectural style, whether of a Gothic revival or modern utilitarianism. The house church movement has produced one pattern (and incidentally it is only in the house church context that the married 'ex-priests' of the Roman Catholic Church are able to fulfil their sacramental role). The elements of the part-time ministry—worker-priests as well as priest-workers—and of the female ministry are all being incorporated in the rebuilding programme. In the mission areas, whether in Britain or abroad, there has been a particularly strong growth of the lay apostolate. It has also, though very tentatively, sprung up in areas where the professional ministry of the churches has been withdrawn for reasons of economy, reorganisation or simply lack of support. But this has usually happened only when the withdrawing minister has prepared the ground for a lay ministry in advance. It is only the more far-sighted, lay-minded of the professional clergy, of whom the churches could certainly do with many more, who can say with any confidence that the churches have more professional ministers than is good for them. The Anglican parish of Holy Trinity, Houslow, for example, on the edge of London Airport, is successful enough in conventional terms to be able to maintain three professional priests; but another mark of its success is that it is no longer the professionals who run the parish. The pastoral cure of souls has been largely taken over by a lay apostolate of men and women, who meet daily to pray and plan the parish's strategy. The three full-time clergymen have thus been released for a wider, extra-parochial ministry.

There is a long way to go before the major churches in Britain will steel themselves to accepting a predominantly lay ministry, but there are many indications of this in the thinking of their wiser strategists. The Church of Scotland's Committee of Forty has outlined its vision of the 'stripped down' church, 'less dependent on expensive buildings and on whole-time salaried workers'. A Roman Catholic priest, Michael Winter, has proposed a basic eucharistic community of about thirty people which would no longer need an expensive building or a full-time, fully-paid priest for its liturgy, but would be led in worship by an ordained, and preferably married wage-earner. 'This simple starting point would, at a stroke, free the laity of many of the financial burdens which now take up the energy of so many committed Church members.' (*The Month*, April 1975.) In the present state of church affairs, all this may seem like so much crying for the moon but, whether the churches' hierarchs and older conservatives like it or not, economics may force such a solution upon them. So let us briefly crystal-gaze at how the churches' ministry could look in the stringent future. Its basis would not be the national institution, but the local worshipping community. The indigenous church would find and elect its own unpaid ministers—pastors and preachers, as well as ministers of the sacraments and of financial resources. It would be a corporate ministry, for the participation of wage-earners and family men and women would make that essential. Of course, the local ministry would need the confirmation and communion of the wider Church, the 'Catholic and Apostolic Church', and it might get this through the supervision of a local bishop, possibly himself part-time, whose diocese would cover no larger area than that of an English district council (the Roman Catholic bishops in England and Wales have now begun to implement a plan for dioceses of between 80,000 and 200,000 Catholics). Conceivably the episcopal supervision of local churches would be exercised by itinerant specialists, rather like the travelling bishops and missionaries of Celtic Britain or of Africa today. Of course, a very great deal would be lost in this do-it-yourself, stripped-down church. The role of the professional clergyman in the secular life of the local community would inevitably be lost. Many large and historic parish churches might have to be sold off. There could well be a drastic fall-off in church attendance and 'civic religion'—the performance of the traditional rites of infant baptism, marriage and committal of the dead—could well cease. The tradition of the cure of souls which theoretically extends far beyond the depleted ranks of the church congregation, in fact the whole submerged influence of the historic churches in British life, would probably wither away. But, short of a financial and vocational miracle to restore the viability and confidence of the churches' professional leadership, it is in the direction of the 'stripped-down church' that present trends must lead.

9

The Question of Government

Compared with the major problems caused by the drift from the churches and the crisis of the clergy, questions of church government are of significantly lesser import. To many Christians, indeed, the devotion of so much energy, time and money by their ordained leaders and most experienced laity to the procedures of deliberation and consultation seems to be a malignant excrescence on the already emaciated body of the missionary Church. This is a view heard especially from two quarters. In the conservative camp, many senior parish clergy regard the new machinery of lay participation in church government as a direct threat to their independence, or at least as the heaping of unnecessary burdens upon them by insensitive bishops and meddling laymen. This view has had much support in the Church of England since the early reforming era of the Church Assembly, set up in 1919, and clergy fears have not been noticeably assuaged by the change to full synodical government half a century later. Similar suspicions have been harboured by senior Roman Catholic clergy since Vatican II and particularly since the late sixties when the Church in Holland was set on a collision course with Rome over powers for the laity. On the other hand, the younger radicals in the British churches are far from enamoured with developments in church government; they tend to be activists in what Dr Coggan called the 'socio-political arena' and for them the growth in ecclesiastical bureaucracy is not just a wasteful irrelevance, but often harmful to the climate of mission. A friend who recently took over the editorship of an influential Catholic journal said that he was determined to devote more space to questions of family and business ethics and far less to discussion of church structures. Disenchantment with the structures is therefore broadly-based, more broadly-based than even the dissatisfaction with the way in which church unity discussions are conducted, although the gamut of dissatisfaction is the same in both cases.

But if all government is at best, as Thomas Paine said, a necessary evil, then church government is an evil thrust upon the religious community by the hard necessities of our times. There certainly does not appear to be any great popular clamour for it. Nor is there much evidence today of the ideological enthusiasm which led groups of seventeenth-century laymen, for example, to suffer persecution for congregational or presbyterian forms of church life. Today, apart from the special interest groups among the articulate middle classes, the great mass of Christian people appear to be acquiescent towards the *status quo* and reluctant to share the responsibilities of the clergy. This is really not surprising. The strongest critics of outdated ecclesiastical structures are to be found among those who have given up regular churchgoing as a lost cause and that is an option which just was not or could not be taken in the seventeenth century. The pressure for spreading the base of ecclesiastical decision-making comes today from the articulate few among the laity, but even more from church leaders themselves, who no longer have either the confidence or the ability to run a clerically-dominated institution. In an age of fast vanishing resources and spiralling costs, the ordained leadership needs the support and advice of the laity more than ever. Radical strategies need to be devised and difficult economies implemented, which depend for their success upon the acceptance of the laity. Specialist lay skills in education, financial management and communication need to be mobilised. And there is always the hope that lay participation in church affairs can become the turning point in the fight against secular-isation and the decline of institutional religion. Then there is the ecumenical dimension which inevitably focuses greater attention on systems of government. In the Church of Scotland talks with the Methodist Church, a great deal of attention has been given to the compatibility of the Methodist circuit and the Kirk's presbyteries.

There is not, however, one single entity in British religion which can be called church government. It comes in many varieties with differing historical pedigrees; indeed, church history is largely made up of disputes and debates about structural questions. Today the unifying concern of all churches is with the greater involvement of the laity in structures which should be as democratic as the modern age demands while not destroying the historical character and mission of the churches. At the one extreme, there is the 'democratic' congregational system in which all important decisions—from the form of worship to the calling of ministers, and even in some important respects the content of Christian belief—are decided by the local church meeting. At the other extreme is the Roman Catholic Church which was described, earlier in this book, in Hans Küng's words, as 'the only absolutist system that survived the French Revolution'. That description may still hold true of papal power but it needs some practical qualification at a lower level in Britain (if not yet in Ireland). The usual way of describing Roman Catholic church government is to say that it is 'monarchical'; the Pope rules, partly through the bishops who are all his appointees, and the participation of the rest of the 'people of God' cannot be anything but consultative. There are good arguments for this, of course, in Catholic theology and in history, for it is a survival of the temporal power of the Popes within the context of European politics. But another reason is that, unlike the Protestant churches which since the Reformation have organised themselves as settled Christian communities, the Roman Catholic Church in Britain at least has regarded itself as a missionary organisation, as the embodiment of the Church Militant, constantly under battle orders. That is still to some extent true. It is moreover no coincidence that the only major Protestant denomination which approaches Rome in denying scope for real popular participation is the Salvation Army.

Among most of the Protestant churches in Britain there have been few major upheavals in church government in the period since the war. Their democratic procedures for electing delegates to their synods, conferences and assemblies have worked tolerably as well as in the past and if the delegations have become dominated by what has been called the 'clericalised laity'—ministers' wives, paid officials and full-time committee persons—to the virtual exclusion of working-class Christians, then this is a reflection of the trend within the local churches as well. However, one would not expect any radical changes to the governing bodies of these churches, short of their uniting with other churches, for it is in the structures of government that these churches have their distinctive character as Presbyterians, Congregationalists, Methodists and so on. The one change that has taken place has been among English Congregationalists who as a consequence of the union with the Presbyterians in the United Reformed Church have adopted a structure of provincial synods and districts along Presbyterian/Methodist lines. For all the Free Churches the successful feature of their government systems is that important decisions are taken mainly at a low level and the national assembly or conference is partly a meeting of spiritual and moral uplift and partly the occasion for discussing broader questions of ethical, national or international concern. Indeed, the General Assembly of the Church of Scotland with its visitation by the Queen's representative, the Lord High Commissioner, together with his suite, and Scottish troops on parade, really takes the place of a Scottish parliament. Whether it will remain unchanged after political devolution is an interesting question.

In contrast, the Church of England has undergone continual structural upheaval within the last century and a half, culminating in the introduction of synodical government in 1969–70. It never was a democratic church, for it is episcopally governed with its bishops claiming the 'apostolic succession' from the New Testament Church. It is also the Church by law established in England with the Queen as its 'Supreme Governor' which means that, following the normal constitutional practice of the state, she on the advice of her Prime Minister appoints the bishops. Descriptions of this strange ecclesiastical beast, part political, part spiritual, have filled many volumes and continue to do so (see the recent works by Mayfield, Beeson and Paul). Suffice it to say here that until 1828 and 1829, when Parliament allowed Nonconformists and Roman Catholics to play a full part in English public and political life, it was Parliament itself which acted as the democratic check upon the activities of the bishops. Since then, fearing that control of Church affairs would pass into the hands of an irresponsible, un-Anglican legislature, the Church of England has been groping its way towards self-government and lately towards a form of representative government. It has been a long, often dispiriting and sometimes chastening process (the biggest subsequent shock came a century later in 1928 and 1929 when Parliament threw out the revised Book of Common Prayer), but ultimately it has borne fruit in the General Synod and diocesan and deanery synods. The main achievements of synodical government for the Church of England have been its acquisition of the power to change its worship without parliamentary approval, a thorough-going revision of worship (described in Chapter Seven) and the beginnings of the mammoth job of restructuring its ministry to make the Anglican system viable in the modern world. But, set against this, the Church still lacks direct control over a major part of its affairs. Its chief officers, the bishops, deans and so on, are still appointed by the Crown; its financial endowments are managed by the Church Commissioners who are partly answerable to Parliament; and it does not have the unfettered power to change either its disciplinary rules (amendments to Canon Law require the Royal Assent) or its basic structures (synodical 'Measures' require parliamentary approval and then the Royal Assent). And yet, despite the smallness of the dent it has made in the Establishment nut, the achievement of the General Synod in its first five-year term up to 1975, has not been insignificant. It is often pointed out that the Church cannot hope to unravel the political tangles of four centuries within half a decade.

Critics of the Synod are not prepared to be so indulgent. They point out that time is running short for institutional religion in Britain and shorter still for the Church of England. It is not only Anglicans who have become disenchanted by the General Synod's preoccupation with institutional questions. A not unsympathetic Roman Catholic, Robert Nowell, spoke for many of them when he reported that 'the impression given by the General Synod is of interminable debates on matters of secondary importance and of enormous difficulty in being able to find time for the crucial issues facing the churches today, as well as of the inability to take clear decisions when these are called for.' (*The Month*, July 1973.) The performance of the General Synod has improved since then, but only marginally. The first difficulty about it is that it is unrepresentative. Its non-ordained members are drawn almost exclusively from the 'clericalised laity' or the leisured classes— the only people who can afford to spend four week days in London or York three times a year, with probably twice that much time also devoted to diocesan synods and committee work. In the first General Synod it was discovered that there was only one true representative of the working class, and he does not appear to have stood for re-election in 1975. Secondly, while the genuine laypeople (excluding clergy wives, deaconesses, paid officials and so on) are underrepresented, all lay people are outnumbered. The 238 members of the House of Laity (70 of them women) are matched by an equal number in the House of Clergy, plus 24 suffragan bishops, deans and provosts, and 43 diocesan bishops (who as the House of Bishops have a reserved power of veto over both other houses). This sort of balance has little theological or other justification beyond the fact that Anglican laypeople have always acquiesced in a subsidiary role. There is, however, inherent in this synodical structure a conflict between what Leslie Paul describes as the 'popular government' of the elected laity and the 'professional government' of the clerics. One can take this further and say that the experience of the General Synod shows that it is really impossible to govern the Church of England while there are so many diverse sources of power—the bishops, the Queen and her Parliament, the parish priest in his freehold benefice, the elected councils and synods, and there still remains a large residue of control in the hands of universities, charitable trusts, missionary and other societies, private patrons and others. Much of the work of the General Synod has been an attempt at the centralisation and rationalisation of these different sources of control. The Synod has seemed at times to be in the position of a helmsman wrestling with the tiller of a ship which has six independent rudders.

However, a great deal of the work of the Synod has been not the spiritual direction of the ship, but the overhaul of its machinery within a scrupulously legal framework. This has led the Synod to model itself very closely upon its secular mentor, Parliament. Thus it has elaborate standing orders (running to 80 pages of a special rule book), a crowded but skilfully managed agenda with provision for the guillotining of debates when a division is needed, and even the presence of bewigged lawyers flanking the Speaker when the Synod is discussing legislative business. A great deal of the real business is done in committee but, unlike Parliament, these committees are not accessible to the rank and file of the assembly and it can take fifteen months or more between the time when a measure is first debated and the time when it receives the Royal Assent. So, despite the high intentions of many of its members, the Synod often finds itself dotting the i's and crossing the t's of measures which laypeople will seldom encounter in their local Christian communities. When sitting at Church House, Westminster, the members have emblazoned above their heads the splendid thought: 'Holy is the true light and passing wonderful, lending radiance to them that endured in the heat of the conflict.' But since the conflict, however heated, is often inconclusive until Parliament across the road has given its subsequent approval, wags of the Church press corps have suggested that the true motto of the Synod should be 'that the question be not now put'.

It is of course easy to list the failings and foibles of the General Synod and difficult to suggest a better forum for a body as spiritually and constitutionally anomalous as the Church of England. The members of the Synod are as aware of the problem as their external critics. In any case, it may yet be too early to pass judgement. There are already signs of development. The General Synod of the Church of England has managed to struggle free of its procedural shackles rather more successfully than have the smaller synods of its sister churches in Wales, Scotland and Ireland; it has largely avoided the settlement of issues along High Church/Low Church party lines; it has evolved a high standard of debate with little opportunity for either preaching or demagogy; and, through its bishops, it has begun to fashion a new style of corporate leadership which depends less on the constitutional checks and balances, or the inherited status of some prelates, than on a determination to see the future predicament of the Church clearly and to argue about it cogently. But perhaps the real worth of Anglican synodical government is not to be found in the statutory bodies of the General Synod and the parochial church councils, but in the intermediate synods of the dioceses and deaneries. Although a few bishops still treat their diocesan synods as briefing sessions for the lower ranks, and some elected lay members have found it difficult to overcome their feelings of deference to his Lordship and his Bishop's Council, yet most diocesan synods have shown a remarkable aptitude for tackling the really important issues of church policy in a businesslike way. Their deliberations, for example, on the ordination of women and on social issues like abortion have shown a surer contact with grassroots opinion than have the General Synod debates on the same issues. But even more interesting are the smaller and less developed deanery synods, which at present have no legal status beyond electing members to the diocesan bodies and discussing matters referred down to them. In the deanery there is the chance for lay men and women in close contact with the local scene to speak out openly about the problems and opportunities of their congregations. The way in which some deanery synods have set about the planning of local structures, often maybe with more enthusiasm than experience, is one of the more hopeful areas of Anglican synodical participation.

The Anglican experiment in participation clearly has a long way to go. It does not have the directness or the scope for concentrating the Church's mind on the wider issues that many of the Free Church assemblies display, but it is being watched with interest, particularly by Roman Catholics. Since the end of the Second Vatican Council, the prospect of all the 'people of God' playing a fuller role in the decisions of the Church has been dangled tantalisingly before Catholics in Britain. The first real change has been within the hierarchy itself, which has transformed its informal meetings into the Bishop's Conference for England and Wales. It now publicises its agenda and many of its findings and has shown a willingness to learn from priests and laymen outside its immediate circle of advisers. Admittedly, under Cardinal Heenan, the Conference did still appear to be an instrument for sanctioning and implementing the party line on certain issues like abortion or clergy discipline, but in 1974 it displayed something of its new spirit by publishing the *Ground Plan* report of a working party (which proposed a much larger number of smaller dioceses) before the hierarchy itself debated it. There could be greater openness in the offing with the decision of Heenan's successor, Cardinal Hume, not to offer himself for the chairmanship of the Bishops' Conference but to become vice-chairman. The other definite change brought about by Vatican II was the establishment in each diocese of a senate of priests, which the Council had commanded in its Decree on Bishops. It may still be too early to judge them, but so far the senates do not appear to have had much impact. The initial criticism was that they were filled with unrepresentative, 'safe' men—the ex-officio diocesan administrators, the canons and senior clergy—but this seems no longer to be the case. Reports from the senates indicate that the proportion of elected and younger priests is rising and also that the bishops are ready to encourage their priests to speak their minds, sometimes by means of a discreet episcopal absence. The problem of the senates, though, is the priests themselves. In many senates, the reports speak of endless discussions taking place on clerical pensions, travel allowances, the wearing of a dog-collar within the parish, or the optimum number of children to muster for a service of confirmation.

Other moves in the direction of participation in the affairs of the Church were not so much commanded by the Vatican Council as commended. This has meant that in a local church as conservative and clerically-dominated as that of England and Wales, innovations have been slow to get started. Parish committees, for example, have varied widely between the elected and the appointed, between the vital forum and the supine or non-existent one, depending upon the willingness of the parish priest to share his pastoral responsibilities with lay people. Diocesan pastoral councils have likewise ranged from the tame assembly (in which the nominees of bodies like the Union of Catholic Mothers have gladly concurred with the bishop's familiar strictures against permissiveness) to those which have zealously involved themselves in strategic issues. One pastoral council is reported to have played an important part in *preventing* the building of a new cathedral which, given the Catholic propensity for constructing first and asking questions later, is a real achievement.

It is at the national level, however, that structures for effective participation between bishops, priests and people have been disappointing. Roman Catholics in Britain have shown a tendency to cling to their international links and to play down their national identity, which is perhaps understandable in a church which owes so much of its strength to immigration and is faced by very nationally-conscious rivals among the Anglicans and Presbyterians. Moreover, it has just not been in character for British Catholics to attempt the radical involvement of lay people in the government of the Church which brought the wrath of the Vatican down upon the Dutch national pastoral conference. In these islands, the prospect of a national pastoral conference being established in the near future remains the rather forlorn hope of a small number of radicals. What does exist in Britain at the national level is a National Conference of Priests—a body which began life in 1970 with a radical explosion of debates on celibacy, authority and the way in which the bishops are appointed, but has since settled down to more genteel discussions. There are also the National Commissions. These are bodies of priests and laity which exist to advise the Bishops' Conference on specific areas of Catholic concern like Justice and Peace, Racial Justice, the role of the Laity, Social Welfare and so forth. It is the Commissions which have become the focal point of lay participation in Roman Catholic affairs, even though they have the limitations of being underfinanced and of being partly representative bodies for the bishops to consult and partly 'think-tanks' to advise and prod the hierarchy into action. According to Dr Michael Hornsby-Smith and Penny Mansfield ('Overview of the Church Commissions', *The Month*, March 1975), they include a high proportion of 'professional Catholics'—the predominantly middle-aged, the single and women—and a surprisingly high proportion of converts. One of the Commissions, that on the Laity, has a membership which is at least half working-class in origin. and that must make it unique among ecclesiastical groups in Britain. *Faut de mieux*, it is with the Commissions that the future of lay participation in the government of British Catholicism lies, but already there is friction over their purely consultative role. The really contentious areas of Catholic life are kept beyond their reach. Education, for example, has its national Catholic Education Council to help the bishops to administer the vast network of schools, colleges and local authority connections, but there is no Education Commission to ask whether this massive devotion of scarce resources really produces the results that the Church desires. And when other bodies like the Laity Commission or the Priests' Conference do so, they are told that is scarcely their business.

The future of lay participation in the government of the Roman Catholic Church in Britain depends upon the willingness of the bishops to delegate. If they go too far in this direction, they may find themselves checked by the Vatican as were Cardinal Alfrink and the Dutch bishops, but as yet there is no sign that the English, Welsh or Scottish bishops are even a quarter of the way down the same road. So how in tune with the needs and aspirations of the people are the Roman Catholic bishops? And would a different method of selecting them change the character of the Church? Similar questions are raised by some of the critics of synodical government within the Church of England, although here the powers of the Anglican bishops are more the powers of initiation than of direct control. So how are they selected and should there be change in the Anglican system?

To lump together the Anglican and Roman Catholic methods of appointing bishops may seem to the latter to be a gross impertinence. As everyone knows the Church of England's bishops are chosen by a Prime Minister, who may not be an Anglican or indeed a practising Christian, whereas Catholic bishops are appointed by the Pope, 'the Vicar of Jesus Christ'. In practice, however, the two systems are not dissimilar. They come up with a similar style of leader and both systems had their origins in the medieval power struggle between kings and popes which had brought episcopal appointments a very long way from the concept of a bishop as a man elected by the local church to exercise oversight (episcope) over it. Although a great deal of modern theology has been devoted to the office of a bishop, both within the ecumenical context and in the Second Vatican Council, much of it is concerned with the pastoral and historical role of bishops, and relatively little with the major administrative role that they now play in the modern Church. The Archbishop of York, Dr Blanch, has said that when he first went to his previous diocese of Liverpool he managed with a part-time secretary three mornings a week, but by 1970 he had two full-time secretaries and even that was before synodical government had really got under weigh.

Until the First World War, the appointment of bishops in both churches was a relatively simple affair, carried out within a charmed circle of people who knew each other personally, or at least through only one or two intermediaries. Queen Victoria and her Prime Ministers took as much care about the selection of their bishops as they did about their Cabinet Ministers; in a later reign, Asquith was particularly interested in episcopal preferments. Both Monarch and

Prime Minister seldom needed to go outside the intimate circle of the archbishops or the Deans of Windsor and Westminster to find a personally vouched-for candidate for a vacant see. In the Roman Catholic Church, a similar inner circle took care of episcopal appointments. After the re-establishment of the Roman hierarchy in England in 1870, the Vatican's Secretary of Propaganda, a Mgr Barnabo, took a personal interest in the new bishops, many of whom had in any case been educated in Rome. But neither system could work so smoothly in the very different social conditions of the 1920s and 1930s, when British Prime Ministers had little knowledge—or perhaps even interest—in the new men coming up in the Church of England and when the Roman Catholic Church was expanding in Britain and producing its own indigenous leaders. It is in this period that the two systems diverged.

The big change for the Church of England was the designation in 1941 of a civil servant as the Prime Minister's Appointments Secretary. His remit covered not only Church appointments, but also Lord Lieutenants, Regius Professors, the Warden of the Cinque Ports, the Poet Laureate and so forth. The last two of the four Appointments Secretaries, Sir John Hewitt and Mr Colin Peterson, have held the office jointly with that of the Lord Chancellor's Ecclesiastical Secretary, thus giving Downing Street control over some 2,000 Crown livings as well as senior Church appointments. From 1941 onwards, the practice of the Appointments Secretary has been to keep a list of possible candidates for bishoprics after consulting widely throughout the Church, particularly when a see became vacant. Having completed his consultations, he would then advise the Prime Minister on a list of three names to be submitted to the Sovereign, who would normally select the first on the list. But the list was never a 'three-card trick': Churchill is known to have excluded Bishop Bell of Chichester from his list for the see of Canterbury, on the death of Temple, and it is said that the Queen had her doubts about Mr Macmillan's placing of Dr Ramsey at the top of the list when Canterbury again became vacant. Further changes in the system took place in 1964 as a result of the Howick Commission on Church and State: this established a Vacancy-in-See Committee to make the views of the diocese known to the Prime Minister and the archbishops, who at the same time acquired their own appointments secretary. There has recently been some friction within the Church over Vacancy-in-See committees, some of whose members assumed that the Crown had a moral obligation to follow their advice. But the constitutional position is clear. However widely the Prime Minister's Appointments Secretary may consult—and lately the practice has been to consult very widely indeed among 'everyone who feels he ought to be consulted'—yet the final choice remains with the Head of State, the Queen advised by her Prime Minister. The cathedral chapter of the diocese is then required to complete the formalities by 'electing' the Sovereign's nominee and if they refuse to do so (as none have in modern times) then it was until recently theoretically possible to invoke the powers of Praemunire against them, sequestering their goods and imprisoning the rebellious canons in the Tower of London (these penalties under the Statutes of Praemunire were quietly dropped in 1967). In fact, vocal discontent with the Crown's appointment of bishops has fluctuated from year to year. In 1974, under Dr Ramsey's leadership, the Anglican General Synod voted by a large majority for talks with the government with a view to the Church obtaining a decisive say in the appointment of its own bishops. But when, in 1976, the new Prime Minister, Mr Callaghan, offered Anglicans much wider consultation on episcopal appointments but ruled out any decisive choice, the Synod voted by an even bigger majority to accept. Both Church and State thus veered away from disestablishment, although the Church has still to decide how wide and open its own internal consultations will be.

In the Roman Catholic Church, the major change in episcopal appointments came in 1938 with the establishment in London of the Pope's personal representative, the Apostolic Delegate. Henceforth it was through him that the Greater Chapter of canons of the vacant diocese would submit their list of three names (the *terna*) to the Pope. The bishops would in any case append their own comments and additional names and from 1971 onwards the Bishops' Conference began to keep a list of suitable candidates in advance of a diocese becoming vacant. Under the present Apostolic Delegate, the Swiss Archbishop Bruno Heim, consultation has become very wide. After the death of Cardinal Heenan, the Delegate took the unprecedented step of inviting comments not only from English and Welsh Catholics but from all interested Christians on the sort of man who should lead the Roman Catholic Church in this country. This led to some well-publicised lobbying for certain candidates, among whom Dom Basil Hume did not often figure.

However, the bald description above of the procedures of both churches for the appointment of bishops leaves out one important feature. To a great extent the episcopal hierarchies of the Church of England and the Roman Catholic Church in England and Wales are self-perpetuating. In recent years, the majority of diocesan appointments in both churches have been from the ranks of the non-diocesan bishops (in the C of E called suffragans or assistant bishops and in the Roman Church coadjutors or auxiliary bishops). In both churches, the practice has been that these secondary bishops are chosen by the diocesan himself; the choice is automatically confirmed by the Pope in the case of Roman Catholics, while in the Church of England the convention is that the Prime Minister ticks the first of the two names submitted to him. Of the last seven diocesan appointments in the Roman Catholic Church in England and Wales, five (Clifton, Hexham and Newcastle, Nottingham, Portsmouth and the new diocese of East Anglia) were from auxiliary bishops, one was a translation (Liverpool) and the seventh was Cardinal Hume. Of the remaining 13 diocesans, 8 had been bishops in their previous jobs, 4 had been diocesan administrators (Vicar-Generals or Chancellors) and only one had come direct from a parish. The Anglican record is not markedly different. In 1975, out of the 43 diocesan bishops, 7 had been translated from other dioceses, 16 had been promoted from suffragans, 4 had been archdeacons, 8 theological college principals or dons, 2 had been missionaries and 6 parish priests. The average age of the Roman Catholic diocesans was 61; of the Church of England bishops 60.

Will either church change its system and opt eventually for directly elected bishops? The arguments against it are formidable: there is the fear of open and contentious lobbying, of diocesan electors always choosing the local man whom they know, of appointments being made according to party persuasions, whether 'High' or 'Low' or progressive or conservative. In the case of the Church of England, opponents of change contend that the Church could not afford to maintain the sort of office which the State now supports in Downing Street and it is said that direct election of Anglican bishops would call into question the whole issue of Establishment, which could tie the government of the Church down for years to come. Moreover, though there is inevitably a tendency for the existing system of episcopal appointments to produce a large number of 'safe' appointments, there have been the inspired exceptions. One cannot imagine an electoral college within the Roman Catholic Church of England and Wales having selected Dom Basil Hume, an abbot relatively unknown outside his own order, as its national leader. Nor could one have expected a body of Anglican electors to have chosen the late Bishop of Durham, Dr Ian Ramsey, who before he made such a mark in the North-East held an obscure professorship of religious philosophy at Oxford. The argument on the other side is simple and for many quite decisive. It was concisely put by a United Reformed Church leader, Dr Kenneth Slack, in a *Church Times* column: 'Quite simply, there is something theologically shocking in the idea that the one body that cannot be trusted to choose (by whatever means) its own leaders is the one which claims to be born of the direct activity of the Holy Spirit.'

10

The Spirit of Inflation

Earlier in this book, we looked at the pentecostal renewal movement as one of the forces which is shaking the institutional churches from within. One writer has called it the 'gale of the Spirit'. But the veritable hurricane of change which has swept through all denominations, flattening long-standing values and structures which will possibly never stand upright again, comes from a very different quarter. It is inflation and, ironically, the original meaning of the word was not far removed from descriptions of the Holy Spirit. Inflation, of course, is no new phenomenon in Western society; it has been eroding the economic strength and social vitality of institutions like the churches for centuries. But the steep fall in purchasing power which followed the 1973 Arab-Israeli war and the subsequent quadrupling of oil prices, has been of a very different order. The report of the Anglican Church Commissioners for 1975 indicates the scale of it:

In 1965/66 the Commissioners' total income was £21.2 million. In 1974/75 the corresponding figure was £34.1 million, an increase over nine years of £12.9 million or 61 per cent. But after allowing for inflation as measured by the rise in the Retail Price Index, the 1974/75 figure was only equivalent to £17.7 million in terms of 1965/66 values, representing a decrease of £3.5 million or 16.5 per cent.

The policy committee of the much smaller Episcopal Church in Scotland put the problem in a wider context:

There will be no return to the former state: the inflationary spiral may (indeed it must) be curbed, and a limited new stability will be attained, but social and financial circumstances will never again be as they were . . . when a more settled pattern of the country and the community emerges, in which our Church must then bear its witness, it will differ greatly from that of the 1950s and 1960s.

It was partly the suddenness and scale of the inflationary shock which followed the events of 1973 but partly also the way in which it singled out the basic weaknesses of Western capitalism that led some Christians to conclude that the crisis was a sign of divine justice. Indeed, the inflationary crisis brought about three quite radical changes in the thinking of churchpeople. It, first, made them sharply aware of their dependence on the fragile financial system. Religious people have always been reticent about money. At a popular level, this meant that older churchmen tended to avert their eyes as they dropped their copper mites into the collection plate; on a loftier plane, it led devout and ordained people to regard money as an unspiritual affair best left to back-vestry laymen to deal with. Before 1973, for example, no Anglican forum, whether the old Church Assembly or the new General Synod, had ever debated the annual reports of the Church Commissioners and to this day there are no provisions for either publishing or debating the financial affairs of the Roman Catholic Church in Britain. However, there is now the beginnings of a new openness about church finances and a popular desire, if not yet the whole-hearted willingness of those in authority, to debate the balance sheet of the churches' economic and spiritual priorities.

Secondly, inflation has led to some radical changes in Christian thinking and organisation which would probably not have taken place so quickly at a time of economic stability. We have already seen some of these changes in the earlier chapter on the ministry. Thirdly, and perhaps most important, the inflationary cyclone which hit the West in the mid-seventies has produced a heightened awareness of the world economic order, and raised in new and more urgent forms many of the moral dilemmas that have continually troubled thinking Christians. There is the dilemma over the churches' inherited treasures —the noble buildings, the vestments and Communion plate—which in an earlier age served in a sacramental way to direct men's attention towards the Divine Majesty but now seem to many to be a major impediment in bringing modern man to God. People should come before buildings, is the current cry. There is the dilemma over church investments in land and the Stock Exchange. Should these investments be regarded mainly as an assured source of income for maintaining the work of the Church, should they be used as an instrument of social and political pressure, or should they be liquidated altogether? The debate goes on. One side finds support in Jesus's warning that earthly treasures are corrupted by moth and rust and are themselves corrupting, while the other side can cite their master's approval of Mary

Magdalene's expenditure of costly ointment upon him and his words 'the poor are with us always'.

What then is the basis of the churches' wealth ? All of the churches in Britain are to some extent capitalists in that they all own property and have investments, but there is a basic distinction to be drawn between the heavily capital-based churches and those which maintain their work almost wholly from the income of congregational giving. The obvious example of the former is the Church of England, which fortunately for our purposes also happens to be the best documented religious body in Britain with regard to its finances (as to most other matters). As the Established Church, it has acquired a great deal of wealth over the centuries, much of which is now managed by the Church Commissioners for England, with august offices at 1 Millbank, opposite the House of Lords. The Commissioners are an anomalous statutory body requiring some introduction. They were established in 1948 by a Measure of the Church Assembly (equivalent to an Act of Parliament) to combine the duties of the Governors of Queen Anne's Bounty (an eighteenth century scheme for helping poor clergy) and the Ecclesiastical Commissioners (a nineteenth century parliamentary device for making the management of Anglican revenues more equitable and more efficient). The 95 Church Commissioners are a microcosm of the British establishment: they include ex-officio all the diocesan bishops and many of the major officers of state, like the Prime Minister, the Chancellor of the Exchequer, the Lord Chief Justice and the Lord Mayors of London and York, 25 members appointed by the General Synod, 4 by the Queen and 2 by the Aldermen of the City of London. But the management of Church assets is mainly in the hands of the three Estates Commissioners, one of whom must be a Member of Parliament. In recent years, the Church Commissioners have become answerable to the General Synod but in the last resort they answer to the Home Secretary and to Parliament, which requires them to publish their accounts annually.

As of 31 March 1975, the Church Commissioners valued their assets at £504.9 million. Four-tenths of the income from these assets came from land and property, three-tenths from equities and convertible stock and three-tenths from gilt-edged, other fixed interest stock and mortgages. But by no means all of the inherited or accumulated wealth of the Church of England has passed into the hands of the Commissioners. The diocese of London, for example, has total assets of nearly £3 million and acts as trustee for a further £2 million. A great deal of this other money, worth about £68 million, is invested through the General Synod's Central Board of Finance and this includes the assets of dioceses, cathedral chapters, parishes, missionary societies, theological colleges and other charitable trusts. Then there is the glebe land, the property and agricultural holdings which in some cases still provides part of the parish priest's stipend but which is now in process, rather controversially, of being brought under the control of diocesan boards of finance. Nobody as yet knows for sure how much glebe there is, but an approximate estimate of 130,000 acres would put a value on it of not less than £40 million (the value per acre being low because most glebe land is subject to long-standing tenancy agreements).

It would be folly, however, to tot up these known valuations and conclude that the Church of England is worth between £600-£700 million, for that would leave out of the sum the Church's two main assets, its buildings and its people. The Church of England owns some 18,000 parish churches, thousands of vicarages, schools and other buildings as well as their ancillary land, like graveyards. Much of this real estate is in prime urban locations: one has only to think of the Christopher Wren churches in the City of London. But is this real estate a saleable asset? Until an American College acquired the Wren Church of St Mary Aldermanbury in 1964 and shipped it block by block to Fulton, Missouri, as a memorial to Sir Winston Churchill, it scarcely seemed conceivable that the Church could actually dispose of its older buildings as buildings. Indeed, it was difficult to put a value on ancient buildings at all (the Roskill Commission on the Third London Airport, which considered the demolition of one of England's finest Norman parish churches, at Stewkley, Bucks, valued it at its fire insurance cover of £50,000). But the sites, rather than the buildings, in certain favoured districts can be an asset. In the seven years after the Pastoral Measure 1968 took effect, 550 churches were declared redundant of which 176 were authorised to be sold, leased or given for other uses and 156 disposed of by sales or by becoming part of the churchyard. These were of course the exceptions, the cases where changes in population had made a separate parish and its church surplus to the Church's pastoral needs. For most Anglican churches, disposal of the building and land is out of the question, except where it is clearly redundant or where it is of no value architecturally and is to be replaced with a modern building. Indeed, rather than being an asset, most ancient church buildings have become a severe economic liability. The ravages of age, pollution, traffic and neglect have caused most ancient churches to be in need now of drastic repair work. The list of current cathedral appeals—Canterbury (£3.5 million), St Paul's (£3 million), York (£2 million), Salisbury (£500,000) and so on—indicates the scale of the problem and also leads to some misconceived criticism of the way the Church of England uses its 'millions'.

The other Anglican major asset is the people who, despite the relentless decline in their numbers, have been contributing much more to the needs of their Church. In 1973, they gave £34.8 million, an increase of 27 per cent over their giving for 1970, but that is still nowhere near enough to meet the needs of inflation. In 1975, the Archbishops' Advisers on Needs and Resources reported to the General Synod that a further £28 million over the 1973 figure would be necessary in 1976, if the Church were to maintain its basic structure, as well as its mission and social work. Of this sum, the Church Commissioners would find an extra £8 million and the people would have to provide the other additional £20 million. The Advisers said rather optimistically that this was an opportunity for the Church to rethink its priorities in a 'challenging and effective way' and, in any case, the additional £20 million meant on average only an extra 20p a week for every person on the Church's electoral rolls. This was optimistic simply because the electoral rolls did not reflect the true state of committed Anglican membership and, moreover, Anglican giving per head of electoral membership in 1973 was only 18p a week. Such is the effect of inflation upon a church which until recently was cushioned against such shocks by its capital assets.

But what about the question concerning the Anglican millions? With all the qualifications and caveats, is not the Church of England a wealthy church and could it not dispose of its vast assets in a more effective, perhaps a more evangelical way? The answers to these questions must be 'Yes' and 'No'. Yes, the Church of England is wealthy to a degree not approached by any other religious or voluntary body in the land. Other churches, like the Church of Scotland or the 'disestablished' Anglican Church of Ireland or Church in Wales, have no such capital assets, though they do have some. And the Roman Catholic Church, which has an active membership as large as that of the Church of England, certainly has no capital endowments of comparable size; and Catholics would leap at the chance to acquire a medieval cathedral, repair bills and all. Thus as an institution the Church of England is far more privileged than its ecumenical peers and its members do not have to shoulder as much of the burden for maintaining their church as other Christians do. But their burden is undoubtedly much larger: as William Temple said, 'the Church of England is the only society which exists for those who aren't members of it'. But whether the Church could use its wealth in a radically different way and, through its wealth, become a more missionary-minded organisation, is extremely doubtful. It is the classic case of an organisation becoming the prisoner of its own historical *raison d'être*. The uses to which the Commissioners' income can be put are severely restricted by statute, being mainly devoted to clergy stipends, housing and pensions; they are not allowed to use their millions for missionary work or repairing cathedrals. And the Commissioners could not dispose of their assets and make the proceeds available for such purposes without considerable difficulty. Synodical and parliamentary approval would be required, and it is doubtful whether it would be forthcoming because of the nature of the trusts in which the assets are held. The Commissioners cannot close down churches under the Pastoral Measure without going through an exhaustive procedure of consultation which can, in the last resort, involve appeal to the Judicial Committee of the Privy Council. Even as a financial institution, comparable in some ways to the large industrial pension funds, the Commissioners operate under restrictions which are unique. On the one hand, they do not receive any contributions year by year with which to increase their capital base and the only way they can do this is by skilful investment management. On the other hand, the Commissioners are prevented by law from using capital gains to augment the income they pay out in clergy stipends. Thus they have become adept at the strange art of trying to boost their assets and their income at the same time, with periodic switches from property into equity and from capital growth stocks into high yield ones. They have gained many admirers in the City of London, though some Anglican clergy view their expertise and success with mixed feelings.

None of the financial institutions attached to the other churches in Britain operates under such stringent laws and conditions as do the Church Commissioners, but all are bound by their status as legal corporations and charitable trusts (which give them tax relief) as well as by the moral obligations they owe to members past, present and future. The Episcopal Church in Scotland in its exhaustive appraisal of how best to survive inflation gave serious consideration to the view that it should liquidate its investments (worth about £3 million) and live off present congregational giving. But it rejected this option for three reasons: it would be failing in its stewardship for the Church of tomorrow if by ridding itself of its investment capital it were to 'eat the seed corn' in order to satisfy today's hunger; it would be morally unjustifiable and probably legally impossible to divert endowments from the benefactors' original purposes to ordinary church maintenance; and, if it were possible to do this, then an overwhelmingly strong claim would emerge in respect of clergy pensions. The Episcopal Church chose instead the option of retrenchment, of cutting back its professional ministry. Yet, despite the serious attention it gave to this issue, the Episcopal Church is not at all as reliant on capital as its bigger sister in England. Its investment income (of some £372,000) is less than half the annual giving of congregations (£768,000).

The larger Church of Scotland has much the same spread of income. According to a report presented to the 1975 General Assembly by Professor J.N. Wolfe, of Edinburgh University, 70 per cent of the Kirk's income derives from 'Christian liberality' and 30 per cent from other sources, including donations, bequests, investments and the endowments of ministerial stipends from tithes and rents ('teinds' and 'feuduties'). These latter (of which there are altogether 23,000 including the controversial 'feu superiorities' which amount to an ancient form of land transaction tax) are the equivalent of the Anglican parson's 'glebe', but there are few other basic similarities between the finances of the two Established Churches. As a Presbyterian Church, the Kirk has no central funds apart from the assessments on presbyteries sanctioned by the annual General Assembly. Its centrally invested assets are held on behalf of congregations and committees, as is the case with the Church of England's Central Board of Finance but not the Church Commissioners. The Kirk's central investments (amounting to some £7.5 million in the long-term General Investment Fund, which is run on unit trust lines, and £4 million in the higher yield short-term deposits) have been severely hit by inflation: the value of the General Investment Fund units dropped by 30 per cent in 1974 (although this compared with a 55 per cent drop in the Financial Times Actuaries Index). These investments, however, provide only a small part of the Kirk's income, when compared with either the glebe income or the contributions of members, the 'liberality' which in 1975 amounted to £10.7 million. Well over half of this (54 per cent) is spent within the parishes, another 19 per cent is spent centrally mainly on maintaining the minimum stipend, and the remaining 27 per cent is spent on extra-parochial work through the Church of Scotland's Mission and Service Fund.

Thus, the Church's normal income is fully committed and the sudden emergency of inflation has had its effect in two different ways. First, to keep pace with inflation, stipends were raised during 1974 by an unprecedented 20 per cent—giving the ministers a minimum stipend of £2,352 a year plus a manse. In typical Church of Scotland fashion, this decision was taken only after considerable agonising over the question of the Kirk giving a national lead by restraining the inflationary demand for ever higher incomes. Secondly, Church leaders were faced with the uncomfortable fact that in order to maintain the Kirk as Scottish people have come to know it, congregations would have to increase their 'liberality' by 12.4 per cent each year and even that might prove insufficient. Moreover, the balance sheets had long concealed another problem. The average per capita giving of the Kirk's 'members' (which in 1974 was £10.1 a year or 19p a week) covered not only widely different degrees of 'liberality' but a very wide spectrum of committed membership. Thus, in assessing the Church's strategy in an inflationary situation, Kirk leaders brought together two tasks: on the one hand, they set out to raise more money and to keep raising it, pressing the tax advantages of covenants for example upon congregations, and at the same time they set out to make membership into a real commitment to the Church. 'The real problem facing the Church is not so much how to increase its income: it is how to awaken its membership to more effective belief in God, one consequence of which will be a greater willingness to give.' And as the Church of Scotland considered this urgent financial and spiritual programme, it also had before it the more radical alternatives of its Committee of Forty, with the picture of the 'stripped-down Church' mentioned in an earlier chapter.

Most of the churches in Britain, however, do not have the fruits of past endowments to enjoy even on the scale of the Church of Scotland, let alone the Church of England. All religious bodies are to some small extent capitalists in the sense that they hold investments against a rainy day, or for a specific project or simply for tax purposes. One can see the motley array of these investments from a study of the Central Register of the Charities Commission: it ranges from the Apostolic Faith Church based in Bournemouth to the Western Union of Unitarian and Free Christian Churches based in Bristol. Yet the revenues derived from these investments are small and most of the

Free Churches in Britain are solidly income-based, maintained and if possible expanded by the giving of their members and adherents, which in a few extreme cases involves tithing (giving a tenth of one's income) or total surrender of one's private wealth to the Church.

The Methodist Church is a typical and even a shining example of how a church can live within its congregational income. According to official Methodist figures, its membership of just over half a million gives on average 50p a week per head, bringing in an annual income of over £10 million. This has enabled the Church to implement a 20 per cent rise in its ministers' stipends for 1974–75, giving each of them a minimum stipend of £2,250, plus a fully rated and decorated house and car and child allowances where appropriate. The Methodist Church feels justifiably proud of the whole-hearted response from its members to the demands of inflation; indeed the response has been so good that Church leaders say that they could afford more ministers if only there were enough candidates coming forward for the ministry. It also prides itself upon being one of the few major churches in Britain which is able to give a house to each retired minister and minister's widow. But there are hidden snags in this record of success. One is that while the 'people called Methodists' have lived up to their tradition of stewardship and responded well in a time of economic emergency, yet the Church's membership is steadily declining and coupled with a continuing though less dramatic rise in the inflation rate this could ultimately put the Methodist Church in the same inflationary predicament facing other churches. A second qualification to the Methodist success is that, while members have rallied to the immediate needs of their local ministers and churches, the needs of wider enterprises, such as the missionary societies, have not been so well met. This is a little surprising in view of the outward-going nature of Methodism, but it does reflect the trend in other British churches. Thirdly, and much more tentatively, it can be argued that the Methodist success in coping with the inflationary crisis is basically a defence of the *status quo*, of its denominational identity, and not in enlarging its missionary field either at home or abroad. It is a church which takes good care to live within its means. It is a principle of Methodist financial stewardship, for example, that no new church building should be erected unless the funds are either already available or firmly pledged by local Methodists. Although this principle is really workable only through help from certain charities like the Rank Foundation or because of the sale of redundant church buildings in other parts of the country, yet it does represent a moral commitment by Methodists to their ideal of financial stewardship. This is a wholly admirable trait within a credit-crazed society and of course it contrasts strongly with the Roman Catholic record of funding their building programmes almost wholly from loans. On the other hand, one cannot avoid wondering whether the Methodist Church has forgotten how to live dangerously, and whether it has not cut itself off from the experience of inflation by society as a whole. One cannot avoid the impression that Methodists may have thus blunted the edge of their traditional social concern and perhaps consolidated the smugness that has been apparent in Methodism throughout the past hundred years. But perhaps these criticisms do not take account of the whole picture which includes areas of church life far beyond the financial. The Methodist Church is a denomination which has to all intents and purposes lost its social constituency and in any case never had a distinctive doctrinal basis; its *raison d'être* now appears to be the ecumenical movement and as we have seen there are intractable problems here.

The last of the four major churches whose financial assets and structures are worth study is at the same time the most interesting and yet the most elusive. The Roman Catholic Church in Britain does not publish its accounts: the only pound signs to be found in the *Catholic Directory for England and Wales* are in the advertisements. For the Roman Catholic rank and file, the finances of their church remain an impenetrable mystery, known only to a few prelates, finance officers and to God. The most that the interested layman can normally expect to be told about Church finances is the cost of the new school or chapel for which he must help raise the cash, although in a few parishes now the clergy are prepared to take the people fully into their confidence with regard to parochial finances. However, open discussion about Catholic finances is rare and certainly does not extend to diocesan or even less national finances.

The obfuscation of Roman Catholic finances is, of course, a world-wide phenomenon and a notorious one. Immense journalistic resources have been spent to little avail on attempting to assess the wealth of the Vatican. But the reasons for the apparent secrecy surrounding the subject may not be as simple as many critics of the Church suggest. It is certainly true that the hierarchies have traditionally viewed finances as something intimately connected with their own spiritual and disciplinary authority. It would be going far beyond the principle of co-responsibility outlined at Vatican II for the diocesan bishop and his advisers to throw open the books, even to the Senate of Priests, let alone to the people at large, and thus allow them to debate the episcopal management of the diocese's hard-earned resources. It was the principle of authority that defeated the small group of Catholic radicals who in the last years of Cardinal Heenan's reign attempted to open up the issue of Westminster diocesan finances. Members of the group maintain that the Cardinal often took important financial decisions entirely off his own bat, with a minimum of consultation even among his immediate advisers, but the radicals also concede that even Heenan could not have known the full picture of the assets and income of the archdiocese.

The fact is that Roman Catholic finances are almost hopelessly fragmented. There is certainly no will to publish consolidated accounts but, even if there were, it is difficult to see how the accounts could be consolidated. The income of the average Roman Catholic diocese comes mainly from congregational giving. Much of this is spent immediately within the parish, and as far as investment income is concerned there is likely to be a multitude of small trusts and endowments, each committed to a specific project, as often as not a building fund. A sample of the 2,000 or so Catholic trusts registered with the Charity Commission (one of the few public sources of information about RC finances) shows the diversity of the Church's assets. They range from the holdings of religious orders, diocesan pension funds, educational trusts and clergy training funds, down to hundreds of local trusts, bringing in an income of some £25 a year perhaps, to be spent usually on the 'advancement of the Roman Catholic religion'. (Some are more specific; for the sending of the sick and aged on pilgrimages to Lourdes, for prizes to the best three acolytes or scholars at a school in Holyhead, £6 a year for altar-boys' shoes, and one for the provision of meals for poor persons, mainly Jews, passing through London on Sabbaths and Holy Days.) Many of these assets are managed by the all-clergy Trustees of the Diocese, of which the bishop is the ex-officio and executive chairman, but many other bequests fall outside the control of the diocese. A grateful Catholic widow, for example, who on the death of her London stockbroker husband has retired to Yorkshire, may have left her property there to her old parish or diocese in the South-East; the southern diocese may well offer the property to the local Catholic Housing Aid Society, or it may simply let it and remit the rents to London, in which case all that local Catholics may know about its ownership is that it is 'owned by the Church'.

A more important clutch of Catholic assets which lie outside diocesan control are those connected with the religious orders, especially the women's orders of which there are 1,270 convents in England and Wales. The religious orders have amassed their wealth broadly in two ways, through the steady accumulation of endowments, bequests and gifts (including collections) over the years and through windfalls, like the sale of a redundant convent, first acquired in the late nineteenth century when suburban land was cheap, but now occupying a valuable development site. Windfalls from redundant property appear to be more common in Lancashire and the Midlands than in the South-East, but they are not always gathered into the Church's larder without difficulty. Recently a group of nuns in London vacated a very desirable convent site next to Westminster Cathedral, which seemed the ideal opportunity for the Archdiocese either to sell off the site for commercial development or to locate its own curial offices there; but both schemes were defeated by careful consideration of the local authority's planning and rating restrictions and the most economical new tenancy turned out to be another order of nuns.

All the same, the assets in land and stocks and shares that remain within the religious orders are considerable, as the Central Register of the Charity Commission shows. The Daughters of the Cross, a nursing order based at Carshalton in Surrey, submitted impeccable accounts to the Commissioners in 1974, showing total assets of £1,498,168, over £900,000 of which was held in property, including a hospital, and £198,000 in Stock Exchange investments; the order declared its annual income to be in the region of £450,000, which of course covered the turnover of the hospital, as well as rents and dividends. A number of other women's orders declared substantial incomes to the Charity Commission—the Ursulines £67,000, the Bernadines £80,000, the Little Sisters of the Assumption £28,000 and the Sisters of Mercy, whose income derives mainly from door-to-door collections, £74,000 in Oldham, £25–£50,000 in Liverpool and £39,000 in Derby. It has to be said that much of this convent income goes immediately into the social and communal work for which Catholic nuns are justifiably renowned. But the figures above are only the tip of the iceberg, for most religious orders in this country do not reveal their current assets even to the Charity Commission and indeed are under no legal obligation to do so. What the figures do indicate, however, is that the wealth of the orders, though unquantifiable *in toto*, is considerable, that a larger proportion of it is held in stocks and shares than is the case with other Roman Catholic assets and that all of this makes the usual estimates of Catholic income, such as that given in the Wells Organisation table on a later page, rather questionable.

A further complication that hinders direct comparison of RC finances with those of other churches is that much of the Catholic Church's financial affairs are operated on a calculated deficit basis. The Archdiocese of Westminster, one of the two largest in England, has a debt of some £6 million, with annual interest payments of £700,000, mainly on schools—and the diocesan debts do not include many which fall directly upon parishes. This means that the assets of whatever origin, which are held or managed by the diocesan trustees, give a misleading picture of the Church's financial position. When the Westminster trustees were first registered with the Charity Commission by Cardinal Hinsley in 1940, the first schedule of assets showed the modest sum of £12,000 worth of shares and £8,500 in cash; the second schedule of assets, however, showed all of the churches, schools, presbyteries and other buildings within the jurisdiction of the trustees throughout North London and the Home Counties, including a large number of plots of land held against future building needs. The distinctive feature of Catholic diocesan finances is that a considerable portion of them are converted into real estate as early as is practicable, often at the price of incurring very large debts which can only be serviced and repaid by intensive fund-raising on the part of the parish clergy.

Until the early nineteen-fifties, much of this fund-raising was directed towards the goal of providing every substantial Catholic community with its own permanent church or Mass Centre, but increasingly from the end of the Second World War onwards the effort has been channelled into schools building. This was, according to Cardinal Heenan in a Pastoral Letter of 1972, not so much a new policy as the reassertion of an old one: 'Never forget that despite their poverty, our ancestors were rich in faith . . . Anxious to provide education for their children they were determined that it should be a Catholic education. That is why they built schools before churches.' That may be so, but one reason why the Roman Catholic Church in this country has been able to undertake such an intensive schools building programme was the passing of the 1944 Education Act, which created the dual State-Church class of 'voluntary-aided' schools. These are in effect Church schools within the State system, for which the government now pays up to 85 per cent of the building costs—but only after the building has been erected. Hence the enormous rolling debts amassed by the Roman Catholic Church. The utility to either the Church or the State of this type of school is a matter of fierce and continuing controversy, which will be reflected elsewhere in this book, but a major element in the controversy is the enormous sums of money that are spent on these ventures, initially by the Church and later in loans and grants by the State. As a well-informed observer put it: 'figures from the Department of Education and Science show grants of £112,796,505 and loans of £22,387,371 between 1953 and 1973; Catholic liabilities since 1944 are estimated at about £70 million and much of this has yet to be paid off' (R. A. Wake, Catholic Education, The Month, April 1975). Mr Wake points out that inflation has increased the burden of schools-building debts by doubling building costs within the past ten years and increasing interest rates by 100 per cent. 'It used to be thought that every parish could carry the debt of a primary school but with inflation even this seems to be getting too much.'

Although inflation has meant that the servicing of the Catholic Church's debts has steadily become more onerous, other inflationary pressures upon the Catholic Church have been less than those upon other churches. The economic crisis of the seventies has not provoked the leadership into serious consideration of radical alternatives to the professional parish ministry—quite the contrary. The basic reason is that to a large extent the Catholic clergy are outside the cash economy. In place of the Protestant minister's stipend, the Catholic priest will receive his board, lodging and working expenses direct from his parishioners (sometimes in kind in the form of direct hospitality and services) and his only cash remuneration will be in effect pocket money. This may amount to some £300 a year for the average parish priest and £200 for his assistants, if they are lucky, to which should be added 'stoll fees' (for marriages), cremation dues, bequests for private masses and so on, in all giving the priest an income of some £700–£800 a year. Clergy who are maintained on this basis can be squeezed much harder in times of economic stringency than can the centrally-financed Anglican vicar, with his wife and three children and probably higher educational and social expectations. It is not at all surprising that inflation has thus hardened the resistance of many senior Catholics to any relaxation of the celibacy rule. How could the overstretched Church *afford* married priests? Inflation has also provided a new defence to the demands that the Roman Catholic Church should provide for lay representation in its government. At present, through the National Catholic Fund, the Church spends £150,000 a year on its central services (mainly upon the Commissions, but £28,000 of it goes towards the Catholic Information Service at Abbots Langley in Hertfordshire). The Church of England, on the other hand, in 1975 spent £1,413,170 on its synodical government and central services. How could the overstretched Catholic Church afford that luxury either?

To sum up this general view of the churches' finances, it is worth quoting from the only published list of the resources of the British churches, published by the Wells Organisation. The Wells Organisation, which has been active in the fund-raising field in this country for almost twenty years, describes the list as in some respects 'arbitrary' with 'many unsupported and probably some very erroneous assumptions and estimates'. Certainly the Anglican and Roman Catholic figures need to be assessed with some reservations. The figures all relate to 1973. (*See opposite page.*)

The economic crisis of the seventies shook the foundations of all the British churches, with varying degrees of seismic intensity. Dangerous cracks appeared in their financial structures, as they did in financial institutions the world over, but for the churches the cracks went deeper, penetrating to their fundamental thinking about the place of the professional ordained ministries and the commitments of church members. For the remainder of the decade and beyond, we can expect to observe church leaders at work busily surveying the damage and overseeing repairs or even complete rebuilding programmes. For one small but influential group of Christians, however, the effects of the economic crisis did not go far enough: they could have wished that inflation had brought the whole edifice of institutional religion crashing down in ruins. These were the Christian radicals, the men and women who are committed to taking their religion into the secular struggles for racial and political justice, for Third World development, for better housing and so on. Until recently, most radicals would have been too actively engaged in their various humanitarian labours to have been much concerned with ecclesiastical economics. But the inflationary crisis presented them with a stark contrast. On the one hand, there were the needs of the world's teeming poor, made considerably poorer by the sequence of events which had followed the 1973 Middle East war, and on the other hand, the behaviour of small groups of Western Christians, apparently hypnotised by their own

Denomination	Total estimated population *thousands*	Income all sources *£ thousand*	Members' offerings *£ thousand*	Total members on roll *thousands*	Churches or congregations
Anglican and Episcopal Churches	28,690	74,060	26,058	3,332	20,703
Roman Catholic	5,481	20,200	15,125	3,025	4,351
Greek Orthodox	140	200	120	25	50
Scottish and Presbyterian	3,071	15,617	11,726	1,393	4,062
Methodist	2,191	7,842	6,180	683	10,391
Congregational (incl. URC)	466	5,015	2,432	301	3,012
Baptist	514	2,130	2,054	280	3,919
Pentecostal	90	800	740	65	1,099
Evangelical and Wesleyan Reform Union	42	240	150	27	555
Lutheran	54	72	35	24	78
Salvation Army	246	650	520	103	1,048
Unitarian and Free Christian Church	36	180	125	23	264
Seventh-Day Adventists	20	1,030	775	12	142
Church of the Nazarene	10	226	216	4	99
Countess of Huntingdon Connexion	5	45	24	3	33
TOTAL	41,263	126,307	66,280	9,478	51,334

economic difficulties. Moreover, the crisis demonstrated that in the wider humanitarian concerns the churches were 'compromised', their hands were unclean. 'We may ask,' wrote one of their critics, 'how far the churches have allowed themselves to become so identified with the structures of injustice that they actually live off them.' (Charles Elliott, *Inflation and the Compromised Church.*)

The radical critique of the churches' economic behaviour in the inflationary seventies was directed at both their sources of investment income and at their levels of spending (where the radicals found ready support from less radical quarters). There were, for example, ecumenical parallels to the Anglican distaste for the growing list of million-pound cathedral restorations. Some Roman Catholics blanched at the £1 million repair and maintenance fund launched in 1976 for West-minster Cathedral, which was only 73 years old and had been described —not so much because of its Byzantine architecture as of its pastoral utility—as a 'mausoleum with music'. And younger Methodists, particularly in the North of England, could not see the necessity for the £750,000 appeal for repairing and restoring Wesley's Chapel in City Road, London. Another object of critical attention was the housing of Anglican bishops. *Private Eye* began a new round of bishop-bashing when it revealed that the cost of adapting a new See House for the Bishops of London was £100,000, and the outraged critics were scarcely mollified by the Church Commissioners' subsequent promise that they were inviting episcopal views on 'the nature and standard of housing which nowadays should be provided for diocesan bishops'. The new Bishop of London was Dr Gerald Ellison, and his successor at Chester, Dr Victor Whitsey, attempted to stem the tide of criticism of episcopal 'life-styles' in a letter to *The Times*:

> The *whole maintenance* of one average Diocesan Bishop, i.e., the official expense of a large service tenancy; of secretarial and administrative assistance; of travelling expenses of 15,000 to 20,000 miles per annum; plus *salary*, amounts to less than £20,000 per annum or £400 per week. If this is compared with any similar position in the professions or industry, or the armed forces or civil service, it can hardly be gainsaid that a Diocesan Bishop would be cheap at double the price.

Debate about the soaring overheads of maintaining the ecclesiastical status quo has long been a feature of British church life. The relatively new element in the debate has been the demand that the churches should thoroughly examine their consciences about where their money comes from and accept that they have at least an indirect responsibility for some of the world's economic injustice. It is not enough in the radical view that the churches should seek the best possible financial return from 'clean' investments. That may be said to be that part of the Church Commissioners' investment policy which avoids shares in companies operating wholly or mainly in armaments, gambling, breweries and distilleries, tobacco, newspapers, publishing and broadcasting, theatre and film, or South Africa (the more positive side of the Commissioners' policy is to accept the responsibility which large investors bear for the general health of society). In the radical view, however, the minimum condition of church involvement in the capitalist system at all (and some are totally opposed to any such involvement), is that it must be actively critical, that the churches must seek wide discussion of the whole impact of the system and engage in 'social audits' of companies in which they are involved:

> Leaving aside the scandalous suggestion that the Church should actually obey its Master and live for the day rather than insure itself for eternity, it is surely mandatory on the Church (and, no less, on all of us Christians) to take a critical, though arguably not a wholly negative, interest in the corporations which use its wealth.

That is the view of Dr Charles Elliott who combines a minor canonry at Norwich Cathedral with an academic post as a development studies economist. He attacks the 'uncritical capitalism' of the churches across a broad front. He points out that almost nothing had been said by the institutional churches in the debates about the distribution of gains from the rising value of urban land, although the churches were major holders of such land. He charges the churches with remaining silent over the safety record of the construction industry, from which much recent ecclesiastical income has come. He even singles out the charitable work of the churches for criticism, arguing that their fund-raising for Third World disaster relief or 'development programmes' had only anaesthetised domestic opinion to the real problem of the exploitative terms of trade in raw materials. In *Inflation and the Compromised Church*, Dr Elliott so liberally sprays the ecclesiastical establishment with radical machine-gun fire that, unsurprisingly, he can see little life left in the enemy trenches at the end of the day.

Other opponents of the churches' 'uncritical capitalism', however, have concentrated on two specific investment areas—housing and South Africa—and these are the sectors of capitalist involvement that have gained most attention.

The churches' record in housing during this century has not been a bad one. The Shelter organisation, which has spearheaded so much of the concern about poor housing in recent years, grew out of the Notting Hill Housing Trust, founded by a former Church of Scotland missionary, Bruce Kenrick. And the churches' entry into low cost housing, through housing associations and other cooperatives, has been very wide. But in the popular imagination, if not in fact, the churches' involvement in housing means the ecclesiastical landlords, which in turn means the Church Commissioners in the first instance. At the end of the last war, the Commissioners found that they had inherited from their predecessors, the Ecclesiastical Commissioners, large areas of low-rental housing, particularly in West London. At the time, their critics went to extraordinary lengths to find evidence of prostitutes living in this Church property. With the bad press that this brought as an additional incentive to their emerging commercial priorities, the Commissioners began their long and profitable entry into post-war office development, often in partnership with undertakings like Sir Max Rayne's London Merchant Securities. The Commissioners also formed their own development company, the Church Estates Development and Improvement Company (CEDIC). The list of property developments in which the Commissioners have been involved would include some of the biggest in central London, including the architecturally-controversial Paternoster Square development near St Paul's and the vast area between the Army and Navy Stores and Victoria Station which ecumenically incorporates the new 'piazza', opening up a view of Westminster Roman Catholic Cathedral. It has been argued that the Commissioners in these schemes have been too uncritical of their partners' social and environmental priorities and, in any case, gave too much away to their partners. This may have been so at first, but the Commissioners appear to have ridden the tiger of the property boom more successfully than many institutions. At any rate, office accommodation now represents two-fifths in value of their property portfolio and almost a fifth of their total income.

The Commissioners' stock of residential property, on the other hand, has probably shrunk to as small a size as it now can and the Church Commissioners are in the commercially unenviable—although socially useful—position of being one of the few large private owners of residential property left in Britain. In 1976, there are 6,000 rented houses and flats under their direct management, 70 per cent of them with rents of less than £10 a week, exclusive of rates, and 50 per cent with rents of less than £5. The Commissioners see this as their 'contribution to the urgent social problem of London's housing'. But it is unfortunate that neither the Commissioners nor the Church of England at large really gets the credit for this vital social service. On the contrary, they continue to attract from certain sections of the media the 'wicked landlord' type of attention. Their last major attempt to develop a significant slice of their residential property, the 160-acre Maida Vale estate in North-west London, shows the difficulties the Commissioners have to contend with. With a steady decline in the estate's residents, the Commissioners put forward an ambitious twenty-year scheme of redevelopment, conservation and landscaping and went to great lengths to explain its implications to both residents and journalists by means of glossy brochures, an exhibition and a film show. The Press reviewed the plans favourably but residents reacted with alarm, seeing evictions and higher rents as the price they would have to pay for the scheme. In the event, the Maida Vale development became a casualty of the economic situation and in 1976 the Commissioners announced with regret that they did not feel able to devote any new funds to residential development. Instead, they offered one of the Maida Vale terraces to a housing association.

While the Anglicans were struggling manfully with their historical social burden and landlord image, a new propertied villain was identified elsewhere in North London. In an interview with the *Catholic Herald*, Fr Oliver McTernan, an Islington parish priest and co-founder of the Angel Housing Advisory Centre, expressed his concern about a terrace of 'dingy', 'leaking' and 'unfit' houses near his church. The special reason for his concern was that fifteen out of seventeen houses in the terrace were owned by A. M. & G. Properties, a company whose chairman was the Most Reverend Thomas Ryan, Bishop of Clonfert, Ireland, and whose profits helped to fund a Catholic boarding school in the West of Ireland. The interview brought a swingeing reply from the bishop across the water, but Fr McTernan was not finished with his revelations about Catholic property ownership. At a conference organised by Shelter, ten months later, he called for an inquiry into property owned by the Church and gave further examples of the reasons for this. There were he said, properties 'in bad physical repair, multi-occupied and lacking in basic amenities' owned by the Archdiocese of Westminster and in Hertford-shire, a local health officer had described as 'unfit for human habita-tion' an old lady's house owned by the Jesuits (a charge later refuted by a spokesman for the Society of Jesus). 'Such examples,' said Fr McTernan, 'reduce to ridicule the statement issued by the Catholic Bishops' Social Welfare Commission in October 1972, calling for adequate housing for all'. The moral of this story, as Fr McTernan conceded, was not that the Roman Catholic Church was a malicious or deliberately bad landlord: it was that the various authorities of the Church probably had little idea of the properties that had come into their possession and even less of the state of repair they were in. Unlike the Anglican Church Commissioners, there was no centralised control over Catholic property ownership. The scandal of Catholic housing was a product of the fragmented state of Catholic finances, described earlier in this chapter.

A similar picture of ignorance and lack of coordination emerged rather more vividly from the other area of radical investigation of Church investments—South Africa. The record of the British churches in supporting their South African counterparts in their courageous stand against *apartheid* is well known. It has produced, for example, a long, purple line of expellees returning to the Church of England from the Republic and from South-West Africa (Namibia). But what of the churches' indirect responsibility for *apartheid* through their investment in British companies having links with South Africa? For a long while, this responsibility was hidden away in the investment portfolios of the different churches. When it was first brought to light in the case of the churches' holdings in Con-solidated Gold Fields (a British company, whose South African asso-ciate had a bad name for its treatment of black workers in the gold mines), then there were cries of injured innocence from the eccle-siastical pursekeepers. The Anglican Central Board of Finance pro-tested that its 70,000 share holding in the company in fact merely represented its stake in a construction company which Consolidated had taken over, and its chairman, Sir Edmund Compton—in a famous outburst—added that he considered it his duty to consider the financial profitability of companies to which the Church lent money, rather than their social impact. The Central Board of Finance later disposed of its original £175,000 holding in Consolidated Gold Fields for £100,000 and adopted the Church Commissioners' policy of avoiding direct investment in South Africa. Many other church bodies did likewise.

The Roman Catholic Archdiocese of Westminster, however, held on to its 30,000 Gold Field shares and became one of the first church institutions to follow a new policy of using shares publicly to press a point of view rather than disposing of them. The initiative came from Mgr Bruce Kent, secretary of the radical Pax Christi group, who in 1975 raised the issue in the diocesan Senate of Priests. A meeting was then arranged between Cardinal Heenan and Christian Concern for South Africa, an independent and ecumenical body which had been set up to advise church institutions with shares in British companies operating in South Africa. CCSA had published a report, accusing Consolidated Gold Fields and its South African associate of paying wages to African workers 'below most current measures of the lowest subsistence level'. After the meeting, the Cardinal announced that he had decided to retain the shares in order to keep a voice in the company's AGM and nominated Mgr Kent to speak there on the diocese's behalf. Mgr Kent did so but, predictably, failed to receive satisfactory answers (Cardinal Heenan died the week before the company's AGM).

Already this approach to South African investments was being out-flanked by another radical group. ELTSA—End Loans to South Africa—was formed by a Methodist minister, David Haslam, to seek more open confrontation between the churches and British companies investing in South Africa, particularly the big banks. In a booklet, *Go Sell*—subtitled 'an investigation into the failure of the British churches to meet the challenge of investment in apartheid'—Mr Haslam accused groups like CCSA of being 'an escape route' for the British church establishment, a buffer for those who wished to avoid confrontation. He himself had been asked by the police to remove himself from Westminster Abbey during a demonstration about South Africa. The particular target of ELTSA was the Midland Bank's participation in a European banking consortium loan to the government of the Republic. The group had inspired the Methodist Conference in 1975 to pass a resolution calling on the bank to withdraw from the consortium and Methodist leaders had had private talks with the bank to no apparent result (as had the Church Commissioners). In their frustration, ELTSA supporters resorted to direct action, including the placing in Midland branches of counterfeit Giro slips overprinted 'Deposit on Apartheid'. Then, to some surprise, the disparate groups critical of the bank's policy suddenly lined up behind one protest action. The initiative came from the Methodist Church's Central Finance Division, who put down a resolution for the Midland AGM calling on the bank to make no further loans to South Africa. In a significant change of policy away from behind-the-scenes diplomacy, the Church Commissioners and the Church of England's Central Board of Finance, holding 750,000 and 150,000 Midland votes respectively, agreed to back the resolution and the United Reformed Church followed suit. ELTSA supporters now began to search the published list of the bank's shareholders in search of other likely religious backers. In many cases, their letters went unanswered but they did receive promises of support from three Roman Catholic religious orders—Holy Cross Abbey in Dorset, the Carmelites of Quidenham in Norfolk and the Presentation Convent of Armagh—as well as from some Catholic dioceses. The Greater London Council also backed the resolution, which was called at the Midland Bank AGM on 7 April 1976, but defeated by 47,404,015 votes to 2,945,759.

Although defeated at the count, the churches' Midland Bank resolution was a significant achievement. It brought together some of the churches' major financial institutions and their radical critics in an alliance which would have been inconceivable two years before. It showed in a dramatic way that the radicals' message about 'social audits', about the international responsibilities implicit in ecclesiastical capitalism, had gone home. It was 'the first time a resolution on a moral issue had been tabled at any annual general meeting in the country,' said the Rev Derek Farrow, general secretary of the Methodist Finance Division. It demonstrated the moral power that could be exerted through the churches' economic wealth, but it also gave some of the backers of the Midland Bank resolution pause for thought. How far should the churches intervene in the capitalist corporations from which their main need is urgent funds with which to keep the churches going? Does not power corrupt and is not economic power, wielded with high moral intent, possibly the most corrupting of all? The churches' action certainly did not go uncriticised both inside the churches and outside.

Writing to the Archbishop of Canterbury—'as one member of the Church of England to another'—the Conservative MP, Eldon Griffiths, asked: 'is any of us entitled, as a Christian, to exalt his own moral conscience so high that he cares little or nothing about the effect his self-righteousness may have on others?' It was a question that had an especially pertinent ring to it in other areas of British church life.

II

The Moral Watchdogs

The area of life in which Christians are most likely to be accused of exalting their moral conscience and of imposing their self-righteousness upon others is not, of course, protest about South Africa or any other political issue, but morality. Not since the mid-Victorian period have questions of morality and particularly sexual morality so dominated the thinking of church people. But the differences of a hundred years are legion. The traditional Christian ethic is now on the defensive; its apologists can no longer hope to control public debate as their forbears did with a few allusive phrases like 'nice girls don't' or the blanket condemnation of 'unnatural practices'. In the modern argument, Christians are expected to define their terms closely and explicitly and are constantly challenged to know at first hand what they are talking about.

However distasteful the learning process may be, the new breed of Christian moral watchdogs have been prepared to do this—to the credit of their courage though not always of their discretion. Research on his report into pornography took the Roman Catholic peer, Lord Longford, into the porn shops and strip clubs of Soho in London and almost ensnared him in the participatory acts of Copenhagen's red light district; Mrs Mary Whitehouse, although she saw only half of the French film *Blow Out* ('La Grande Bouffe'), later went into a court of law to protest explicitly about scenes of masturbation and anal intercourse. For their troubles, Lord Longford was voted by one newspaper the most caricatured figure of 1971 and Mrs Whitehouse had a porn magazine named after her.

In the circumstances, it is hardly surprising that the morality campainers have descended into the morality arena, determined to offer no quarter. They see little room for accommodation with their humanist adversaries. The appeasement doctrine of the 'new moralists' of the sixties, like Bishop Robinson and the authors of *Soundings*, who believed that a coming together was possible between the youthful counter-culture and the moral authority of the churches, has been rejected totally. The notable feature of the moral campaigners is their abrasiveness, which has its counterpart perhaps in the abrasiveness of British politics in the seventies (the Conservatives under Mrs Thatcher have made common cause on a number of issues with the moralists under Mrs Whitehouse). But this abrasiveness is not confined to the campaigns against pornography and indecency on TV and film. Evidence of it can be seen in the other related issues which will be considered in this chapter—sex education, contraception, abortion, divorce law reform and homosexuality.

Their abrasiveness apart, other common features of these morality campaigns have been the lay initiative that brought most of them into being, the prominent role that is played in them by women and the fact that they are, after their fashion, ecumenical. One group which has been active in the campaign against abortion-on-demand has been the so-called Order of Christian Unity, which describes itself as 'Christians of all denominations, united by belief in Jesus as God and Saviour and together upholding his Commandments, particularly in family life, education and medical ethics'. (Its driving force is the Roman Catholic Marchioness of Lothian.) 'Upholding the Commandments' and reasserting the authority of the Church and the Bible over personal and social morality is a central theme of all of these morality campaigns. They have inevitably come into conflict with the intellectual leadership of the churches, who in their view have sold the pass on authority and the basic certainties of the Christian faith. In her autobiography, *Who Does She Think She Is?*, Mrs Whitehouse tells of coming into the school where she taught at the height of the 'Honest to God' debate and hearing the reaction of her fourth form girls to a television discussion between a psychologist, a bishop's wife, a headmistress and a clergyman who 'although none of them dare say it outright . . . seemed in favour of sex before marriage if certain conditions were fulfilled'.

Thus, alongside the abrasive attitude towards secular adversaries, there often goes an impatience with less resolute Christians amounting almost to hostility. There is an attitude of 'those who are not for us are against us', which has caused consternation and division in all the churches. The proponents of a more liberal ethic who were so evident in the sixties have tended to run for cover before the moral onslaught of the new puritans. Others, who see the Church's role in the social field as being more concerned with pastoral care than proclamation of moral standards have been greatly perplexed by the reactionary movement. It was for them that the writer on mysticism, Monica Furlong, spoke in 1974 in a series of articles in the *Church Times* covering much the same ground as this chapter. In the first article she confessed that with most of the moral issues of current concern—abortion, divorce, homosexuality and so on—she had not got them worked out to anything like her own satisfaction. 'Of course, I know that even to wonder and puzzle about them causes offence in certain quarters—the quarters where there is a "Christian answer" to every question. But what worries me about "Christian answers" is that they nearly always seem to be "tough" (not to say brutal) answers, giving blanket commands to people to do what often turns out to be the impossible; and my experience of life does not lead me to think that this is the way of love.' Mrs Furlong went on to 'stick her neck out' and to doubt whether there were in fact 'Christian answers' to anything at all: 'All that is available to us is a "human answer", one that exists in the same way for those who are not practising Christians as for those who are; and it is an answer (if I have understood Christ at all) which tries to set prejudgements on one side and see what is the most loving solution for the greatest number of people.'

Monica Furlong had ventured into a minefield where in recent years few of the churchs' professional moral guides have trod with any confidence. What made the path particularly perilous was the rapidity and extent of social change in Britain since the mid-fifties. It is unnecessary to expand here on the profound changes in the attitudes to sex, marriage and related issues, which have taken place, particularly among the young, in the past two decades. But one feature of this change that is worth comment is the accumulation of legislation since the late fifties, much of which had the intention of withdrawing legal scrutiny and legal sanctions from large areas of public behaviour. Much of this new legislation had the prior approval of specialist groups within the churches who drew a distinction between the Church's pastoral ministry to the sinner and the code of conduct for its members who must be taught to avoid sin. This distinction was made by the evidence of the Church of England Moral Welfare Council to the Wolfenden Committee on Homosexual Offences and Prostitution in 1956 and ten years later the Archbishop of Canterbury's Commission on Divorce (*Putting Asunder*, 1966) drew a careful distinction between what the Church should require of its members and what it thought should be the law of the land in the twentieth century. These two reports—along with similar statements from other Protestant churches

—went a considerable way towards helping Parliament to decide in favour of changes in the law.

But what the report writers did not foresee was the degree to which permissive legislation would itself change social attitudes, both outside and inside the churches. Nor did they appreciate the scope that permissive legislation would offer to commercial exploitation. Shows like *Hair* and *O Calcutta!* might perhaps have been expected as a consequence of the Lord Chancellor's withdrawal from censorship over the theatre. But few observers in the sixties could have foreseen that the Obscene Publications Act, 1959, would eventually lead to the display of sex manuals and girlie magazines in almost every corner newsagent's shop in Britain or that the Abortion Act, 1967, would within a few years turn London into 'the abortion capital of Europe'. In the eyes of the new puritans, the permissive trend of legislation in Britain had set not just new limits to moral behaviour but new norms of behaviour. Their campaigns for closer adherence to Christian values therefore embodied a double concern about authority: on the one hand, they were trying to bring the nation back to the authority of the Bible and the Church as the only sure ground for moral behaviour and, on the other, they were at war with those social authorities that had abdicated from their responsibility to maintain moral standards. This applied not only to Church leaders and theologians but also to the BBC for bringing indecent television programmes into people's homes, to school teachers for encouraging a hedonist (or even 'Marxist') attitude towards sex, to the police for not enforcing the existing laws with rigour and to Parliament for sanctioning permissive laws in a negligent manner. During the campaign for the October 1974 election, the Marchioness of Lothian, whose organisation had sought the views of all election candidates on certain moral issues, pointed out that the two major Acts of the 1960s, 'the abortion so-called reform' and the 'divorce so-called reform' had received the active support of 262 and 183 Members of Parliament respectively out of a total of 630.

The first that most British newspaper readers and television viewers knew about the Christian counter-attack against the permissive society was the huge Festival of Light rally in Trafalgar Square in 1971. As we saw in an earlier chapter, the impression was given by the Festival's organisers that this was a spontaneous uprising of outraged youth against the 'moral pollution' of the age, whereas the truth lay in the confession of its secretary to *The Times* that the rally crowds consisted almost entirely of invited coach parties from evangelical church groups. We have listed some of the achievements of the Festival of Light in terms of spiritual uplift elsewhere in this book; but in terms of its crusade against 'moral pollution' it appears to have achieved very little. After 1971, the big names—Muggeridge, Longford, and so on—drifted away and the Nationwide Festival of Light (as it then was) became just another evangelical pressure group, sending out guest speakers to preach to the converted from an address in South Woodford, East London.

Mary Whitehouse's successive campaigns against sexual licence on the large and the small screens have proved to be a much more resilient phenomenon. They began with similar *éclat* to the Festival of Light at a series of mass meetings in Birmingham and the West Midlands and with a petition of half a million signatures, protesting at the low moral standards of certain television programmes. From these events the 'Clean Up TV Campaign' was born in 1964, receiving the support among other bodies of the Catholic Teachers' Federation. Three years later, Mrs Whitehouse (herself an Anglican with strong past associations with Moral Rearmament) put her campaign on a more permanent footing with the establishment of the National Viewers and Listeners' Association; she became its honorary general secretary (the president was the retired Chief Constable of Lincolnshire) and by 1975 Mrs Whitehouse said that there were 31,000 individual members. The NVALA was conceived as a watchdog upon the standards of all the broadcasting media but it soon concentrated its attention upon the peak-hour viewing of BBC TV. Mrs Whitehouse's love-hate relationship with the BBC is well known: she has frequently castigated it for failing in its duty as a public service to uphold the Reithian standards that she had known in her girlhood, but she has also at times defended the Corporation, for example from the Labour Party's criticisms of bias during the 1974 elections. Over the years, she has developed a quite sophisticated regard for her adversary. 'We are faced with a great divide,' she wrote in 1974, 'the gap between those who produce and those who receive programmes. That the gap is polluted by a great deal of misunderstanding, resentment and even bitterness, cannot be doubted, certainly in Britain. It is ironic that this is not unconnected with the very expertise which makes British television the envy of the world.' ('Controlling the Explosive Influence' *The Spectator*.) The BBC and the IBA for their part have refrained from entering into any special relationship with Mrs Whitehouse and the NVALA, which they regard as just one viewers' pressure group among many. And on the main demand of the NVALA, for a Broad-casting Council which would exercise the same lay oversight of tele-vision and radio that the Press Council does for newspapers, there has been a marked lack of enthusiasm from the broadcasting authorities and the Government.

So what are the achievements of Mrs Whitehouse? In terms of 'improving' the standards of television, they are hard to verify. There has certainly been a change in the style and content of BBC television programmes since the daring and satirical sixties, but whether because of pressure from the NVALA and similar groups or because of internal programme judgements within the Corporation it is difficult to say. However, Mrs Whitehouse has certainly gained a following within the churches. The Church of England's report, *Broadcasting, Society and the Church*, (1975) which demanded that the broadcasting authorities should pay attention to Christian moral principles which are 'of universal and eternal validity', owed much to pressure groups like the NVALA (although one Anglican bishop described it as 'inaccurate, biased, and in the long run likely to lose us confidence with the broadcasting authorities'.). Mrs Whitehouse has also become a public figure in her own right, contributing frequent articles to newspapers and the weeklies (latterly more on sex education and the dangers of free contraception than on broadcasting). She has had her own advice column in the magazine *TV Life* and she has become a frequent guest speaker to bodies outside the churches. Although spurned by officialdom and by many of the churches' intellectual leaders, she has undoubtedly gained herself the ear of a not inconsider-able section of the population, particularly the middle-aged. With them, she was on the same wave-length when she declared to the Royal Society of Health in 1974 that over the years the unthinkable had been made thinkable by the media—the thinkable had become see-able and the see-able had then become do-able—and it was a short step from the do-able to the done and from the done to the done-thing.

The Earl of Longford (Knight of the Garter, prison reformer and former Socialist Minister) is the most engaging of the crusaders against pornography in the seventies and he chose a particularly engaging way of fighting his crusade. The Longford Commission, which was modelled upon a government Royal Commission—though with all its fifty-three members chosen by the Earl himself—was a novel device for attempting a broadly-based study of the problem as the prelude to

changes in the law. It was perhaps too broadly based. After its formation in May 1971, there were defections from the ranks of the Commission, particularly as a few members began to realise that Lord
Longford already had very firm ideas about the corrupting effects of
pornography and a well-formed taste for publicity. The trip to
Copenhagen in August of the same year showed the Earl's taste for
publicity at its most dangerous. He had given advance notice to the
British press of his intention to visit two sex clubs in the Danish
capital and, on arriving at the second club (as he described in his
autobiographical volume, *The Grain of Wheat*) he found 'newspapers,
cameras and television were much in evidence'. But Lord Longford
had not reckoned on the degree of audience participation. He and his
party were in ringside seats when 'a tall, rangy, dynamic female, completely nude' descended into the audience. 'I was becoming aware that
no action which did not involve me visibly would satisfy. Now the lady
was on my neighbour's lap, caressing him indescribably, amidst
mounting response from the audience. The cameras were all too
obviously getting ready for her next move. But my next move was still
more obvious to me. At one moment, as seen through the eyes of one
of the many newspapers that depicted the scene, I was sitting there like
a stage professor in a house of ill-fame. The next my seat was empty.'
According to Lord Longford, the Copenhagen episode achieved three
things: publicity for his campaign, the closing a year later of all but a
handful of the Danish clubs and a chance for him to vindicate himself.
'Up till then I was never far from the innuendo that I was actually
enjoying the pornography I affected to detest. Once and for all, I felt
that I had nailed that falsehood in every honest mind.'

Unfortunately, the Copenhagen episode remained better imprinted
upon the public mind than did the recommendations of the Longford
Commission which were published in paperback form in September
1972. These were that there should be a new legal definition of
obscenity—replacing the definition of an article which is liable to
corrupt or deprave (which had become difficult to prove, because
policemen are by and large incorruptible) with something of which the
'effect, taken as a whole, is to outrage contemporary standards of
decency or humanity accepted by the public at large'. The Longford
Report also recommended stiffer penalties, the prohibition of indecent
displays and the bringing of sex education material within the scope of
the obscenity laws. Sex education, said the Commission, was primarily
a matter for parents. The Longford Report, which was signed by only

forty-two of the original fifty-three members (including Dr Coggan, then Archbishop of York, the Roman Catholic Bishop Butler and the Methodist Lord Soper), was not however universally acclaimed by the secular press. *The Times* described it as 'lacking in thoroughness, coherence and detachment' and thought it 'good campaigning stuff but not an adequate preliminary to legislation'. In fact, four years later, none of the recommendations of the Commission have become law; there has been a Private Member's Bill which sought to ban indecent displays in shops, cinemas and so on, but this Bill died with the February 1974 general election.

The Longford Report was a splendid, though flawed, attempt to curb pornography and indecency by linking them to the outrage of the public at large. It did not achieve its main objective and more success in the Christian crusades against pornography was won by individuals who took their objections to the courts rather than to public opinion. The campaign in the courts had its set-backs—Mrs Whitehouse lost her *Blow Out* case as did a Hertfordshire Roman Catholic supporter of the Festival of Light who tried physically to stop the screening of *Last Tango in Paris*—but eventually it achieved more effective action by the Metropolitan Police against porn shops and a change in the Greater London Council's policy of licensing films. The legal campaigns go on.

The anti-pornography crusaders are worth the space that has been devoted to them in this chapter, if only because for a decade they have dominated the thinking of certain quarters of the churches and inevitably coloured the view that the world takes of the Church. It is natural that pornography should excite this attention among churchgoers, for the existence and even more the experience of pornography is shocking to most Christians. Hardly any church people would wish to excuse the phenomenon and most would condemn it as a symptom of a sick society. But is it worse than that? Does it in fact corrupt its viewers and lead to any more harmful social behaviour than masturbation (which admittedly many Christians, including the Vatican, condemn as against God's laws)? Here the evidence is inconclusive and conflicting. The evidence of an American congressional committee which concluded that pornography was socially harmful, was rejected by the President's health and social advisers. Even the evidence about the effects of television upon people's behaviour is quite inconclusive. What we are left with for sure is the shock and outrage of certain Christians and others when faced with the fact of pornography, and perhaps their own personal fears of the phenomenon. The Director of the Festival of Light, Mr O. R. Johnston, advised readers of the *Church of England Newspaper* that, when preparing for a prosecution of a film or magazine, it was necessary for a small group actually to have seen it: 'this viewing should be done by two or three mature Christians *together*, with much prayer before, during and after what is certain to be for them—particularly for any Christian women involved—a very unpleasant experience.' To many Christians, however, this approach would appear ludicrous and they would agree with Monica Furlong's attitude that the best way of dealing with pornography is to laugh at it and to regard it as a not unhelpful sign that, as a society and individuals, we have failed to make normal life real and satisfying.

By the mid-seventies, the campaign against pornography and sexual licence on TV and film was slackening and its supporters were turning more to other causes, particularly to the question of sex education in schools. The Longford Commission was concerned with this issue, as have been Mrs Whitehouse and the Festival of Light, and it has given rise to its own pressure groups, including the so-called Responsible Society and the Social Morality Council. The watchdogs were awakened to what appeared to them to be moral subversion in the nation's classrooms by a series of unrelated events from *The Little Red School Book* in 1971 to Dr Martin Cole's sex education film, *Growing Up*, and the activities of *Grapevine*—a group of young people, sponsored by the Family Planning Association who disseminated sex and contraceptive information in informal surroundings. But by 1974, the attention of the moralists had become focused on the activities of the FPA itself which, according to Mrs Whitehouse, were 'increasingly causing alarm'. In a *Spectator* article, she wrote: 'The Family Planning Association, which is increasingly taking over sex education in our schools, has a very negative (contraceptive) approach to the subject and appears very reluctant to give any reasoned support to the idea of chastity before marriage or to develop a positive scheme centred round the whole development of children towards manhood and womanhood. It sees sex education as a means of solving social problems rather than one in which the individual can be encouraged to develop to full capacity, mentally, morally and spiritually.'

These charges (which were strongly contested by the Assistant Director (Education) of the FPA) raise a number of important issues for Christians. Unlike pornography, sex education—and particularly the question of how much and when to teach children about contraception—is a matter of immediate concern to all Christian parents. Ideally, most of them would probably wish their children to learn all that needs to be learned within the family environment and to have no need of contraceptive precautions before marriage. But the parent who believes that this is sufficient preparation for the average teenager in Britain today is out of touch with reality. This is no longer a morally ideal world and because of that, I would hazard a guess that many Christians support the idea of sex education being given to their children in the schools, by mature speakers like the visiting lecturers of the FPA. The latter's case is that unless there is adequate sex education in schools then there is little hope of reducing the number of illegitimate births, abortions and shotgun teenage marriages. It has to be admitted that, with contraception now available on the National Health Service in Britain, there is a danger of family planning aids being distributed across the counter, without sufficient attention being paid to counselling on the wider implications of their use. But counselling in personal relationships is one of the main aims of the FPA's education programme and it is surely reasonable to expect Christians to join the FPA in this and not to oppose it.

That would be a reasonable course, were it not for the fact that the dangers of 'a negative (contraceptive) approach' to sex is not the whole story. There are a number of hidden innuendos in the puritan case against 'sex education', one of which shows the political standpoint of many of its critics. As Mrs Whitehouse wrote in her *Spectator* article: 'the sex educators and the sexual left use sex education as a channel of propaganda. They see the family as repressive and as the base of Christianity and capitalism, and work for the destruction of all three.' A similar point, though without the political overtones, was made in a Responsible Society publication *Sex Education, its Uses and Abuses* by a Roman Catholic probation officer, K.H.Kavanagh, who accused most local education authorities of trying to 'manipulate' the behaviour and values of children through sex education and of offering them plentiful advice about contraception while virtually ignoring marriage. The fears for the survival of marriage as a Christian and social institution, of course, go very deep: they have been reinforced by the incorporation of the doctrine of marriage breakdown in the 1969 Divorce Act and by the growing trend towards cohabitation instead of formal marriage among young people. But another hidden innuendo of the campaign against sex education is the total disapproval of all forms of contraception, inside and outside marriage, by a substantial body of Christians, particularly Roman Catholics. The increasingly strident official Catholic statements on the subject which have appeared since the papal encyclical, *Humanae Vitae*, have been utilised by non-Catholics in their campaigns. There is an ecumenical twist to it also. The Community and Race Relations Unit of the British Council of Churches has felt obliged to review its grants to family planning groups like *Grapevine* in black areas, because of the disapproval of such groups by Roman Catholics who are not in fact members of the BCC.

The Roman Catholic involvement in the campaign against sex education is a by-product of that Church's own dilemma over contraception. Unlike their counterparts in the United States, British Catholics have not played a prominent role in trying to limit the state's provision of family planning services: during the passage through Parliament of the National Health Service (Family Planning) Act, 1967 which first made it possible for local authorities to set up family planning clinics, not a single Catholic or other MP voted against the Bill. This silence, which contrasts with the strident tones of recent debate, may in part be explained by the well-known reluctance of Catholics to become involved in controversy about national affairs. But 1967 was the year before *Humanae Vitae* and there was an air of nervous anticipation abroad. Few Catholics perhaps dared to hope that the Vatican would relax its contraceptive ban completely and follow the 1958 Anglican Lambeth Conference and other non-Catholic Western churches in affirming that 'the responsibility for deciding the number and frequency of children has been laid by God upon the consciences of parents', but many did hope for some modification to the ban, perhaps to include the Pill in the same category as the 'safe period' as acceptable forms of family planning. Instead, there came *Humanae Vitae* and the traumas that that entailed for individual Catholics and even more for many of their pastors. The crisis that this caused for the authority of the Church in Britain has been noted elsewhere in this book. The controversy of course rages on, constantly fuelled by utterances from one side or the other (like the publication in 1975 of an uncensored English version of *The Population Problem*, sponsored by the Conference of International Catholic Organisations but very much disapproved of by the Vatican). And in Britain there has been no decisive episcopal move to end the controversy, either in the direction of leaving the decision on contraception to the informed consciences of married couples (as the West German bishops did in May 1975), or in adopting a hard-line interpretation of *Humanae Vitae* (as the Irish bishops did also in May 1975, when they stated that 'the contraceptive mentality is characterised by a lack of generosity of spirit and of readiness to assume responsibility'). Contraception remains a source of deep division for British Catholics and one on which they tend to line up with like-minded non-Catholics on one side or the other. The campaign against sex education has given the papal loyalists on birth control something of the ecumenical support which they have lacked up to now.

The support of non-Catholics has also been important in the anti-abortion campaign which followed the passing of the 1967 Abortion Act. The parallels with contraception are ironic for as the obstetrician, Sir John Stallworthy, and many others have pointed out, the best answer to abortion is an effective system of birth control. This is amply demonstrated in the experience of Italy where, under pressure from the Roman Catholic Church, contraceptive advice is banned and where illegal abortion has become the common alternative. The World Health Organisation has estimated that there have been a million and a half abortions a year in Italy, although some observers have put the figures considerably higher—a state of affairs that led to a politically dangerous referendum on the subject which was only headed off by Italy's 1976 election. In Britain, however, the legalisation of abortion in 1967 passed off quietly with few overt protests from the churches, even from the Roman Catholics. Catholics remained quiet because, as the late Cardinal Heenan said, they did not wish to be accused of imposing their view that abortion is in all circumstances wrong upon society at large. But the other churches in Britain had to some extent prepared the ground for changes in the law. The 1965 report *Abortion : an Ethical Discussion* by the Church of England's Board for Social Responsibility (the successor to the Moral Welfare Council) led the way for change by allowing that in certain circumstances, like risk to the life or health of the mother, the risk of a deformed child or conception after rape, abortion could be morally justifiable. But at the same time, as Dr Ramsey told the Convocation of Canterbury in 1967, the general inviolability of the foetus had to be protected: 'We shall be right to continue to see as one of Christianity's great gifts to the world the belief that the human foetus is to be reverenced as the embryo of a life capable of coming to reflect the glory of God whatever trials it may be going to face.' A similar attitude was taken by the Church of Scotland's Social and Moral Welfare Board in 1966 and by the Methodist Church's Department of Christian Citizenship in the same year. In general, the larger non-Roman Catholic churches agreed upon the limited need for legalised abortion to safeguard the life or physical and mental health of the mother and the sponsor of the 1967 Act, the Liberal MP David Steel (the son of a prominent Church of Scotland minister) took these views seriously into account. But in the run-up to the Bill, there remained some important differences between the churches and the Bill's parliamentary backers over the so-called 'social clause', which extended legal abortion to consideration of the 'patient's total environment actual or reasonably foreseeable'. It was this clause which prevented the British Council of Churches from giving the Bill anything more than its grudging support and caused it to demand that there should be a review of the Act after five years. The Roman Catholic Church, for reasons already mentioned, remained outside the debate: its ethical position was and still is quite clear, that since the first century A D the Church has regarded abortion as not only a sin but as homicide. But there were other Christian voices raised against the new Act, notably from the Salvation Army, the Free Church of Scotland, the Assemblies of God and the Protestant Anti-abortion Group—consisting largely of Pentecostalists in the Midlands.

After the passing of the Act, however, the form of the debate changed dramatically. The main reason for this was the quite unexpected number of abortions which took place in the years following 1967 as the Act came to be interpreted in a more permissive way. In 1968, there were 37,000 abortions, but by 1973 there were 160,000, of which just under a third were performed upon women from abroad in private clinics. This form of 'abortion-on-demand' had become possible because of a late change to the wording of the Act while it was passing through the House of Lords: the wording of the 'social clause' had originally said that abortion should be legal if the risk to the health of the mother was 'grave', but the Upper House had substituted the clause that abortion should be legal, *inter alia*, if to continue the pregnancy involved a risk to the woman's health, physical or mental, greater than if the pregnancy were terminated. It seemed to offer some surgeons *carte blanche* for abortion on demand. There was also great concern in the years following 1967 at the activities of a few abortion-only clinics, at taxi drivers who touted for business among foreign girls at airports and at the alleged racketeering that had sprung up around legalised abortion.

Another new element in the debate was the formation of an effective inter-denominational group, resolutely opposed to the 1967 Act. This was the Society for the Protection of the Unborn Child (SPUC), founded in 1967 by a group of non-Catholics, among whom a prominent member was the journalist Phyllis Court (Mrs Phyllis Bowman) who was later received into the Roman Catholic Church. The Catholic Church itself gave SPUC considerable backing from 1970 onwards. On the other side of the debate, there has also been a significant change. The Abortion Law Reform Association and similar groups, which before 1967 had campaigned for legalisation on humanitarian grounds, were progressively taken over by feminist groups who demanded abortion without any restriction for all women as a right. Increasingly, as the seventies progressed, the debate became less concerned with the realisation of the original purposes of the 1967 Act than with confrontation of the rival ideologies of these two sides. As an embryologist observed, in a letter to *The Times*, opinion had become 'polarised and absolutist: the feminist on her platform claims unquestionable rights over her own body, while the theologian in his library equates deliberate destruction of the fertilised egg with murder. These two views pre-empt further discussion and only obfuscate the problems of abortion decision-making.'

But the decision-making had to go on, as the promised five-year review of the Act became due. This was carried out by a committee headed by Mrs Justice Lane, which recommended ministerial action to stop the well-known abuses of the 1967 Act but concluded that by and large it had produced a relief of human suffering, had stamped out illegal abortion and fulfilled the original intentions of Parliament. Action was taken by the Department of Health and Social Security against the racketeering clinics and all referral agencies were required to be licensed by the Department. In addition, the enactment of legislation similar to the British Act (and in some cases more liberal) by Britain's neighbours—France, Holland, Denmark, Sweden, Austria, Norway and Finland—and also by the United States, reduced the number of foreign women coming to Britain in search of abortion. The one outstanding and major cause for concern among moderate observers of legal abortion was the discrimination that was taking place within the National Health Service against doctors and nurses who refused to take part in the termination of pregnancies on conscientious grounds. But there was also moderate concern that in certain parts of the country, like Liverpool and Glasgow, where Roman Catholics formed a substantial proportion of Health Service staff, it was proving difficult for women in need to obtain abortions except through private clinics.

These considerations figured prominently in the propaganda of the pro- and anti-abortion lobbies, but they were in effect incidental to the major struggle for substantial changes in the law in one direction or the other. In 1974 and again in 1975, both sides staged massive rallies in London in order to influence Parliament, which had before it a Private Member's Bill, sponsored by a Glasgow MP, James White, seeking to restrict legal abortion and to put the onus of proof of need for the operation upon the doctor rather than the objector. The rallies and demonstrations produced the inevitable claims and counter-claims about numbers. A SPUC rally in Hyde Park in October 1975, which was supported by the Nationwide Festival of Light and the Order of Christian Unity, claimed attendances of 80,000. There was also evidence of smear tactics. According to a report in the *Catholic Herald*, a pro-abortion rally in June 1975 was described by a SPUC observer as being 'a solid phalanx of red banners, Communist Youth, International Socialists, Anarchists' Association, the Gay Liberation Front and Sappho, a lesbian group'. There did seem to be many diverse groups climbing aboard the bandwagon, but whether they justified the *Catholic Herald*'s headline 'A Day Out for the Reds' is open to question. The smear from the other side was that SPUC was really a 'front' for the Vatican's intervention in British politics, which was equally unjustified in view of the strong lay and non-Catholic initiative which had brought the Society into being. SPUC counter-claimed that it represented 'the silent majority' against abortion on demand and certainly its restrained behaviour in public contrasted strongly with the activities of similar 'Life' groups in the United States (during the early primaries in the 1976 Presidential contest, one Democratic candidate, Senator Birch Bayh, complained that his meetings were being broken up by hysterical demonstrators, dressed in hospital gowns smeared with red paint). There were other injudicious excesses. Cardinal Heenan's domino theory, that contraception leads to demographic suicide and that abortion leads to euthanasia, was one. Another was the publication of the book, *Babies for Burning*, by two Roman Catholic researchers, Michael Litchfield and Susan Kentish, in which they repeated their allegations, first made in the *News of the World*, that aborted foetuses were being used for medical research and in one case boiled down to make soap. The book had a profound influence on the parliamentary Select Committee, set up to consider Mr White's Bill, but was strongly contested by many parts of the medical profession and not just the pro-abortion sections of it.

The emotionally-charged, disputatious attitude to the abortion debate has dominated popular discussion of the subject in Britain, and particularly discussion in the secular and religious press. In defence of this way of airing the subject, it can be argued that the contending lobbies have succeeded in drawing attention to the major social implications of the 1967 Act which were not adequately explored before it became law. The SPUC in particular can claim to have exposed abuses of the Act which might otherwise have remained hidden and it has consistently argued that indifference on the part of Christians has played into the hands of the exploiters of legalised pregnancy termination. But when all that has been said, there remain very serious grounds for concern about the way in which the lobbies and the churches have handled the debate. Most Christians regard abortion as shocking and as contrary to the will of God, but behind these feelings of common distaste there are theological and social differences which cannot be glossed over. The Roman Catholic Church believes that the fertilised egg is already human life which God has visited with a soul and that abortion in all cases is therefore tantamount to murder; the Protestant churches do not share this belief and, although they regard the foetus as something to be protected and reverenced, few non-Catholics believe that it is fully human until it is viable outside the womb. But even if all church people were to agree that abortion is homicide, there would still remain the occasion when the Christian doctor or parent would have to decide between the life of the foetus and the life of the mother. For Roman Catholics, who accept the teaching of their church, there is no dilemma; for most other Christians the dilemma is very real and it was this which led many non-Catholics to give qualified support to the 1967 Act. But there is a further problem of conscience over homicide itself for Christians do not regard killing as always wrong. Indeed the Roman Catholic Church has been more reluctant than most churches to condemn capital punishment and war as wrong in every case. Commenting on this aspect of the debate, a Catholic mother wrote to *The Times* to complain about the difficulty of dissenting from the teaching of her church on abortion: 'Men understand war; so they have no difficulty in accepting that to kill in a just war is not to deny the "right to life". Women (mothers especially) understand birth; so they have no difficulty in accepting that to kill the foetus for good and generous reason is not to deny the "right to life". I myself cannot accept that capital punishment and killing in war are sometimes acceptable, but abortion never.'

The possibility of honest diversity in the Christian attitude to abortion has been one casualty of the partisan approach to the debate by lobbies like the Society for the Protection of the Unborn Child. Again, as with other morality campaigns, it has become a matter of those who are not for us are against us; indeed, with abortion the accusation has often been that doubt is near to being an accessory before the fact of murder. This absolutist element in the abortion debate has put a considerable strain on the unity of Christians. In the summer of 1975, the Church of England's Board for Social Responsibility withheld publication from a joint Anglican-Methodist report because it was not critical enough of the 1967 Abortion Act. The decision suggested that there might be an unexpected gulf between the two churches on important ethical questions and that the Church of England might be paying more attention to academic moral theology and to its ecumenical relations with Rome than to the social conscience of the individual. In the event, the Church's General Synod entered upon a debate about Mr James White's Abortion (Amendment) Bill with no adequate study document before its members and in a highly emotional debate, it gave support to a motion calling for radical changes in the 1967 Act. The keynote of the debate was the challenge of the Bishop of Leicester, Dr R. R. Williams, who asked 'are we to allow the Roman Catholic Church alone to uphold the sanctity of life?' Put in those terms, the abortion issue has appeared to many Christians to be a form of moral blackmail.

Another major casualty of the abortion debate has been the policy of sensitive cooperation between theologians, doctors, lawyers and social workers in trying to build an acceptable ethic for the moral difficulties of our day. The policy has a venerable history and has been particularly evident in the reports of the Church of England, Church of Scotland and Methodist Church since the fifties on a wide range of issues from homosexuality and contraception to the care of the dying and of the incurably malformed. In these discussions, the theologians have tried to leave behind the image of themselves as censorious moralists and, instead, to encourage the treatment of patients as 'whole persons in their social context'. That phrase is from a paper given to the Royal Society of Medicine in 1975 by Dr J.S.Habgood, the Bishop of Durham, on social attitudes towards Venereal Disease. 'Morality, as well as medicine, is about wholeness. Moral insight begins as we consider individual actions in relation to a whole life and in the broadest possible context. Religious morality widens and changes the context by the perception of a spiritual dimension.' It is this approach to religious-medical ethics which has been damaged by the confrontation tactics to the abortion issue. To label all doctors who perform abortions as murderers is a total negation of the Christian concern for the 'whole person'.

The two remaining moral issues to be dealt with in this chapter can be treated more briefly, for they have both progressed beyond the stage of gaining legal sanction and social acceptance and have become, for the churches, largely a matter of internal discipline among their members. But even this generalisation needs qualification, for neither change is universal throughout Britain. The concept of marriage breakdown, incorporated in the 1969 Divorce Act, is still not law in Scotland, and homosexual acts between consenting adults over 21 in private are still illegal in Northern Ireland. Over most of Britain, however, neither the experience of a broken marriage nor involvement in an active homosexual relationship is particularly uncommon nor cause for overt discrimination. But not so within the churches.

Divorce has long been a problem for the churches. In Anglican Canon Law, it simply does not exist for marriage is there described as 'indissoluble, save by death'. And upholding this ideal of marriage as a life-long commitment in a society which has progressively debased the institution by easier divorce laws and other ways has become, for some Christians, one of the few worthwhile tasks before the Church. For other Christians, however, the Church's ministry to the divorced person, as someone in need of forgiveness and a new start, is as important if not more important than the ideal. And moreover, the changes in social attitudes towards marriage have been reflected in Church thinking about the purposes of marriage and the fulfilment which ought to be expected within it. The focus of this conflict between standards and change is the Church of England, which as the Established Church is the place in which most religious marriage services are solemnised. In 1936, Archbishop Lang's famous broadcast about the intention of the King to marry a divorced woman had the majority backing of Anglican and national opinion; but, when in 1976,

Buckingham Palace announced that Princess Margaret and her husband, Lord Snowdon, were to separate, Archbishop Coggan was careful to stay out of the limelight, though of course the question of royal remarriage was not mooted. The conflict in the Church's behaviour can be seen in a hundred less public ways. In 1973, the Mothers' Union —for long the bastion of the ideal of marriage for life—agreed to admit divorced persons to membership, but in 1976 the Bishop of Worcester demanded and got the resignation of a parish priest who had announced his intention to marry his divorced housekeeper. Indeed, the Church of England's inquiry bureau has said that questions relating to remarriage in church represent the biggest single subject on which its advice is sought.

In 1973, this confused state of affairs came to a head with the publication of a report *Marriage, Divorce and the Church*, which recommended that under certain conditions the Church of England should permit its parish clergy to remarry divorced persons in church, and not as at present simply bless their civil ceremonies. The report led to a fierce controversy, in which it was claimed a majority of church members favoured the change but were opposed by a majority of the bishops. The proposed change came before the General Synod in November 1973, when it was lost by a single vote, and again in November 1974 when a move to pass it to the diocesan synods for consideration was also defeated. Since then, the Church of England has set up another commission on the subject. In the meantime, divorced Anglicans have had to content themselves with either a service of blessing following a civil remarriage, with finding a priest who is willing to break Canon Law or with a second marriage in the Methodist Church, which has relaxed its rule on remarriage (the Methodist Church marries some 1,200 divorcees a year of whom about half are Anglicans).

One reason given by conservative Anglicans for resisting the change in its marriage discipline is that it would complicate relations with the Roman Catholic Church. But a curious thing has been happening to the marriage discipline of Rome since the Second Vatican Council. The Roman Catholic Church does not, of course, recognise divorce but it does grant annulments through its marriage courts, which have been described as being thought of in the popular imagination 'as slow, expensive, narrow-minded and ever so slightly corrupt'. In September 1975, however, the canon lawyers of Great Britain and Ireland decided to break their habitual silence and show, not only that these criticisms were largely unfounded, but that the grounds for Catholic annulments had been considerably changed in the past ten years, particularly in the area of 'due discretion'. Some twenty cases a month are now dealt with by the matrimonial court of Westminster, which caters also for the British Armed Forces and for the dioceses of Plymouth, Northampton and Brentwood. The basis on which the canon lawyers work is that all marriages are valid until proved otherwise, but that the discovery of a flaw in the marriage from the beginning, perhaps even a psychological flaw, is *prima facie* grounds for an annulment. In some ways, the change has made a nonsense of the Church's stand against divorce. In the Republic of Ireland, where under pressure from the Church there is no divorce, Church annulments are increasing rapidly year by year; but the 'remarriages' in Roman Catholic churches which result from these annulments are regarded by the state as bigamous, whereas second marriages by civil ceremonies following a divorce in the English courts are recognised. In order to remain within the laws of his Church and his state, the Irish Catholic therefore requires both a Catholic annulment and an English divorce. Meanwhile, in 1976, the Anglican Church of Ireland agreed to a proposal that divorcees may be remarried in church, which seemed the simplest solution.

The position about homosexuals within the British churches is far less complex but many times more explosive. As we saw at the beginning of this chapter, the churches played their part during the fifties in preparing the way for the recommendations of the Wolfendon Committee on homosexual practices and the subsequent changes in the law. A major contribution here was that of Dr Derrick Sherwin Bailey, secretary of the Church of England's Moral Welfare Council, who in his book *Homosexuality in the Western Christian Tradition* (1955) showed that traditional Church and state attitudes towards homosexuals were savage, inconsistent (in that they penalised male homosexuals far more than either lesbians or the most heinous heterosexual transgressors) and also theologically erroneous. The historical destruction of Sodom and Gomorrah, in fact, had nothing to do with the homosexual practices for which God is reported to have devastated the Cities of the Plain. The theologians of the fifties called for compassion, understanding and justice for the homosexual and even for recognition that there can be love within a physical homosexual relationship, but they stopped short at giving their blessing to these relationships as in any way comparable to married, heterosexual love. This is the frontier on which the contentious moral battle of the seventies is being fought. With the emergence of all sorts of homo-sexual rights groups, notably the activist and often outrageous Gay Liberation Front, there have also appeared a number of Gay Christian groups calling for similar recognition and acceptance. There is Reach, an interdenominational gay group led by a Church of England priest from Essex and another priest of the same diocese, the Vicar of Thaxted, was in 1976 elected president of the Gay Christian Move-ment; Quest is a group of Roman Catholic homosexuals; the Open Church Group, originated with Methodists, Inter-group with gay Unitarians, The Friends' Homosexual Fellowship with Quakers and so on. Their common aim, as the coordinator of the Open Church Group, who is a Methodist local preacher, put it, is that 'not wanting mere pity or tolerance for gay people, we seek full and open acceptance for homosexual Christians within their own churches'. Or as a member of Quest put it: 'Homosexual Catholics are not asking the Church to give them *carte blanche* to indulge themselves in undisciplined sexual relations, nor for any special treatment whatever. They desire merely to be accepted for what they are, what the Lord made them, with the sexuality which he gave them.' In 1974, the Church of England's Board for Social Responsibility set up a working party to study the changing attitudes of society towards homosexuality and it promises to be one of the most contentious documents the Church has received since the fifties. As a spokesman for the Board admitted, 'the subject of this study is one which is deeply divisive and which is likely to create tension both within the Church and outside it.'

That may be putting it mildly, for as yet the mustering forces in the British churches have not reached open confrontation. If the ex-perience of Christians in other countries is anything to go by then there is a very fierce storm brewing. In Italy, the Vatican's condemna-tion of homosexual relations as a 'serious depravity' and 'intrinsically disordered' led to a storm of personal abuse against the Pope by gay (though not necessarily Christian) groups. In the United States, the United Presbyterian Church deferred the request for ordination of professed homosexuals on the grounds that it could find no guidance in the Presbyterian Book of Order, or Book of Confessions, but it was clear that if the request was granted many older Presbyterians were prepared to secede. And opposition to churches' acceptance of homo-sexual relationships as 'normal' is not confined to the expected moral watchdogs, like Mrs Whitehouse and the Festival of Light; it comes also from many of the non-practising homosexual Christians, who for years have sublimated their sexual proclivities within the traditional Christian ethic and remained celibate. Is their sacrifice of a lifetime now to be pronounced futile by gay groups or a theologians' report? Perhaps it was with these people in mind that the anonymous writer of the preface to *Crockford's Clerical Directory* wrote in 1977: 'In this as in other matters a special standard can reasonably be expected of the clergy, who are so often entrusted with the care of the young and with counselling about marriage; and although church history shows how much can be contributed by priests "who are not the marrying sort" we are also convinced by church history that the only alternatives can, and ought to be, either faithful marriage or faithful chastity.'

In her *Church Times* articles, Monica Furlong pronounced homo-sexuality to be the 'acid test' of whether Christians believe in the goodness of sex as such. 'What seems strikingly obvious about all this is not how sad it is (most homosexuals are no sadder than anyone else) but how absurd it all is. *How* absurd that thousands of people are somehow "not acceptable", sexually speaking, when all they want to do is something as relatively harmless as sex.' But if all Christians in Britain believed that, there would not have been the decade of confrontation, bitterness and resentment that we have tried to chart in this chapter.

12

Politics and Conscience

Few Christians would dispute the importance of the moral issues discussed in the last chapter. Many, however, would question the pre-occupation with them to the virtual exclusion of other social concerns which is evident in some church circles and they would also feel some concern about the way that the handling of these issues has coloured what Dr Coggan called the churches' 'entry into the socio-political arena'. A common criticism of the morality campaigners is that they give a partial and over-simplified view of the churches' role in national affairs: many causes of distress within society arise not from the decline or confusion of moral standards (to which arguably there are 'Christian answers') but in morally 'grey' areas, like housing, employ-ment, crime and punishment or social and political justice. Here the direct application of 'God's Commandments' or of principles derived from the natural law of creation is far from being an adequate guide. The issues are too complex, too modern, too sociological; Christian insights here need to be interpreted in the light of what is possible and practicable, in other words of politics. The churches' entry into this particular arena has not been helped by the absolutism of the moralists who, despite their own frequent links with conservative politics, tend to argue that the 'Church ought to keep out of politics'. So there emerges a clear division of opinion between those who see the Church's role primarily as the moral guide and conscience of the nation and those who see the necessity for it to become politically involved in order to achieve Christian objectives. With few exceptions (Dr Coggan for one and perhaps Lord Longford) there is little overlap between the two camps. There being no good theological reason for this, one is left with the explanation that it is a question of social genes such as W. S. Gilbert described in *Iolanthe*:

> Nature always does contrive
> That every boy and every gal
> That's born into this world alive

Is either a little Liberal
Or else a little Conservative.

The distinction between moralists and politicos is an important one in the study of the evolution of Church activity in the seventies but it is already being consigned to the theologian's study by the increasing politicisation of events in Britain. The fashionable talk of the churches entering the political arena ignores the fact that they are already deeply implicated in political affairs and political controversy. In the seventies, this has been notably true in three areas—education, Northern Ireland and race—where, of course, the churches' involvement predates by many generations the current political controversy surrounding these issues. The three are linked in other ways. The debate in Britain about the desirability of denominational schools is an even more contentious matter in Northern Ireland; and the churches' support, albeit only of a humanitarian nature, for 'freedom-fighting' guerrilla groups in southern Africa is bitterly resented by the close observers of guerrilla violence in Northern Ireland. In 1976, the General Assembly of the Presbyterian Church in Ireland narrowly defeated a motion to disaffiliate from the World Council of Churches because of the latter's 'Programme to Combat Racism'.

At a deeper level, however, all three of these issues—education, Northern Ireland and race—have raised in an uncomfortably immediate way the classic Christian dilemma between equality and élitism, between selection or election and universality. Despite its aristocratic and often rigidly hierarchical character, and the unquestioning support which the Church has given to many undemocratic and repressive regimes, there has always been within Christianity a disconcertingly egalitarian strain. A famous statement of it is in St Paul's Letter to the Galatians where he writes of the love of God, in which 'there is neither Jew nor Greek, neither slave nor free, neither male nor female.' If all men are equal in God's love and the redemption of Jesus is for all, then should not the churches be preaching and practising equality in their social attitudes—for example in their education policy, as between the clever and the dull children of both rich and poor parents, or in Northern Ireland as between Protestants and Catholics or everywhere as between the races? The 'ideology' of the Gospels is unambiguous and, for the younger generation of Christian radicals, very persuasive. In practice, however, the churches have always found good reason for behaving very differently. All men may indeed be equal in God's love, but it is obvious that not all men are created equal in their talents or in the place within society where God has 'set' them. And there are other considerations. The fact that most private education in Britain is run by the churches themselves or with considerable support from their ordained ministers is justified in many ways, ranging from support for the freedom of parents to choose to pay for their children's education to the argument that, in an increasingly secular society, religion may survive only within the private educational sector. And if private education produces an élite, then it is surely better that it should be a Christian rather than a non-Christian élite. The ministry of the Church of England is still heavily dependent upon the products of the English public (private) schools. Not dissimilar arguments have been used in Northern Ireland and Africa to justify other forms of religiously legitimised discrimination. But more and more this sort of reasoning has been condemned within the churches and their record over equality has become the occasion for self-criticism and the racking of consciences.

> The Christian community, engaged and involved with a sinful world at every turn, has only too frequently throughout its history failed to express this equality in her own life. Sometimes, it has even contrived to be an opponent of rather than a witness to this equality. That is undeniable. What is no less undeniable is that, whenever it returns to its origins in the New Testament, it is called again to have that mind 'which was in Christ Jesus' and it cannot have that mind without discovering and expressing among its members the equality which is in Christ. (David Edwards in *Equality and Excellence* by Daniel Jenkins.)

The first problem that arises from the study of the churches and education is not so much their support for unjustifiable privilege within the educational system, so much as the charge that the Christian religion is accorded a privileged place in the system which is no longer justifiable in terms of the churches' support among the adult population. As far as Church opinion is concerned this is a recent problem. Education in Britain began with the Church and was largely in the control of the Church—or later the churches—until the end of the nineteenth century. Even the dissolution of the monasteries and the Reformation only transferred secondary and higher education in Britain from one group of churchmen (the monks and brothers) to another (the Oxford and Cambridge educated clergy of the Church of

England and, in Scotland, the dominies appointed by the Kirk or burghs). With education thus integrated into institutional religion, its practitioners saw little reason to distinguish between the imparting of information in subjects like mathematics, history, the Bible and so on, and the inculcation of spiritual and moral values. But as the state took a larger share in the running of the nation's schools, the distinction between religious and secular education became increasingly apparent and controversial. It was already controversial before 1944, when Mr R. A. Butler's Education Act gave a guaranteed place to religion within the state system, by providing for a daily act of Christian worship and an 'agreed syllabus' of religious instruction to be worked out by consultation between the local education authority, the teachers and the churches. This was a unique development with no parallel in the state schools of comparable countries, like the United States or France. It was acceptable in Britain mainly because of the widespread assumptions (strong in the post-war years) that (*a*) Britain was basically still a Christian country and (*b*) moral and religious education were inseparable.

The questioning of both of these assumptions in the 1970s and the demand for changes in the provision for religious education in state schools have come as something of a shock to many churchpeople. Is this yet another assault by the secularisers upon the Christian standards of Britain, such as has been seen in the moral field? But the answer has to be no, for the debate about religious education is neither sudden nor wholly secularist in origin. Demands for change in the 1944 provision of RE have come not only from the British Humanists' Association and other predictable bodies, but also from the Religious Education Council (on which the churches are represented) and from working parties of the British Council of Churches and the Free Church Federal Council. There have been a number of factors at work.

In the first place, it has become undeniable that Christianity in the 1970s does not have anything like the support that it enjoyed in Britain in the 1940s. Not only does it have fewer adherents, but there is also more questioning of its basic theological and moral teaching, even by its professional leaders like bishops. Secondly, Christianity no longer enjoys the position of being the one unchallenged spiritual culture which motivates the inhabitants of Britain—immigration and the hippy movement have introduced a greater interest in non-Christian world religions and in the world at large there has been a resurgence of Marxist and other secular ideologies which have also had an appeal within Britain. Thirdly, it has become obvious that compulsory religion in state schools has become the Cinderella of the curriculum, a subject in which few pupils take exams, in which all too few teachers have either strong personal convictions and/or educational ability, in other words the perfect occasion for a generalised 'liberal studies' discussion lesson far removed from the spirit of the 1944 Act.

But fourthly, and perhaps least understood by lay Christians, there have been changes in educational practice and aims so that these are no longer in tune with the old ideas of religious education. In 1945, the Surrey Agreed Syllabus could state quite confidently that, through RE, children 'may gain knowledge of the common Christian faith held by their fathers for nearly 2,000 years; may seek for themselves in Christianity principles which give a purpose to life and a guide to all its problems; and may find inspiration, power and courage to work for their own welfare, for that of their fellow creatures and for the growth of God's kingdom.' Even in 1954, the Sunderland Agreed Syllabus was able to say that the school 'ought to do its positive best to guide children into church membership'. But by the seventies, not only the guidance towards church membership but also reference to religion as 'the guide to all life's problems' had gone. The lofty moral justification had given way to the need for RE to justify itself on the same 'open ground' as other subjects on the school curriculum; it had to show its 'own inherent educational value' in the words of a Durham County report of 1970, which had considered the traditional justifications of RE based on the Christian cultural tradition and on moral principle and found them lacking in force. RE could no longer be seen as a way of handing down unquestionable adult values, for that was now seen as a form of 'indoctrination'. It had to be both intellectually honest and also in tune with the daily experience and personal development of children. Like other subjects taught in schools, RE had to be related more and more to children's needs, but even more than mathematics, spelling or cookery, for the majority of children, particularly in urban areas, would have had no family or personal contact with 'the Christian faith held by their fathers for nearly 2000 years'. Moreover, increasing attention has been given in recent years to moral education in its own right, removed from its traditional base in religion. Thus, at a time when the aims and the resources of education as a whole are under scrutiny, the unique place of religion is being even more closely scrutinised. It has figured in all the major education reports in Britain—Crowther, Newsom and Plowden—all of which showed themselves sensitively aware of the need to make religion educationally acceptable in a pluralistic society without at the same time destroying or impeding the development of what Crowther identified as 'a faith to live by'. The same problem has occupied many of the best professional men and women in the churches and, although it may be desirable that more of the laity should be actively aware of the educational problems of religion in schools, it is fortunate that the debate has not become the ecclesiastical football that many of the moral issues of the seventies have become. Undoubtedly, there will be changes in RE, probably along the lines of the report of the Free Church Federal Council—with school worship less frequent but better prepared and RE lessons 'reluctantly' retained although with broader horizons. Many churchpeople will dislike this intensely, but the obvious lesson is the one drawn by the Free Churches that the transmission of the Christian faith belongs not to the schools but to the churches.

The RE debate mainly concerns state-schools, for private and church-owned schools in Britain have their own methods of teaching and practising religion. But they are far from unaffected by the RE debate within the state sector. On the one hand, it has been seen as a warning to the private sector. At the Headmasters' Conference in 1975, its chairman, Fr Patrick Barry, OSB, the Head of Ampleforth, warned that any new Education Act would be unlikely to treat Christianity as 'anything more than a minority interest' and that the future of Christian education would inevitably rest with the independent schools and a number of 'voluntary aided' schools and eventually perhaps only with the independent schools. Something of what Fr Barry had in mind was evident in the Catholic response to the government's withdrawal of financial support from the direct grant schools (which, although private grammar schools, received the fees for the majority of their pupils from the local education authorities). In 1975, there were fifty-four Roman Catholic direct grant schools, most of them in the north-west of England, and the choice before them was to become fully independent and fee-paying or to become 'aided' comprehensives within the state system. The Catholic Education Council and the bishops strongly recommended the latter course (which almost all the schools in the end took) and argued that this was really a change in the schools' financial status rather than fundamental educational principle. But for many Catholic parents it was not that simple. Their social objections to comprehensives apart, they could see that the change would bring the schools one step closer to the state system in which RE was so seriously under threat. If in no other way, the change would be from grammar schools, usually run by religious orders, to much larger establishments under lay control, where the majority of the teachers would probably be non-Catholics. Indeed, it was already a cause of serious concern that the 'voluntary aided' schools were losing their religious ethos. Religion was being left more and more to the specialist teacher or the visiting priest and the schools were no longer fulfilling their original aim of being a bridge between the family community and the church. In addition to these problems, RE in Catholic schools faced similar educational difficulties to those faced by RE in the state sector.

The 'voluntary aided' schools were in fact another innovation of the 1944 Act. Part of the controversy which has always surrounded them is that they are restricted mainly to two denominations. While most of the churches for a variety of reasons have maintained their own private and boarding schools (including the Methodists, Friends and even Christian Science), the 'voluntary aided' schools are almost exclusively the property of the Church of England and the Roman Catholic Church.

The principle of giving state aid to church schools was established in 1902, when it created a political storm from the Nonconformist Liberals—Lloyd George said it was 'more loot for the bishops' and others described it as 'Rome on the rates'. The 1944 Act built on this principle by incorporating the church schools within the state system, making available to them a guaranteed share of public funds for their building and expansion (50 per cent in 1944, 85 per cent now) and paying the salaries of their staff; but the majority of the school governors or managers are appointed by the church, the head teacher is usually a member of that church and the church retains control over religion in the school. In the 1930s, this type of school accounted for almost half of the schools in England and Wales; in 1975 they accounted for less than 18 per cent. The decline was almost wholly due to the shrinking number of Anglican village schools, which because of changes of population and economic viability had been amalgamated or gone into the state system as 'maintained' schools. Although there are voices within the Church of England calling for an end to this decline and also for firmer policies regarding the Church's colleges of education, the declining trend seems inevitable. But the number of Roman Catholic 'aided' schools, often in crowded urban areas, has gone on increasing since the war. At the present there is no sign of population changes forcing any change in this trend, as there has been for example in the United States.

The current problems of the Roman Catholic 'aided' schools (of which there are some 2,640 in England and Wales as against a slightly smaller number of Church of England 'aided' schools) focus upon three issues—money, their value in transmitting the faith to a new Catholic generation, and the degree to which they fulfil the aim of a place in a Catholic school for every Catholic child. As we have seen, there are acute and continuing financial problems regarding the debt burden of the schools policy upon individual Catholic congregations and the Church at large, and there have also been serious doubts expressed by Catholic researchers about the efficacy of this policy in preventing the disaffection of senior pupils from the ministrations of the Church. It is worth noting, however, that in the United States where there have been similar problems about teenage 'leakage', Andrew Greeley, the guru of American Catholic education, has pointed out that the disaffection is greater among young Catholics attending secular schools than those in church schools. Recently, in Britain, however, there has been equal concern that the schools policy should have run into these serious difficulties at a time when it has only half fulfilled its broader aims, when only 62 per cent of Roman Catholic children are in Catholic schools. In the circumstances, should the Roman Catholic dioceses press ahead regardless with their current policy, when many of them have no realistic hope of catering for the education of even half their children without considerable financial help from outside the diocese? Or should the bishops consider drastic change in a policy which, in some respects, has only succeeded in duplicating the state's education and in practice measures its success not in terms of attendance at Mass but of university places and GCE passes? One writer on Catholic schools took as his text a question asked by a visiting church educationalist: 'Apart from the crucifix on almost every wall, in what way does this place differ from a maintained one?' These are questions which concern Catholics in Britain deeply; the fact that they are not given such a thorough or public airing as some other social issues can be explained by the unswerving commitment to the present policy by the bishops and by the heroic sacrifices of so many congregations.

The Catholic Church is thus locked into its own educational policy with little prospect of early release and even research into the policy's failings becomes impossible. In September 1976, the National Conference of Priests put forward to the bishops a carefully-costed programme of research to discover (*a*) the reasons why children from Catholic schools leave the Church (£34,700), (*b*) the obstacles that exist to closer cooperation between the local Church, the parents and the teachers (£12,500) and (*c*) the problems faced by Catholic children in non-Catholic schools (£12,500). The bishops, although not totally unreceptive to the idea, turned it down as too expensive.

Criticism of the official educational policy of the Roman Catholic Church in Britain has, therefore, to be diplomatic in the extreme if it is to gain a hearing. It was in this manner and with the explicit denial of wishing to be in any way 'iconoclastic' that Fr David Konstant, director of the Westminster Religious Education Centre, put forward what amounted to a revolutionary plan for change in Catholic education. His starting point was that, indeed, Catholic education must be for all but to make it revolve around the child, instead of the person (adult and child) had perverted the policy and led to all the familiar problems. Education is the continuing need of all Christians, said Father Konstant, religious and priestly as well as lay, and particularly for certain groups like the family and the teachers. This was best carried out in small groups and by the use of all the educational facilities available including state facilities like adult education institutes. Father Konstant then tentatively outlined a new strategy, which included a 'holding operation' on all new school building, coupled with a five–ten year plan to pay off the Church's school debts, and then devotion of new resources to a much broader type of education. 'The strategy proposed involves using all available resources . . . developing better facilities for on-going adult education for a variety of groups; and breaking away from the school as the beginning and all too often the end of our education programme.' (*The Tablet*, 31 January 1976.) It was a blueprint for the kind of education that could well have appealed to Free Churchmen in its emphasis upon the education of the adult Christian, as in the Methodist 'class' system.

Coincidentally with Father Konstant's new strategy, which at least provoked wide comment even though its chances of being acted upon look slim, there appeared a much more open attack upon the Catholic schools system. The aim of 'All Children Together', founded in 1975 by a group of young and mainly professional Catholics and Protestants in Northern Ireland, was to break down the sectarian divisions of the province by tackling them at the place where they are being created.

The group's aim was an integrated school system. Although this inevitably meant changes in the teaching and strongly Protestant ethos of Northern Ireland's state schools, the first target of the group was inevitably the Catholic schools, most of them 'voluntary aided'. As one of the group's leaders, Anthony Spencer of Queen's University, Belfast had written: 'the church-controlled schools ensure that the culture transmitted from one generation to the next not only protects the power of the Church over its own members but also the very strong group solidarity and its concomitant ethnocentricity and xenophobia.' (*The Month*, January 1973.) 'All Children Together' has claimed that the majority of parents in the province, Catholic and Protestant, give general support to the idea of integrated schools, but they have expected and received stiff opposition from the Roman Catholic hierarchy. Members of the group who have withdrawn their children from Church schools and sent them to state establishments have been accused of being anti-Catholic and have been ostracised by their parish priests. In 1977, the women's peace movement took up the fight against segregated schooling and offered to provide minibuses to enable children to travel across Belfast to take part in extracurricular activities, like sport, with children of the opposite religion.

How far religious indoctrination and indeed religion itself have contributed to the troubles of Northern Ireland is a question that has lain heavily upon the consciences of church leaders throughout the British Isles. When the Northern Irish in 1968–69 first thrust themselves violently upon the attention of an unknowing world and an uncaring Britain, they did so under the unqualified sectarian labels of 'Catholic' and 'Protestant'. The reaction of British Christians was one of shock and profound dismay. Could it really be Christianity in any shape or form that lay behind this violence and hatred? As one English Catholic wrote later: 'When such crimes as individual murder have to be identified by reference to the religious profession of the transgressor and the victim, the credibility of the Gospel itself seems to be challenged.' The secular press in Britain went further and accused the people of Northern Ireland of religious extremism, of bigotry, sectarianism, and of rekindling the religious violence of the seventeenth century under the folk banners of King Billy and the Pope (the fact that the Pope of the day probably gave diplomatic support to William III against the Catholic King James was beside the point!). The vehemence and wildness of some of the accusations brought an understandable response from church leaders in Northern Ireland. However justified the charges of past religious intolerance may have been, the present troubles were not religious in origin, but political, economic and social. The 'Protestant' and 'Catholic' labels did not tell the whole truth. In the case of the extremists and the gunmen, they were positively inaccurate, since these people seldom set foot inside a church. In any case, had not Cardinal Conway excommunicated all members of the Provisional IRA? It was only a short step from this line of argument to maintaining that Northern Ireland's troubles were not religious in character at all, and this became the conventional wisdom of many church leaders on both sides of the Irish Sea in the early seventies. (In much the same manner some internationally-minded Christians later maintained that religion had nothing to do with the 'Christian' and 'Muslim' conflict in the Lebanon.)

This religious disclaimer, which was seldom heard from church people most closely involved in the search for peace in Northern Ireland, has subsequently come in for devastating analysis. 'Our attempts to exonerate ourselves as churches are very suspect,' wrote a Presbyterian Church in Ireland minister, 'in view of our long and intricate involvement in the formation of the bent of people's minds in Ireland. Have we not played a part in encouraging, exalting, and extending the kind of tribal, sectarian, self-righteousness which forms a culture in which violence easily multiplies?' (John Morrow, *The Captivity of the Irish Churches*.) Others drew attention to the cultural and linguistic inheritance from religion shown by the extremists on both sides. The Rev Steven Mackie, a Church of Scotland university chaplain, who wrote about Northern Ireland for the British Council of Churches, concluded that there were clear Old Testament and Exodus overtones in the Protestant celebrations of the Twelfth of July, making it a sort of Ulster Passover, and also Messianic overtones in the Catholic celebration of the Eastern Rising of 1916. A former Catholic chaplain in Northern Ireland drew the author's attention to the parallels between IRA language and Catholic preaching about 'climbing the hill to Calvary' and 'being bathed in the blood', while Loyalists tended to think of their campaign in the Old Testament terms of 'going out to slay the Canaanites'. More fundamentally, Anthony Spencer in his widely-discussed article in *The Month*, saw a major cause of the violence in the alliance between the Catholic Church and Irish nationalism—'Catholicism is the key to Irish nationalism, as the clergy never tired of insisting'—and in the alliance between the Protestant churches and Loyalism. 'In Ireland both ethnic communities have used religion to define national identity, to sanctify political institutions, and to legitimate the hatred, discrimination and injustice which each community shows towards the other. In both, religion and national identity became so firmly linked together that they have never been prised apart.' In Spencer's view, the churches had become prisoners of the political divisions that they had sanctified. Catholic bishops, under pressure from Rome, might condemn the violence but their condemnations were too little and too late. Irish Catholicism had in the process been emptied of its specifically Christian ethic of universal love.

It was strong stuff and, of course, resented but it was a view with which many English Catholics felt an instinctive sympathy: the Irish origins of English Catholicism were a cause for deep gratitude but on its native soil Irish Catholicism had become perverted. On the other side, it was less easy to accuse the Protestant churches of legitimising the violence, since they were fragmented among different denominations and had clearly never had the power over their people that the Catholic bishops had. What English Protestants did find particularly unpalatable was the direct involvement in sectarian politics of clergy like the Rev Ian Paisley, of the 'Free Presbyterian Church' and the Rev Martin Smyth, a Presbyterian Church in Ireland minister who was Grand Master of the Orange Order. This was a point taken up by Professor Ronald Hanson (himself a former Church of Ireland bishop) in one of his regular columns in *The Times*. In a later column, Professor Hanson wrote about what he saw as the basic flaw in Irish Christianity: 'the reason why the different versions of Christianity in Northern Ireland are today the helpless captives of political ideology is because critical religion, reflecting religion, religion appealing to the intellect and not only to the emotions, has been almost unknown there.' Other Christians and many non-Christian observers concluded that Northern Ireland's problem was that it had too much religion of any sort. What it needed was a thorough secularisation of its politics and social life—the census returns quoted in an earlier chapter indicate that many Irish agree with this.

Many of these criticisms were well-founded and acknowledged as such by Northern Ireland church leaders. But men and women in the front line of a quasi-civil war do not relish having their guilt thrown up in their faces by uninvolved spectators, however well-meaning. In any case, it did not need the latter-day analysis of English and Scottish churchmen to make the Northern Ireland Christians aware of their guilt. In 1966, the General Assembly of the Presbyterian Church had publicly sought forgiveness 'for any attitudes and actions towards our Roman Catholic fellow-countrymen which have been unworthy of our calling as followers of Jesus Christ'. This was the era of Captain Terence O'Neill's policy of détente, when the first contacts were opened between Belfast and Dublin and also between the churches, taking up the spirit of Vatican II. It was the time when the Corrymeela Community was founded in County Antrim to promote and pray for reconciliation between the two religious communities. In their way, these pioneering contacts paved the way for the civil rights movement of 1968 which had such a tragic aftermath. But the onset of the violence and the drawing of the sectarian battle lines did not bring a halt to the inter-church contacts, in fact quite the reverse. In the dark days of the communal rioting of 1969–70, representatives of all the churches forged stronger bonds of cooperation as they tried to calm the fears and tensions of people living along the 'peace lines'. The evacuation and rehousing of intimidated families and the rescue of children from the environment of violence became a particular area of what in Britain would be called 'ecumenical' activity. When a visiting archbishop chided Cardinal Conway on the lack of formal ecumenical relations in Northern Ireland, His Eminence asked the English prelate how often he met his Protestant counterparts—'about twice a year'—'Well, I meet mine about twice a week,' said Conway. Formal meetings between the various churches were initiated in September 1973 at the Irish Church Leaders Conference in Dundalk; then and again in the following three years, the leaders set about identifying the major causes of division and friction between them and there was a great deal of discussion about the Catholic rules on mixed marriages (but significantly, out of respect perhaps to the joint chairman, Cardinal Conway, there was little discussion of segregated education). This sort of 'full and frank exchange of views' was new and uneasy territory. Where the church leaders found their new cooperation easier was in the Irish Churches Joint Peace Campaign in December 1974 when over a million posters and stickers proclaiming 'Think—Pray—Talk Peace' were distributed. The Campaign was a masterpiece of ecumenical planning and for a while had a profound impact on the life of the province (the women's peace movement of 1976 was a continuation of the process). One well-publicised event during the campaign was the meeting between prominent Protestant clergy and leading members of the Provisional IRA at Feakle, which led to the IRA's fifteen day Christmas truce. If only the church leaders could have taken their people with them (and all of their clergy), then there would now be peace in Northern Ireland.

Contrary to the beliefs of some British critics, however, it is not possible for Irish church leaders to decree peace from the pulpit. The intimate and perhaps culpable alliance between religion and politics suffered a number of sudden and rude shocks in the events of the late sixties. In 1969, the Roman Catholic Bishop of Down and Connor, Dr Philbin (who is nobody's idea of a post-Vatican II progressive) was jeered by the Catholics of Ballymurphy when he asked them to remove barricades thrown across the streets. In the working class 'ghetto' areas of Northern Ireland, particularly in Belfast, a new spirit of populist solidarity has arisen, which holds little brief for the traditional authority of the churches. Other professional groups—teachers, social workers and especially politicians—have experienced the same alienation towards them. One consequence of the troubles, therefore, has been the emergence of ghetto leaders with little time for the historical paternalism of the churches and with respect for religion only when it comes to them on their terms. Some clergy have been prepared to do this—notably Desmond Wilson formerly in Ballymurphy and Brian Smeaton, a Church of Ireland priest in the Protestant Shankhill Road area—but only at the price of cutting themselves adrift from the institutional churches (both Wilson and Smeaton received financial backing from a London-based group called 'Community Projects', one of whose leaders was an American Jesuit priest). One result of the communal troubles of Northern Ireland was to open up a gulf between the churches and an important section of their laity which had not been known in Northern Ireland before, even in the grim days of early industrialisation.

Most of these events went little noticed in Britain. Only the stigma of 'religious conflict' remained as a lasting impression among Christians on the other side of the water. To the people of Northern Ireland, it seemed that criticisms from this quarter were often founded upon a fundamental lack of understanding and sympathy. This was not, admittedly, the whole story. Many British Church leaders went over to Belfast to judge for themselves the religious element in the conflict and they often kept in touch with people they had met there. Corrymeela, the Irish School of Ecumenics based in Dublin, and many of the projects for mutual help like British holidays for children from Northern Ireland, all found considerable support among Christian groups in England, Scotland and Wales. There was also a modest but inspired scheme for Scottish ministers to exchange parishes with their Northern Ireland Presbyterian cousins and some of the Kirk ministers confessed that they found a deeper sense of living religion in violent Belfast than they did in tranquil Scotland. But all too often, Northern Irish Christians were given the impression that theirs was a foreign problem, having little to do with the even tenor of British church life. This attitude was at best unfeeling, but it was often hypocritical. The British churches certainly bore some of the responsibility for the injustices of Northern Ireland and yet they had taken little interest in the province and put no pressure on the British government before the onset of violence. And were there not instances of intolerance and discrimination in Britain too? Remarking on the title of Steven Mackie's book for the British Council of Churches, one Northern Ireland Presbyterian said: 'it shouldn't have been called *Ireland's Conflict Diminishes Me*, but *Ireland's Conflict Mirrors My Own*.'

The parallels with the attitudes of the British churches over the race issue are instructive. Here too there is evidence of ignorance, apathy and even hypocrisy; there is evidence again of a determination to keep the problem at a safe distance from British church life. On the face of it, however, the British churches have a good record over race. The British missionary tradition was on the whole an enlightened one that is still valued in the former mission fields; Christian Aid, raising some £5 million a year for Third World development and relief, is Britain's fastest growing charity; and all the major churches have expressed their solidarity with the causes of racial justice and equality. But, until recently, race was seen by most churchpeople in Britain as an overseas problem and one that caught their imaginations (if at all) only after Britain had liquidated her direct colonial responsibilities over non-white peoples or, in the case of Rhodesia, been effectively dispossessed of them. One can see this in the roll-call of the British churches' heroes in the racial conflict—Trevor Huddleston, Martin Luther King, Dean ffrench-Beytaugh, Cosmas Desmond, Colin Winter—mostly white men, all non-violent and all of them active outside Britain. The only two priests one can think of who have made a name in British race relations are Michael Hollings (whose candidature for the archbishopric of Westminster drew attention to his work among the Sikh community of Southall) and Wilfred Wood (who is probably better known to black non-Christians than to his fellow-Anglicans in South London).

Moreover, British church attitudes—again until recently—were founded upon a very real ignorance of the thinking of people who are racially oppressed. All the evidence collected by the British Council of Churches (in *Combatting Racism* by Kenneth Sansbury) shows that white congregations have little understanding of what is known by 'racism' and, taking their cue from the interest of the British press in southern Africa, tend to equate it with *apartheid*. The accusation made by Dr Philip Potter, the (black) general secretary of the World Council of Churches, that Britain is racist because of its immigration policies was greeted with incomprehension. Even within the restricted frame of southern Africa, there is little understanding among British Christians of why their African co-religionists should be turning more and more to non-liberal, and often revolutionary, solutions to their problems. The ignorance of churchpeople over this is, of course, in line with the ignorance of the population at large but, in view of their churches' official concern with racism, one can argue that this ought not to be the case. An Anglican diocesan secretary of education commenting on the WCC's controversial Programme to Combat Racism, said that nothing about the PCR had ever come to him in his official capacity: 'we are failing grievously to educate the laity and it is not therefore surprising that they too often react in accordance with their unexamined prejudices, when they hear about the PCR, for instance, and polarisation results. Communication through the press and other mass media is not education.' The attitudes of British churchpeople are still rooted in the missionary paternalism of twenty years ago, before the dawn of an independent Third World, and because of this many of them find it difficult to comprehend, even less to play a constructive part in, the race dialogue which figures so large in international politics today. This is pre-eminently true of the discussion about 'liberation' and liberation movements. As the Rev R. Elliott Kendall, Africa Secretary of the Council of British Missionary Societies, has put it: 'liberation movements have not got across to the British public. As an imperial power, defending its gains, we have an instinctive reaction against those who rise against white authority. There is deep colonial race prejudice in Britain, of very interesting historic origin. The common stand is not for liberation and equality of the black, but for humanitarian or mission help.'

These deeply-ingrained attitudes were rudely disturbed in the late sixties by a number of happenings inside and outside Britain, of which by far the most important was the extended debate over the so-called Programme to Combat Racism. The issue of racism (an unfamiliar and in some ways offensive word to most British Christians) became apparent at the Fourth Assembly of the World Council of Churches, held at Uppsala in Sweden in 1968. In the background to this momentous meeting, which showed a determination to meet racism with action and not just verbal condemnations, was the emerging struggle in southern Africa where white Rhodesians had seized their independence three years before and where guerrilla action against the Portuguese had turned into serious warfare. But there was also a new racial climate in the United States, where inner cities were burning, where Martin Luther King had been assassinated, the Selma march had been met with police violence and the black community was demanding huge guilt payments from the churches. These American experiences were brought to Uppsala in a forceful speech by James Baldwin, who described himself as 'one of God's creatures, whom the Christian Church most betrayed'. Bishop Sansbury, who was at Uppsala, says that this speech and the outpourings of guilt from other American delegates made a profound impression upon the Assembly, which then went on to make the following declaration:

Contemporary racism robs all human rights of their meaning, and is an imminent danger to world peace. The crucial nature of the present situation is emphasised by the official policies of certain governments, racial violence in many countries, and the racial component in the gap between rich and poor nations. Only immediate action directed to root causes can avoid widespread violence or war.

Racism, therefore, was not confined to southern Africa; it had root causes throughout the world and was economic as well as political. Moreover, the talk of imminent violence was all too evident in the tone of many of the speeches at Uppsala. This was carried over into two highly-charged meetings held in Britain in the following year. The first was an 'International Consultation on Racism' held at the ecumenical centre in Notting Hill, West London, which was alternately interrupted by black militants and by the National Front. The second was at Canterbury, where the WCC Central Committee met to set up the Programme to Combat Racism. British church leaders and activists were well represented at both of these meetings as they were on the WCC Executive Committee, which in 1970 made the notorious first grants from the PCR's Special Fund to African liberation groups. It is clear that many of these churchmen were swept along on a black tide of which they had little real knowledge: for them it was often a crash course in consciousness-raising about the humiliation of being black and the consequent guilt of being white. Many of them, according to Bishop Sansbury, felt that there were 'ominous portents that the racial turmoil of other countries could only too easily be repeated in Britain if matters were allowed to drift.' The impression made by these meetings upon ecumenical 'insiders' was profound. But the first that the mass of Christian people in Britain knew about all this was the revelation by the newspapers that the WCC Special Fund to Combat Racism was to give grants to groups committed to armed struggle and revolution in places like Rhodesia and Mozambique. Most of the newspapers sensationalised the news, though some of them also pointed out that the WCC had received assurances that the grants would be used for humanitarian and not military purposes. However, neither the British Council of Churches nor the individual denominations were given advance warning of the announcement from Geneva and, although the grants represented only a small part of the PCR Fund and an even smaller part of the World Council's Third World grants, the damage done was fundamental and long-lasting. As Kenneth Slack, director of Christian Aid, put it: 'I do not think that the programme has quite recovered from that among British churchpeople.'

Despite misgivings about the grants and the nature of the announcement, the British Council of Churches at its meetings in 1970 and 1971 urged member churches to support the PCR Special Fund. The gap between the 'responsible' ecumenically-minded leaders and the rest of the churches can be gauged from the response to those appeals. With the exception of the Methodist Church, which contributed substantially to the Special Fund through the Methodist Missionary Society, the other denominations officially gave almost nothing. It was in most cases left to individuals and congregations to support the Fund. Indeed, the Church of England, after a series of heated debates on the Fund within the General Synod, showed its disapproval of the PCR by voting in 1974 to cut £1,000 from the Anglican contribution to the forthcoming Nairobi Assembly of the World Council. However, a move to withhold the whole of the Church's contribution was defeated decisively and the £1,000 shortfall was later made up by a voluntary appeal, organised by the bishops of Warrington and Chelmsford.

From all this, it might be concluded that the British churches were —as their critics maintained—displaying their inherent racism and were under the sway of the sort of right-wing backlash shown by the *Daily Telegraph* (this newspaper constantly attacked what it called the policy of 'grants to guerrillas' and also managed to bring into this category Christian Aid and other church bodies with no connection whatsoever with the PCR). But this would be an unfair criticism. Many of those who opposed official church grants to the PCR did so on the grounds that while they opposed racism they were far from satisfied with the wisdom of the World Council's approach and doubted the political competence of the PCR's closest supporters. Others were put off by the truculent tone of PCR's supporters: 'nobody's support and sympathy were ever reinforced by kicking them in the teeth,' wrote Margaret Duggan in the *Church Times*, after attending a tempestuous discussion involving a PCR staff member. It was also widely recognised that some PCR activists and many recipients of its grants were Marxist-inspired, and this was true not only of the African liberation movements. There was particular concern at the $10,000 grant to an organisation in Britain known as Towards Racial Justice, in order to subsidise publication of the magazine *Race Today*. The tone of this 'clearly Marxist paper', as the Bishop of Bristol described it, can be judged by the complaints made by the Commissioner of the Metropolitan Police at publication of an article by a black schoolgirl calling for communal resistance to 'the pigs'.

But the greatest concern over the Programme to Combat Racism was directed at its links with violence. The grants to African guerrilla groups in Mozambique, Angola, Namibia, Rhodesia and South Africa might not in fact be 'grants to guerrillas', since they were earmarked for medical and educational programmes among the civilian populations away from the fighting, but they did, even in a tenuous way, link the British churches with revolutionary violence. And that at a time when revolutionary violence throughout the world appeared to be becoming an end in itself (viz Northern Ireland). Indeed, some Third World churchmen went much further than the official policy of the World Council and the PCR. In May 1974, Canon Burgess Carr, secretary general of the All Africa Conference of Churches, said that the liberation movements had helped the Church to learn that the Cross sanctified violence into an instrument of redemption. This, said the chairman of the Anglican Pacifist Fellowship, was turning 'the fundamental truth of the Christian Gospel completely back to front.' Many Christians in Britain felt the same about the cult of the 'theology of revolution', associated with the Colombian priest-guerrillero, Camilo Torres. And referring to a much closer instance of this worrying phenomenon, the Roman Catholic Bishop of Derry, Dr Edward Daley, told an ecumenical congregation in St Giles's Cathedral, Edinburgh, that perhaps Christians ought to stop arguing the theological pros and cons of 'just wars' and 'just rebellions' and go back to some form of pacifism.

Although the PCR, as an offshoot of the World Council of Churches did not concern Roman Catholics directly, that Church had its own worries about racism, liberation movements and tacit support for violence. Again, as with the Protestant churches, the official record was good: Pope Paul's two encyclicals *Pacem in Terris* and *Popularium Progressio* gave heart to Catholics all over the world who had identified themselves with the human rights and racial struggle, but they stopped far short of endorsing political violence. And this was the dilemma of a church which had given traditional support to established governments and the rule of law and order. For a church as heavily involved in focal areas of revolutionary ferment—Latin America, the Middle East, Africa and, of course, Ireland—Rome was acutely affected by the whole debate about liberation and violence. What attitude should the Church take and indeed was a single, universal attitude possible? From the response of different hierarchies, it seemed not. No doubt the bishops in Mozambique erred too much in one direction when they maintained a total silence during the world's outrage at the Portuguese Wiriyamu massacre. But how far should the Church go in the other direction, as far as Monsignor Hilarion Capucci, the Greek Catholic archbishop of Jerusalem, who was imprisoned by the Israelis on charges of smuggling arms to Palestinian liberation groups? The Fourth World Synod of Bishops in Rome heard from the Bishop of Mar del Plata in Argentina of the 'dramatic temptation' which violence represented to many Latin American Christians, and the Archbishop of Foraleza in Brazil, Mgr Lorsheider, said: 'there are nations in which the Church is being asked to involve itself in political controversies in a kind of revolution—often violent—which is sometimes presented as the only valid opportunity for evangelisation.' It was a familiar dilemma for Protestants embroiled in the controversy over the World Council's Programme to Combat Racism.

The PCR's grants to liberation movements continue to divide the churches in Britain, as in other European countries, but since the early seventies much of the heat has gone out of the issue. The PCR which had originally been a five-year programme was in 1974 put on a permanent footing with a budget of £150,000, much of it provided not by the divided churches but by the governments of Holland, Sweden and Norway. Inevitably, the PCR was debated at the Fifth World Council Assembly at Nairobi in 1975, when the case against the Christian sanctification of violence was forcefully put by the Bishop of Truro, Dr Graham Leonard. But Nairobi was notable for widening out the debate over racism and discrimination to take account on the one hand of the economic injustices of the world's North-South trade and, on the other, of the question of human rights in the Communist-ruled countries, an issue which had been severely neglected during the period when the WCC was preoccupied with 'white racism'. The British churches took up both of these themes: Dr Coggan and other church leaders have been consistently preaching the 'theology of enough'—that there is a level of living standards beyond which it is not decent or Christian for Western society to strive—and at the same time a working party of the British Council of Churches produced a report in depth on Christianity under Communism (*Discretion and Valour*). The more forthright policy of the British churches over investment in southern Africa was another result of the more reasoned consideration of racism at Nairobi and, in June 1976, taking up another point made in the renewal document of the PCR, there occurred the first British church demonstration against the sale of arms overseas—a subject which is increasingly exercising the churches.

But what of race relations in Britain itself? One of the aims of the PCR (as defined in its 1974 renewal document) was 'to involve more fully member churches and regional ecumenical organisations in programmes to eradicate racism particularly in their own areas'. This aspect of the programme had been somewhat ignored in the welter of argument and counter-argument about liberation groups. Critics of the British churches did not find this surprising and openly accused them of racism on their own doorstep, a point with which some British churchmen felt obliged to agree. 'PCR has confronted the British churches with the racial question in a form which compelled the disclosure of British racial prejudices,' wrote Canon D.M.Paton of Gloucester. What was certainly true was that during the period when the World Council's policies towards southern Africa received almost daily attention in church debates and letters to the *Daily Telegraph* and *The Times*, few churchpeople paid attention to the views or the problems of Britain's own racial minorities. Speaking in the Anglican General Synod in 1975, the Earl of March (secretary of the WCC Finance Committee) said: 'it seems extraordinary to me that over the last seven years, the General Synod and the Church Assembly never once debated Racism in England or Human Rights in the United Kingdom, both topics which were constantly at the centre of WCC debates and also of growing concern to the people of this country.'

The root cause of this state of affairs was that the major churches in Britain had lost touch with the immigrant and coloured population. This was partly a matter of geography. In many of the most 'churchy' parts of Britain—rural Herefordshire, the Scottish Highlands, mid-Wales and the prosperous outer suburbs of most cities in the United Kingdom—there are comparatively few immigrants and little evidence of racial tension. The statistics of religious activity show that where the churches are strong there are few immigrants and where immigrants and second- and third-generation black citizens are numerous the churches are correspondingly weak. An obvious reason for this is that many of the most recent immigrants have been Muslims, Hindus and Sikhs, for whom religion may be the most important thing in their lives but does not relate to the established Christian churches. Moreover, the older black communities, mainly from the heavily missionised West Indies, appear to have drifted away from British Christianity in considerable numbers. Pentecostalists apart, there are few thriving black congregations, even in London and Birmingham, to give the sort of importance to black Christianity that the churches of Harlem in New York or of Johannesburg provide. West Indians appear to have chosen social and communal centres as the focus of their cultural life in preference to the churches. There is also a feeling among the West Indian community that British religion is inhospitable and even strongly prejudiced against them. The experience of the Roman Catholic Church is relevant here. In 1975, the Commission on Racial Justice for England and Wales found clear evidence of what it called 'institutional race prejudice' in Catholic voluntary aided schools in four different areas: what was meant by this phrase was that the schools had disproportionately fewer black pupils than did the local county schools, even though there was no reason to suppose that the black Catholic population was smaller. The Commission attributed this not to any policies or behaviour of 'obvious prejudice' but to the fact that Catholic teachers and priests did not go out of their way to see that black Catholic parents were offered Catholic school places. 'Over and over,' said one member of the Commission, 'we heard "back in St Lucia (or Dominica), it wasn't like this; the priests knew us and there was no question of being left out or ignored".'

One thing that the Programme to Combat Racism might have done was to throw some sort of bridge across the chasm between the black communities in Britain and the churches. The involvement of white Christians in issues which were near to the heart of all blacks might have given the latter some faith in the caring ministry of British Christianity. This did in fact happen in the Methodist Church, whose early support for the Special Fund to Combat Racism gave it an entry into many black groups and a greater credibility in the eyes of black communal leaders. There was also respect for individual church leaders who took a sympathetic stand over the PCR, particularly for members of the British Council of Churches. But in general the black communities in Britain were disappointed, if not surprised, by the reaction of the British churches. 'Initially PCR raised high hopes,' wrote Abdul Minty, secretary of the Anti-Apartheid Movement, 'that WCC policy would wear off on to British churches and create a new atmosphere in a country which is so important both in respect to southern Africa and also to its own growing expressions of racism.' What did happen in fact was that the liberation groups issue dominated the British churches' debate about the PCR and once that had died down after the World Council Assembly in Nairobi, the mass of British people concluded that the racism issue had resolved itself. Those churchpeople who were closely involved with the black communities, particularly through the Community and Race Relations Unit of the British Council of Churches, knew otherwise.

Away from the headlines and the limelight of public debate, race relations in Britain were gradually deteriorating. The economic crisis of 1974–75 and the rising level of unemployment had a particularly serious effect on black school-leavers. There were periodic clashes with the police over the rising figures of black crime and all the while some British politicians were pressing for stricter curbs on immigration and for the repatriation of part of the immigrant population. It took the re-emergence of race into the secular newspaper headlines to show the churches how little they knew about the sensitivity of these issues. Spurred into comment by a spate of demonstrations by the National Front and also by certain inter-racial incidents and deaths, the Archbishop of Canterbury made a series of dramatic statements on the issue in 1976. He condemned all demonstrations by racists as a disgrace to Britain and likely to do 'incalculable harm' to community relations and family life, and he showed a sympathetic understanding of the generation gap which existed in many black families. That was fine and Dr Coggan was commended, among others by the *Methodist Recorder*, as a courageous and forthright churchman. But when a month later, in his diocesan newsletter, Dr Coggan attempted to set out guidelines for Christians to speak out more clearly on race relations, he was forced to take account of the less than enlightened attitude of most white Christians in Britain. He therefore reaffirmed his belief in Britain as a multi-racial society but at the same time called for a clearly defined limit on the number of immigrants allowed into the country. Criticisms from black communities and from white clergy active in the racial field poured down upon the archbishop's head. And their feelings of disappointment were hardly assuaged by Dr Coggan's later explanation to the General Synod that he thought it important 'that Christians should have, and should spread, a balanced approach to this difficult matter of race relations which can so easily blow up'.

Nobody can doubt the difficulties of the race issue or of many others which Christians are likely to encounter when they enter the political arena. But the unfortunate feature of church debates about the issues of race, Northern Ireland and education is that they reveal the wide gulf of understanding which has opened up between well-intentioned and responsible church leaders and the people who are actively engaged in the field. Less than two decades ago, one could have argued convincingly that all three of these issues were close to the churches' hearts, that Christians and their leaders were in closer contact with these issues than most secular politicians, and that there existed within the British churches a special understanding and expertise on these matters. But the confusion of so many recent ecclesiastical utterances on these issues shows just how far the churches have been left behind by the rapid pace of political change.

13

Hope and Despair

It is a cliché to say that for years Western society has been under a barrage of change and that its institutions have been shaken to their foundations. But nowhere is the cliché less avoidable than in the case of institutional religion. The churches are by no means an easy subject on which to pronounce judgement for the evidence is abundant, perplexing and often contradictory, but the uncommitted observer often arrives at the conclusion that they are far gone on the path to obsolescence. 'The Churches are dying' is the common expression of this view. And the statistics of membership and religious practice, which so preoccupy the present generation of church leaders, all seem to point in that direction. Regular adherents of the Church of England and the Free Churches have been falling away steadily since before the First World War; the membership of the Presbyterian churches in Scotland, Northern Ireland and Wales have all gone into decline since the mid-fifties; and the Roman Catholic church, which for long cultivated an impression of immunity from this Protestant sickness, is now being made statistically aware of the serious problem it faces with its teenage drop-outs and the lost allegiance of immigrants from countries like Ireland.

Moreover, the capacity of the churches to cope with other problems —such as the erosion of their moral authority, theological doubts and diversity, inflation, the difficulties of maintaining plant and personnel and the insistent demands for justice, equality and participation—do not give the observer much confidence in their chances of survival. It is incidentally, worth recalling that the demand that the churches should embrace the cause of social justice not only covers the vexed question of involvement in political issues like racism and economic policy, but events much nearer home—like the demand of a disciplined priest that he should have a full and fair hearing before his bishop or the grievance of parsonage families whose economic sacrifices in the cause of the Gospel have now become a scandal. The problems come crowding in like the complications in a terminal illness and, from the introversion displayed in many church debates, one begins to wonder whether the patient really has the will to survive. And in the final analysis, he is on his own. The crisis affecting the credibility of the churches is more serious than that affecting other institutions, like Parliament, the police and the schools, for there will be no votes, no statutory provisions and no Exchequer 'lame duck' grants to keep the churches going if they appear in danger of collapse. Churches have to rely on their members and they are no longer numerous.

There is much truth in this familiar evidence of ecclesiastical decline but taken as a whole the doom-laden scenario does not really add up. Despite their many serious difficulties, the churches in Britain are clearly not about to fade away. There is a great power of resilience and inertia in them and identifying where this lies is a more fruitful exercise than going over the familiar ground of declining membership. Of the other factors that have to be taken into account, perhaps the most important is faith (a quite separate issue from morale, which has recently been as low as it has ever been). The faith of Christians in the Church means that they see it as something more than a mere social convenience, like an angling club or the Ancient Order of Buffaloes friendly society. To Christians the Church is the body of Christ, an organisation which is divinely appointed and constantly renewed through the power of the Holy Spirit. There is plenty of circumstantial evidence to support this ancient dogma—in the brief but revolutionary reign of Pope John, for example, which he described as the 'New Pentecost', or in the ecumenical and charismatic movements that have transformed the life of the churches since the early sixties. The trouble is that many Christians appear to rely upon this divine intervention and the success of renewal movements to the neglect of the painstaking action which they themselves must take to renew the churches. There is a tendency to keep belief in the everlasting Church —the Body of Christ—in a quite separate compartment from feelings about the actual Church. It is interesting that two of the more famous ecclesiastical drop-outs of recent years—Nicolas Stacey, the Anglican ex-rector of Woolwich, and Charles Davis, formerly the leading Roman Catholic theologian in Britain—both concluded their devastating criticisms of the Church as they knew it with expressions of faith in the Church as the everlasting Body of Christ. One may be excused perhaps from wondering what is meant by faith in the Body of Christ but rejection of the visible Church.

However, another aspect of the power of Christian faith within the churches is their capacity for survival against all odds, including persecution. The outstanding instance of this in the modern world is to be found not in Britain, of course, but under Communist rule in the Soviet Union and Eastern Europe. The reports that have been reaching the West in recent years of a vigorous Christian life in Russia, of crowds packing the churches for the Orthodox Easter, for example, and even of overt criticism of the régime by Christian leaders—as in the impassioned letter from two Russians which had such an effect on the World Council of Churches Assembly at Nairobi—have made a profound impression on Christians in Britain. Their admiration and sympathy have been aroused, but so too have their envy and despair at the very different quality of church life in the West. Michael Bourdeaux, director of Keston College (the interdenominational centre in Kent for the study of religion and Communism) wrote in his annual review: 'I have not counted the number of times in 1975 that I have been struck dumb with wonder at the spiritual power leaping across the terminals from east to west. The charge of electricity activates us directly—but always too soon we recoil into ourselves, paralysed at our impotence . . . we have been deeply impressed by the relevance of the Russian Christian revival to our own situation.' British Christians have been shamed by their incapacity to respond and the salt has been rubbed into the wound of Western self-criticism by Alexander Solzhenitsyn. All this has led some Christians to wonder whether a dose of persecution might not be a bad thing for Christianity here: a Roman Catholic bishop said that totalitarian government in Britain would probably be the surest and quickest instrument for achieving church unity.

But it does not need such drastic adversity to demonstrate that religious institutions have great reserves of resilience and survival. The many Christian sects and smaller churches which are dotted up and down the length of Britain illustrate just that. While the modern charismatic movement has gained followers in all the major churches, including Roman Catholics, without as yet propagating its own sects in Britain, the relics of earlier pentecostal revivals are still there in the Apostolic Church, the Assemblies of God and the Elim Foursquare churches. More conventional revivals have left their mark in the independent Evangelical churches, the gospel and mission halls, often intended for extinct social situations, like the London City Mission which took the message of Sankey and Moody to the metropolitan working classes in the 1890s and still survives in different social surroundings. There are the obstinate remnants of the tiny schismatic denominations—the Free Church of England, the Catholic Episcopal Church, the Free Methodists—and the many rump churches left behind by unity schemes among Baptists, Methodists, Congregationalists and Presbyterians. There are the sects with distinctive doctrines and practices like the Brethren, the Unitarians, Jehovah's Witnesses, Mormons, Adventists and the more recent imports of Scientology and the so-called Unification Church of the Korean millionaire, Mr Sun Myong Moon. What is it which enables these often tiny religious groups to survive in a society which has little sympathy for sectarianism and has forgotten, if it ever knew, the disputes that brought them into being? Part of the answer is their members' faith and commitment, including extensive financial commitment, which is often missing in the life of the larger churches. But there are other elements too—exclusivity of beliefs and membership, strict discipline and a fairly wide-ranging rejection of the secular world along with its systems of morality and government. In the popular mind, it is this rejectionism which distinguishes the sects from other religious bodies—the Witnesses' rejection of military service and medical attention, the Mormons' rejection of all drugs including tea and coffee, the rejection even of family ties by the Brethren, the Scientologists and the misnamed Church of Unification. A church which is by no means as extreme as these bodies is the Free Presbyterian Church of Scotland, but at its 1975 General Assembly the two major items on the agenda were prohibitions on members entering other churches and on ministers serving on secular councils. Rejectionism is an important factor in the life of the sects, but exclusivity is the key—the belief that they and they alone are right.

The example of sectarian religion presents mainstream Christianity with both a temptation and a warning. Although for most purposes the major churches ignore the very existence of the sects, the temptation for them to take up similar conservative attitudes in an attempt to rally the faithful is strong. Christians of whatever denomination are on the whole conservatives; in a constantly changing world they flee to the Rock of Ages, to the unchanging Gospel, and take comfort in the unchanging ministrations of the everlasting Church. Or rather they would do so, but for the fact that the Church itself is changing, just as rapidly and often in the exact footsteps of secular change. The churches' moral authority has been relaxed, discipline has gone by the board, worship has been de-mystified, theological doubt and diversity are tolerated and even encouraged, indeed much that the ordinary Christian of the past would have identified as central to the Churches' existence has been thrown out of the window. Complaints of this nature are often heard from the conservative members of the major churches, but they can equally be found in the anti-church editorials in the Witnesses' magazine, *The Watchtower*. The enemy of the conservative Christians everywhere is the creeping secularisation of religion by the progressives who have allegedly taken over the churches' leadership.

The conservative reaction to secularised religion has come in many forms in the past decade. The most vigorous of them has been the new puritanism which has sought to reaffirm 'Christian answers' to the dilemmas raised by the permissive society of the sixties. The Festival of Light, Lord Longford, Mrs Whitehouse, and many other groups and individuals have campaigned determinedly against the 'moral pollution' of Britain, particularly as expressed in pornography. In their wake have come further campaigns against the relaxation of the laws of Britain regarding abortion, divorce, homosexuality, contraception, religious education and so on. Implicit in many of these campaigns has been the belief that the churches are facing not just a drift into moral chaos, but a concerted, Marxist-inspired conspiracy to pervert the nation through the infiltration of the media and the teaching profession. These are all familiar enemies of conservative churchpeople—secularisation, permissiveness, Marxism—but what of the other enemy, the ecumenical movement? One of the interesting things about the morality campaigns described above is that they have embraced members of all the churches and have given a vigorous impression of ecumenism. But true ecumenism, in the sense of the pursuit of organic church unity and not merely *ad hoc* alliances against common adversaries, is far from their intentions. The inauguration of one conservative group in November 1974 demonstrated this. The Christian Affirmation Campaign, which brought together members of the Anglican, Roman Catholic and Free churches, was described by the Religious Affairs Correspondent of *The Times* as 'a landmark in the progress of the so-called "right-wing backlash" in the English churches, a growing protest movement against change, against new theological ideas, and against the current leftish slant of church involvement in social and political questions'. The Christian Affirmation Campaign was particularly active in its loathing of the World

Council of Churches which it believed 'to be embarked on a watering down of the Christian gospel, a search for lowest common denominator religion with non-Christian faiths, and a dangerous enthusiasm for Marxist ideas on political ethics', and quite naturally it went on to lambast the movement for church unity in Britain. 'Anti-ecumenical ecumenism at first boggles a bit,' commented Fr John Coventry SJ in *The Month*, 'but surely it is only one more demonstration that like-minded people associate together, and that being at home in conservatism is more a matter of character, politics and educational background than of faithful witness to a Christian tradition.'

Quite so, and a major drawback of the conservative prescription for the ills of the churches in Britain is that it appeals only to people of a certain type of character and often those of a restricted social background. The conservative campaigns have been a deliberate attempt to revive the religious paternalism of the past and to break off negotiating contact with the secular society. This attitude, however, takes little account of British society's very real pluralism and not surprisingly it has been a provocation to student and left-wing groups. The emphasis on 'reaffirming' existing Christian answers and dogmas also flies in the face of much recent thinking about the nature of the Church itself. 'The pilgrim Church' was the phrase that came out of the Second Vatican Council or, as Bishop Christopher Butler put it, the Church is 'not primarily introspective and conservative, but primarily an indomitable adventurer into new fields'. One of the more heartening things for non-Christians is that some church people actually seem to believe these phrases and are prepared to act upon the blueprint of the Church as a pilgrim-venturer. There are radicals and others not so radical who are prepared to push out the boundaries of institutional religion to try to make contact with political issues, with the secular morality and with those who do not share the traditional faith and values of Christendom. These are the pioneers, so to speak, of twentieth century Christianity. But they could not exist in the sort of Church which the conservatives are striving for, where the main emphasis would be not on seeking answers to new questions but on reaffirming old answers. Indeed, the radicals barely exist at all in the sects and they did so only on sufferance before Vatican II in the Roman Catholic Church, which particularly in Britain maintained a closed, 'fortress Church' attitude towards the secular world and maintained that few spiritual or moral truths were to be found outside its walls.

The main Christian tradition in Britain, however, has been quite different from that. For all its failings (and they are legion), the tradition has been that of an open religion, which attempted to minister to the nation as a whole and not just to an exclusive band of believers or members. The essence of the tradition was partnership between the religious and secular views of society and the cross-fertilisation of ideas and contacts, and this was given formal expression in the Crown's links with the established churches of England and Scotland, the presence of Anglican bishops in the House of Lords, in the role of the Church in state education, and so on. It is a unique tradition, quite unlike the less equitable balance between Church and state in other countries, where for example a polarisation has occurred as the result of the Roman Catholic Church's direct role in the politics of Latin nations and where the Protestant churches have appeared to be merely endorsing the capitalist or social democratic political systems of the United States and Scandinavia. But the real value of the British tradition has been not in its national character, so much as at the local level, where many non-Christians still regard the neighbourhood church as in some ways 'their' church and where there is still little evidence of anti-religious or anti-clerical feeling.

The whole tradition is now being put in jeopardy by the conservative reaction which is evident in many parts of the British churches. The essence of the tradition is that if society goes through radical change, then the churches must themselves adapt to this or at least learn to reinterpret their message to cope with it. But this the conservatives cannot do. The periodic attempts of revivalist preachers to bring Britain back to its 'Christian origins' may well be understood within the tradition, but the determined controversialism of recent years is alien to it. The abortion issue is a case in point. Whatever its ethical merits and de-merits, abortion has become for many Christians the occasion on which to make a last stand against the permissiveness of society as a whole. There have been charges and countercharges of minority opinions being forced upon the majority. Debate has given way to propaganda and rhetoric, and in the eyes of many church-people abortion has become a make-or-break issue for the churches' influence upon the nation. The danger is that if abortion and similar questions are blown up into such an issue, they could very easily have precisely that effect. There is also the risk that the tradition will be jeopardised by another form of ecclesiastical exclusivism, that which seeks to make the churches more self-sufficient and self-regarding. The lack of a social gospel among the charismatics is one aspect of this.

Another is the desire of many Anglicans to cut off the untidy, inconvenient roots which the Church of England extends into secular society—for example, by giving it independent control over the appointment of its own bishops or by denying the rite of Baptism to non-churchgoers who for social reasons want to have their children 'done'. Both of these changes would arguably help to transform the Church into a more tightly organised, self-supporting and perhaps more committed body, but the danger is that they could easily be a step towards the transformation of a national church into a sect. Whether the churches in Britain at a time when their support is declining, can afford to erect new barriers between themselves and the non-practising majority of the population is a matter of keen debate. The question at the centre of the debate is whether the churches exist for their members only or for the world. There is no doubt where the majority of the church leaders stand on this question, but the people do not appear to be of the same mind.

A further danger and one that is implicit in much of what has been said above is that the churches in Britain are now entering a painful period in which schism and division are becoming all too possible. At a time when unity talks and ecumenical co-operation is so much the vogue, the dangers of schism may seem far-fetched. But the danger signs are there and in other countries, comparable with Britain, the signs have already become reality. The United States is of course renowned as a forcing ground for sectarian religion and many of the sects which it has exported across the Atlantic have failed to take root here, but the new schismatic tendencies within the major churches could be rather different. The charismatic movement, for example, which has radically transformed the American view of the 'Secular City' (the title of the book by Harvey Cox on religion and modern America) has already become a fragmented force; it is split between non-denominational 'uplift' groups (like the Full Gospel Businessmen's Fellowship International), pentecostal groups which are working within the established denominations and others which are already developing sectarian rules and leaderships of their own. There is in Britain a similar tendency, though by no means so advanced, in the mushroom growth of charismatic 'house churches' whose members regard the local 'official' churches as not just literally unregenerate but often as the main enemy of their true, spirit-filled religion.

Another issue which has already split the American churches is the ordination of women. After a long procedural wrangle over the rights of ministers to dissent from United Presbyterian Church policy on this issue, several of them left the church with their congregations and joined one of the smaller Presbyterian denominations, but that did not settle the dispute which still goes on. In the Protestant Episcopal Church, a number of conservative Anglican clergy also left—even though the American bishops had sought to defer judgement on the ordination of women and only agreed to the ordination of women in 1976 in order to avoid a larger schism by progressives. It is significant that most of the disenchanted Anglicans sought refuge with the Orthodox rather than the Roman Catholic Church, for the latter is itself becoming agitated by demands for the ordination of women and is in many ways more confused and divided over the degree to which it can accommodate change than any other church in America. In Britain the ordination of women is likewise an explosive issue, though largely confined here to the Church of England. There the pressures for and against women priests have been building up steadily throughout the seventies while the English bishops have tried to prevent the crisis from coming prematurely to a head by the device of asking the dioceses to vote on two separate issues; whether there is any insurmountable obstacle to the ordination of women and whether the Church should immediately go ahead and ordain them. On the second question, the Church has still not made up its mind, but already a number of senior clergy have stated that they will resign their orders if the Church of England goes ahead to ordain women.

The issue of women priests is not yet a divisive one in the Roman Catholic Church. There are other formidable obstacles to be overcome before that one is faced. The fullest airing so far given to the question of ordaining women was in the ill-fated Dutch Pastoral Council in 1970, when it was overshadowed by the more urgent question of whether priests should be allowed to marry and whether married men could be ordained. But since 1970, pressure has been building up steadily for a full and frank discussion of women priests, particularly in the United States. The Catholic Church in North American is divided by many issues and merited, as such, a cover story in *Time* magazine, entitled 'The Divided Church'. The divisions stem from the changes following the Second Vatican Council, which introduced an unsettling element of movement into a Church that for centuries had given the impression of being immobile and steadfast, 'Petrine', like a rock. Among American and other Catholics, there are many who cling to the ideal of the past and devoutly desire the Church to stop moving, there are those who loyally accept the degree of change sanctioned by the hierarchy and there are yet others who wish to move very much faster. Since this last group feels that the whole Church will some day catch up with them, they are now engaged on a free-booting style of Catholicism which profoundly disturbs the Catholic bishops. One area of Catholic life in which this disparity is most evident is obedience to the Church's moral teaching on birth control as handed down in the encyclical *Humanae Vitae*. In the new atmosphere of American Catholicism, *Humanae Vitae* has become more honoured in the breach than in the observance. Thus the President of the US Bishops' Conference, Archbishop Joseph Bernadin of Cincinnati, told the magazine *US Catholic*: 'So many consider themselves good Catholics, even though their beliefs and practices seem to conflict with the official teaching in the Church—this is almost a new concept of what it means to be a Catholic today.'

Elsewhere in the world, particularly in the Third World, there is clearly no single concept of what it means to be a Catholic today. Indeed, Catholics often take extreme, diametrically-opposed stances on social and political issues. Take for example the issue of political revolution: Catholics, under avowedly Catholic labels and banners, are to be found in the vanguard of the revolutionary left and in the reactionary vanguard opposing them. In Argentina, for example, in 1975, there was an attempted coup against the ailing régime of President Isabelita Peron by a group of right-wing airforce officers, wearing crucifixes and calling themselves the 'Fraternity of St Thomas Aquinas'; in 1976, a similar military group, pledged to the purging of Communists from the Church, murdered three left-wing priests and seminarians upon the altar of a church. In the same year in Spain, another reactionary assassination squad operated under the name of the 'Warriors of Christ the King', while a left-wing group was campaigning for the autonomy of Catalonia under the name of 'Pax Christi'. And in the Middle East, while Archbishop Hilarion Capucci languished in an Israeli prison because of his support for the Palestinian cause, his Catholic co-religionists in Lebanon were fighting the Palestinians with weapons decorated with pictures of the Virgin Mary and the Sacred Heart of Jesus.

There is, of course, nothing new in the spectacle of Christian fighting Christian in the name of Christ. It happened in mediaeval Europe in crusade after crusade and it became the dominant theme of European politics for a century and a half after the Reformation. But that was power politics under a religious label, a form of tribalism which had been imbued with and sanctified by religion. With certain notable exceptions, the religious warriors of the seventeenth century were not fighting for their personal beliefs but for political and social power. All this changed, of course, in the centuries that followed and both politics and religion became 'civilised', the former by becoming progressively independent of religious conviction and a religious constituency and the latter by becoming a matter of personal, as opposed to public, morality and piety. Religious tribal warfare was kept out of civilised Europe, banished to its fringes as in Ireland or exported to the mission fields as in Uganda. This still seems to be the case, with European Christians learning to live in peace and brotherhood while the more bitter aspects of their religion are manifest only in less developed countries. The truth of the matter is otherwise. Divisions between Christians exist as much in Britain and Western Europe as they do in the Middle East or Argentina and they are of similar origin. The main cause of religious divisiveness today is not tribal, but ideological: it is a reflection, a result of the major division in the world at large between the 'haves' and the 'have-nots', the conservatives who mean to hang on to the privileges and heritage of the past and to resist change, and the progressives and revolutionaries who demand change, and demand it now.

Naturally, this division is nowhere near so pronounced in a country like Britain as it is in the Third World but it lurks behind most of the controversies which are affecting the churches in Britain today. The debates about public morality and the law, which have become particularly heated in the case of abortion and divorce, are one symptom of what we are talking about; another is the debate within the Roman Catholic Church over the changes in the Mass. Neither of these controversies can be fully explained without some recognition of deeper-rooted attitudes and anxieties about the direction in which a rapidly changing world is moving and the direction in which the churches are being obliged to follow. A much clearer instance of this division is seen in the churches' debate about racism. This then is the real pluralism, the wide divergence in basic values, which affects all the churches. It is not just a matter of marginal diversity on minor matters among people who hold the same basic convictions. The divisions of the churches today go deeper than that: they are ideological and they cut across the denominational boundaries. As has been often noted, the real divisions of the churches are not between the denominations but within them, and within nearly all of them to a similar degree. It is the major inescapable feature of institutional religion in Britain and many other countries today.

The intention of this book has been descriptive rather than prescriptive—to attempt to explain what is going on in the churches rather than to presume to tell them how to run their affairs. The latter course would be superfluous, for no one could pretend that today's generation of church leaders lacks advice or criticism. But it is inevitable that, at the conclusion of a work like this, there should be some attempt to identify the areas to which the official churches must pay special and urgent attention, if they are to face the future with realistic confidence. There are indeed three such areas.

The first is unity, not the so-called ecumenical quest for interdenominational amalgamation (though that is not unimportant), but the need for the churches to maintain the unity which they now possess and not to become further fragmented. The missionary task of the churches is often expressed in terms of reconciling men to God and to each other. There is certainly a great need for this service in the modern world, where divisiveness and confrontation have become endemic (a curious instance of how the churches can help is the employment of a parson by Cleveland County Council to teach officials to talk to each other). But the credibility of the churches in this ministry of reconciliation will be considerably lessened if they now enter a period of acrimonious schism and fragmentation. At the time of writing this seems a possibility over many issues, including the Mass, the ordination of women, attitudes towards abortion and homosexuality and so on. The Christian community is becoming as diverse in its practices and as pluralistic in its values as the non-Christian world which it seeks to evangelise; divisive tensions and antagonisms are increasing in both. The churches' first priority then is to reconcile their members to each other and to the need for dialogue and humility, instead of confrontation and walk-outs. Their Lord commanded them, after all, to testify not just to truth but to the Truth which is Love.

The churches' second need is to refashion and revitalise their forms of leadership. There are a number of aspects to this requirement. One is the result of the wholesale distaste in which authority and authoritarianism are now held in the Western world and the demand that leadership, if it is to be credible, must be exercised through persuasion, consensus and participation, particularly when things are going badly. Moreover, participation and democracy can easily degenerate into bureaucracy and committee government, a condition which now afflicts all the churches. So, as many people now recognise, the churches face the big task of regenerating a genuine lay leadership at all levels of their life, especially at the level of the parish or local worshipping community. It will not be an easy task after so many centuries of clerical dominance and lay passivity but it can no longer be avoided now that it is an urgent economic as well as a spiritual necessity. But if the new leadership cadres at the grassroots are not to become yet another cause of fragmentation within the churches, they must be reconciled together in the wider leadership of the Universal, Catholic Church. Here one arrives on the familiar, controversial battleground which is strewn with the competing claims of popes, bishops, synods, presbyteries and conferences. It is here that the historical denominational divisions of the Church are staked out. Yet even here there are reasons for hope. One is the new light being shed by the theologians on the old entrenched spectres of controversy. Thus the Anglican/Roman Catholic International Commission on centralised authority in the Church: 'Primacy fulfills its purpose by helping the churches to listen to one another; to grow in love and unity, and to strive together towards the fullness of Christian life and witness; it respects and promotes Christian freedom and spontaneity; it does not seek uniformity where diversity is legitimate or centralise administration to the detriment of local churches.' Some of the new generation of church leaders in Britain appear to be acting in the spirit of that declaration but it will take more than a generation before the words of the theologians become a description of the *actual* as distinct from the *ideal* Church.

The third and perhaps most daunting task before the churches is to reconcile two divergent strands within their own life, the 'secular' and the 'religious'. In the period since the second world war, the two strands have appeared to be diverging so rapidly that they are no longer thought to be within hailing distance of each other. In one sense, the secularisation of Christianity is far advanced. This is the sense in which secularisation has been forced upon the churches by a society which no longer pays much regard to traditional religion and has assigned belief in the supernatural to the optional margins of modern life. The secularisation of Christianity in Britain is also far advanced in another sense, in the activity of theologians and others who have tried to refashion faith in the absence of traditional 'religious' supports. This has led to radical reassessment of many central attributes of the churches' character, including their worship and piety, their discipline, their theology and dogma, even their justification for setting apart certain objects and people as channels of divine grace. Sacraments and prayer, as well as priests and ritual, all have to be justified afresh in the modern world. Christianity is thus in a state of constant reassessment, with the object of making it more relevant to a world which has lost its regard for religion, which has 'come of age' and has been emptied of spirituality. But is this in fact the case? Is the secularising diagnosis of the modern world a viable one? Has not the modern style of rational, humanistic religion itself been discredited? There certainly appears to be strong grounds for reassessment here too. As official Christianity in the West has become more secularised and 'religionless', as it has turned away from the mysterious to the rational, from the emotional side of life to the more intellectual, its place has been taken by other religious movements, ranging from Hari Krishna, transcendental meditation and Zen to drug cultures and exclusivist sects like the 'Moonies'. Within and on the fringe of the churches, new religious groups and movements have sprung up like the Jesus Movement and the charismatic or pentecostal renewal. These have been a reaction to the excessive rationalism of much else that is going on in the churches. There has been a similar reaction in the Roman Catholic Church among traditionalists, who are particularly strong on the older forms of piety, against the secularising changes introduced since Vatican II.

So how can these divergent strands be brought into harmony so that they can work together to regenerate the Church rather than threatening to pull it apart? The answer lies partly in leadership, partly in frank acceptance of diversity, but partly also in theology. It is in effect the theologians who have set up the antithesis between the secular and the religious camps. But there is no inherent contradiction in the testimony of one Christian through tongues and ecstasy and the testimony of another through social action or political involvement: their common enemy is the arid self-sufficiency so often displayed by institutional religion. It is therefore the task of the theologians to reunite them, to re-present Christianity as a faith which is 'in the world but not of the world', which caters for the 'whole man', which teaches him not to live by bread alone but which also cares about his lack of daily bread. The only way in which this can be done is by starting, not from current problems, but from the life of Jesus. In his latest and most important book, *On Being a Christian*, Professor Hans Küng does not begin with a restatement of a radical's complaints against Vatican institutionalism but with a detailed reconstruction of the historical figure of Jesus of Nazareth. What is wrong with the churches, says Professor Küng, is that they are not Christian enough: they must strive much more to be like Jesus himself. It is a theme which is being taken up by many theologians and church leaders and it is the best hope for the churches as a whole. It is only by returning to their beginnings that the churches today can be sure of a continuing future.

Books and Periodicals
Referred to in the Text

W. Abbott and J. Gallagher (editors) *The Documents of Vatican II* (Geoffrey Chapman, London 1966)

D. Sherwin Bailey *Homosexuality and the Western Christian Tradition* (Longmans, London 1955)

The Baptist Union Directory 1975 and 1976

James Barr *The Bible in the Modern World* (SCM, London 1973)

Trevor Beeson *The Church of England in Crisis* (Davis-Poynter, London 1973)
(editor) *Discretion and Valour* (Collins, London 1974)

David Blatherwick *Adventures in Unity* (British Council of Churches 1975)

Dietrich Bonhoeffer *Letters and Papers from Prison* (SCM, London 1971)

J. M. Bonino *Revolutionary Theology comes of Age* (SPCK, London 1975)

Michael Bourdeaux (editor) *Keston News Service* (Keston College, Heathfield Road, Keston, Kent BR2 6BA)

F. D. Bruner *A Theology of the Holy Spirit* (Hodder and Stoughton, London 1971)

C. O. Buchanan, E. L. Mascall, J. I. Packer and Leonard Graham *Growing into Union* (SPCK, London 1970)

B. C. Butler *Searchings* (Geoffrey Chapman, London 1975)

John Capon . . . *and there was light* (Lutterworth, London 1972)

The Catholic Directory for England and Wales 1976

The Catholic Directory for Scotland 1976

Catholic Herald weekly

Church Commissioners Report and Accounts 1975 for England

Church of England Newspaper weekly

Church of England Reports (Church Information Office, London):
Towards the Conversion of England (1946)
Marriage, Divorce and the Royal Commission (1956)
Sexual Offences and Social Punishment (1956)
Deployment and Payment of the Clergy (the Paul Report—1964)
Crown Appointments and the Church (the Howick Report—1964)
Putting Asunder (1966)
Partners in Ministry (the Morley Report—1967)
Intercommunion Today (1968)
Abortion: an Ethical Discussion (1968)
Marriage, Divorce and the Church (1973)
Broadcasting, Society and the Church (1975)

Church of England Yearbook 1976

Church of Scotland *Reports of the General Assembly* (Blue Book) 1975

Church Times weekly

David Collyer *Double Zero* (Fontana, London 1973) *The Common Catechism* (Search Press, London 1975)

Harvey Cox *The Secular City* (SCM, London 1965)

Crockford's Clerical Directory 1975–1976

Daily Telegraph daily

Charles Davis *A Question of Conscience* (Hodder and Stoughton, London 1967)

Gregory Dix *The Shape of the Liturgy* (Dacre Press, London 1945)

Anthony D. Duncan *The Fourth Dimension* (Mowbrays, London 1975)

David Edwards *Religion and Change* (SCM London 1974)

Charles Elliott *Inflation and the Compromised Church* (Christian Journals, Belfast 1975)

Episcopal Church in Scotland *Second Paper of the Policy Committee* (March 1975)

Monica Furlong *Contemplating Now* (Hodder and Stoughton, London 1971)

John Gaine *Young Adults Today and the Future of the Faith* (private circulation, 1975)

R. F. R. Gardner *Abortion: the Personal Dilemma* (Paternoster Press Exeter, 1972)

Aelred Graham *Zen Catholicism* (Harcourt Brace, London 1963)

Kenneth C. Greet *When the Spirit Moves* (Epworth Press, London 1975)

Bede Griffiths *The Christian Ashram* (Darton, Longman and Todd, London 1966)

The Guardian daily

Michael Harper *As at the Beginning* (Hodder and Stoughton, London 1965) *None Can Guess* (Hodder and Stoughton, London 1971)

Adrian Hastings *The Faces of God* (Geoffrey Chapman, London 1975)

Peter Hebblethwaite *The Runaway Church* (Collins, London 1975)

Gabriel Hebert *The Parish Communion* (Blackman, London 1937)

Cardinal J. C. Heenan *Council and Clergy* (Geoffrey Chapman, London 1966)

Ian Henderson *Power without Glory* (Hutchinson, London 1967)

Dorothy Irvine *From Witchcraft to Christ* (Hodder and Stoughton, London 1973)

Michael Jacob *Pop Goes Jesus* (Hodder and Stoughton, London 1972)

Daniel Jenkins *Equality and Excellence* (SCM, London 1961) *The British: Their Identity and their Religion* (SCM, London 1975)

K. H. Kavanagh *Sex Education, its Uses and Abuses* (The Responsible Society, London 1974)

Hans Küng *Infallible?* (Fontana, London 1971) *On Being a Christian* (Collins, London 1977)

Kenneth Leech *Youthquake* (Sheldon Press, London 1973) *A Practical Guide to the Drug Scene* (Sheldon Press, London 1974)

Michael Litchfield and Susan Kentish *Babies for Burning* (Serpentine Press, London 1971)

Eric Lord and Charles Bailey (editors) *A Reader in Religious and Moral Education* (SCM, London 1973)

Lord Longford *The Grain of Wheat* (Collins, London 1974)

David Martin *A Sociology of English Religion* (Heinemann, London 1967) *The Religious and the Secular* (Routledge and Kegan Paul, London 1969)

Steven G. Mackie *Ireland's Conflict Dimishes Me* (British Council of Churches 1974)

John Macquarrie *Christian Unity and Christian Diversity* (SCM, London 1975)

Alf McCreary *Corrymeela: The Search for Peace* (Christian Journals, Belfast 1975)

Guy Mayfield *The Church of England, its Members and its Business* (OUP, London 1958)

Methodist Conference Minutes and Yearbook 1976

Methodist Recorder weekly

Thomas Merton *Seeds of Contemplation* (A. Clarke, London 1972)

The Month Jesuit monthly

Morning Star daily

John Morrow *The Captivity of the Irish Churches* (Audenshaw Papers, No 45 1974)

New Fire, quarterly of the Society of St John the Evangelist, Oxford

Cardinal J. H. Newman *Essay on the Development of Christian Doctrine* (1845)

The Observer weekly

Leslie Paul *A Church by Daylight* (Geoffrey Chapman, London 1973)

Edward E. Plowman *The Jesus Movement* (Hodder and Stoughton, London 1972)

Private Eye weekly

John Robinson *Honest to God* (SCM, London 1962) with David Edwards *The Honest to God Debate* (SCM, London 1963)

Bertrand Russell *Has Religion Made a Useful Contribution to Civilisation?* (1930) *Education and the Social Order* (1932) *What I Believe* (1935) *Human Society in Ethics and Politics* (1954) SEE: *The Basic Writings of Bertrand Russell 1903–1959* edited by Robert E. Egner and Leslie E. Demonn (Allen and Unwin, London 1961)

Kenneth Sansbury *Combatting Racism* (British Council of Churches, London 1975)

Herbert Slade *Exploration into Contemplative Prayer* (Darton, Longman and Todd 1975)

The Spectator weekly

Nicolas Stacey *Who Cares* (Blond, London 1971)

Norman St John Stevas *The Agonising Choice* (Eyre and Spottiswoode, London, 1971)

Cardinal L. J. Suenens *Co-responsibility in the Church* (Burns and Oates, London 1969) *The New Pentecost?* (Darton, Longman and Todd, London, 1975)

Sunday Times weekly

The Tablet weekly

Barry Till *The Churches Search for Unity* (Penguin, London 1972)

Time weekly

The Times daily

Pierre Teilhard de Chardin *Prayer of the Universe* (Fontana, London 1973)

United Reformed Church Yearbook 1975 and 1976

Paul van Buren *The Secular Meaning of the Gospel* (SCM, London 1963)

Alec Vidler (editor) *Soundings: essays concerning Christian Understanding* (CUP, Cambridge 1962) *Objections to Christian Belief* (Constable, London 1963)

Wells Collection *A 1973 Supplemental edition of the 1971 Wells Collection of UK Charitable Giving Reports* (Wells Group, London 1973)

Mary Whitehouse *Who Does She Think She Is?* (New English Library, London 1971)

Bryan Wilson *Religion in Secular Society* (Watts, London 1966)

Index